HYMN FRAGMENTS EMBEDDED IN THE NEW TESTAMENT

Hellenistic Jewish and Greco-Roman Parallels

HYMN FRAGMENTS EMBEDDED IN THE NEW TESTAMENT

Hellenistic Jewish and Greco-Roman Parallels

Lawrence DiPaolo, Jr.

With a Foreword by
Thomas H. Tobin

The Edwin Mellen Press
Lewiston•Queenston•Lampeter

Library of Congress Cataloging-in-Publication Data

DiPaolo, Lawrence.
  Hymn fragments embedded in the New Testament : Hellenistic Jewish and Greco-Roman parallels / Lawrence DiPaolo, Jr. ; with a foreword by Thomas Tobin.
      p. cm. -- (Hors serie)
  Includes bibliographical references and indexes.
  ISBN-13: 978-0-7734-4923-7
  ISBN-10: 0-7734-4923-X
  1. Jesus Christ--History of doctrines--Early church, ca. 30-600. 2. Hymns in the Bible. 3. Bible. N.T.--Theology. 4. Wisdom literature--Criticism, interpretation, etc. 5. Greek literature--Relation to the New Testament. I. Title.
  BT203.D55 2008
  225.6'6--dc22
                                2008042891
hors série.

A CIP catalog record for this book is available from the British Library.

Front cover: Mosaic of Christ, 4th Century, The Church of Santa Pudenziana, Rome, Italy
          Photo by Dr. Frances Panchok

The Edwin Mellen Press   The Edwin Mellen Press
        Box 450   Box 67
  Lewiston, New York   Queenston, Ontario
  USA 14092-0450   CANADA L0S 1L0

The Edwin Mellen Press, Ltd.
Lampeter, Ceredigion, Wales
UNITED KINGDOM SA48 8LT

Printed in the United States of America

This book is dedicated to the men and women of the 2nd Marine Logistics Group, 8th Engineering Support Battalion, Explosive Ordinance Disposal Detachment and all who have given their lives in defense of our country while serving in the Armed Forces of the United States of America.

Semper Fidelis

TABLE OF CONTENTS

ABBREVIATIONS

FOREWORD by Thomas H. Tobin   i

ACKNOWLEGEMENTS   iv

INTRODUCTION   1

CHAPTER ONE: Are There Hymns in the New Testament?   15
    Prose Hymns: A Brief Word on Aelius Aristides   23
    The One Source of the Christ Hymns   24

CHAPTER TWO: Hymnic Elements in the New Testament   31
    The Hymnic Fragments   31
    The Pre-Existent Christ   33
    The Pre-Existent Christ and the Question of Provenance   40
    Christ the Creator   49
    Christ the Creator and Language: Contemporary Parallels   54
    The Image of Christ the Incarnate Divinity   57
    The Image of Christ the Incarnate Divinity and Provenance   61

CHAPTER THREE: Jewish Wisdom Speculation and the Hymns   69
    Origins of Divine Wisdom in the Book of Proverbs   71
    Echoes of Divine Wisdom in Other Religious Traditions   73
    Divine Wisdom Domesticated in Sirach   77
    The Wisdom of Solomon   79
    The Intersection of Hellenistic Philosophy and Religion   84
    Middle Platonism and the Metaphysics of Prepositions   89
    Philo of Alexandria and the Logos   93

CHAPTER FOUR: The God as Flesh   105
    The God in Human Form   107
        A. Homer   110
        B. The Homeric Hymn to Demeter   111
        C. Euripides   112
        D. Apollodorus, Isidorus, Plutarch, Pausanias   113
        E. Latin Writers: Suetonius, Virgil, Ovid   116
    The Language of Transformation   117
    The God as Slave   120
        A. Apollo   120

B. Heracles   123
C. Athena in Herodotus' *Histories*   127
The God as Flesh   128
    A. Plato, Aristotle, Euripides   129
    B. Epictetus and Josephus   131
    C. The New Testament Usage of Σάρξ   133

CHAPTER FIVE: The Appropriated God and the People of the Hymns 137
    Philippians 2:6-11   138
    1 Corinthians 8:6   139
    Colossians 1:15-20   140
    John 1:1-18   140
    Hebrews 1:3-4   142
    1 Timothy 3:16   143
    Conclusions   144
    Questions for Further Study   149
    The Appropriated God   153

APPENDIX A   155

BIBLIOGRAPHY   159

INDEX OF ANCIENT SOURCES   173

INDEX OF MODERN AUTHORS   182

SUBJECT INDEX   184

ABBREVIATIONS

AB	Anchor Bible
ABD	Anchor Bible Dictionary
A. D.	Anno Domini (i.e. after the birth of Christ)
Aen.	Virgil, *Aeneid*
A.J.	Josephus, *Antiquitates Judaicae* ("Antiquities of the Jews")
Alc.	Euripides, *Alcestis*
Alex.	Plutarch, *Alexander*
Aug.	Suetonius, *Augustus*, in *Lives of the Caesars*
Bacc.	Euripides, *The Bacchae*
B.C.	Before Christ
B. C.E.	Before the Common Era
BDB	F. Brown –S.R. Driver – C.A. Briggs, A Hebrew and English Lexicon of the Old Testament (Oxford 1952)
B.J.	Josephus, *Bellum Judaicum* ("The War of the Jews")
CBQ	*Catholic Biblical Quarterly*
C.E.	Common Era
Cher.	Philo, *De Cherubim*
Chr	Chronicles
Col	Colossians
Conf.	Philo, *Confusione Linguarum*
Cor	Corinthians
Cycl.	Euripides, *Cyclops*
Dan	Daniel
De. Isid.	Plutarch, *De Iside et Osiride*
Descr.	Pausanias, *Description of Greece*
Det.	Philo, *Quod Deterius Potiori Insidiari Gratia*
Deus.	Philo, *Quod Deus Sit Immutabilis*
Deut	Deuteronomy
Dial. Mort.	Lucian, *Dialogi Mortuorum*
Diatr.	Epictetus, *Diatribes*
Ditt. Or.	Orientis Graecae Inscriptiones, ed. by W. Dittinger
Dn	Daniel
Ebr.	Philo, *De Ebrietate*
Ed.	Editor, edited by
El.	Euripides, *Electra*

Ep.	Seneca, *Epistulae*
Eph	Ephesians
Epist. Moral.	Marcus Aurelius, *Epistulae Morales*
Eth. nic.	Aristotle, *Ethica Nichomachea*
ExpT	*Expository Times*
Ez	Ezekiel
FRLANT	Forschungen zur Religion und Literatur des Alten und Neuen Testaments
Fug.	Philo, *De Fuga et Inventione*
Gal	Galatians
Gen	Genesis
Gn	Genesis
Gorg.	Plato, *Gorgias*
Heb	Hebrews
Hec.	Euripides, *Hecuba*
Hel.	Euripides, *Helen*
Her.	Philo, *Quis Rerum Divinarum Heres Sit*
Heracl.	Euripides, *Heraclidae*
Herc. fur.	Euripides, *Hercules furens*
Hipp.	Euripides, *Hippolytus*
Hist.	Histories
Hos	Hosea
HTR	*Harvard Theological Review*
Il.	*The Iliad*
Is	Isaiah
Isa	Isaiah
Jb	Job
JBL	*Journal of Biblical Literature*
Jdg	Judges
JETS	*Journal of the Evangelical Theological Society*
JHL	*Journal of Hellenic Studies*
JSNT	*Journal for the Study of the New Testament*
JSNTS	*Journal for the Study of the New Testament Supplement*
JSOT	*Journal for the Study of the Old Testament*
Jupp. Conf.	Lucian, *Jupiter Confutatis*
JTS	*Journal of Theological Studies*
Kgdms	Kingdoms
L.A.	Philo, *Legum Allegoriarum*
LCL	Loeb Classical Library
Leg.	Plato, *Laws*
Lib.	Apollodorus, *The Library*
Lk	Luke
LXX	Septuagint
Matt	Matthew
Med.	Euripides, *Medea*
Metam.	Ovid, *Metamorphoses*

Metaph.	Aristotle, *Metaphysics*
Mk	Mark
Mt	Matthew
MT	Masoretic Text
Mut.	Philo, *De Mutatione Nominum*
NT	New Testament
NTD	Das Neue Testament Deutch
NTS	New Testament Studies
OCD	Oxford Classical Dictionary
Od.	*The Odyssey*
OLZ	Orientalische Literaturzeitung
Op.	Philo, *De Opificio Mundi*
OT	Old Testament
Parm.	Plato, *Parmenides*
Pet	Peter
P. Fay.	*Fayyum Papyri*
Phaedr.	Plato, *Phaedrus*
Phil	Philippians
Phoen.	Euripides, *Phoenissae*
Plant.	Philo, *De Plantatione*
Poet.	Aristotle, *Poetics*
Post.	Philo, *De Posteritate Caini*
Protr.	Clement of Alexandria, *Exhortation to the Greeks*
Prov	Proverbs
Ps	Psalms
Q	if preceded by a no. refers to a Qumran document (e.g., 1QS)
Q.E.	*Philo, Quaestiones et Solutiones in Exodum*
Q.G.	*Philo, Quaestiones et Solutiones in Genesim*
RB	*Revue Biblique*
Resp.	Plato, *The Republic*
Rhet.	Aristotle, *Rhetorica*
Rom	Romans
SBL	*Society of Biblical Literature*
Scut.	Hesiod, *Scutum*
Sir	Sirach
SNT	Studien zum Neuen Testament
Soph.	Plato, *Sophista*
Som.	Lucian, *Somnium*
Somn.	Philo, *De Somniis*
Spec. leg.	Philo, *De Specialibus Legibus*
St.	Saint
Suppl.	Euripides, *The Suppliants*
SUNT	Studien zur Umwelt des Neuen Testaments
Symp.	Plato, *Symposium*

TDNT	*Theological Dictionary of the New Testament* (ed. G. Friedrich; English translation/editor G. Bromiley, Grand Rapids, MI. 1964-1976)
Theog.	Hesiod, *Theogony*
Thes.	Plutarch, *Theseus*
Thess	Thessalonians
Tim	Timothy
trans.	translator
Tro.	Euripides, *Trojan Women*
Virt.	Philo, *De Virtutibus*
VT	Vetus Testamentum
War	Josephus, *Bellum Judaicum* ("The War of the Jews")
Wis	Wisdom
WMANT	Wissenschaftliche Monographien zum Alten und Neuen Testament
WUNT	Wissenschaftliche Untersuchungen zum Neuen Testament
ZNW	*Zeitschift für Theologie und Kirche*

FOREWORD

Some of the most important texts in the New Testament for the development of early Christian belief in Christ are either hymns or at least hymnic fragments (e.g. Phil 2:6–11; 1 Cor 8:6; Col 1:15–20; John 1:1–18; Heb 1:3–4; 1 Tim 3:16). They reflect beliefs in early Christianity held in common and probably used in some way in common worship. But these texts are also some of the most puzzling and disputed in New Testament interpretation. The reasons for this situation are varied. None of them is freestanding; all appear as part of larger texts. Because of this the original contexts for this material have been lost. We really have no very specific sense of how these texts functioned in early Christian communities. In addition, some of these texts are fragmentary (1 Cor 8:6; Heb 1:3–4; 1 Tim 3:16); we have only fragments of the hymns. Others have probably been added to when they were joined to the larger texts in which they are now found (Phil 2:6–11; John 1:1–18).

But there are also several other levels of questions concerning these texts. The first asks what it means to call them hymns at all. Although in Greek, none of them is in any recognizable Greek meter. Another broader level of questions concerns the thought worlds from which these hymns emerged and of which they were a part. Because these hymns were so influential in the development of Christian thought over the next four centuries, it has often been a temptation to interpret them in the light of that later thought. Of course, everyone knows that this is not legitimate, but it has still often proved hard to avoid.

In this book Lawrence DiPaolo has dealt, I think, successfully with some of these issues in a very insightful and sophisticated way. There are a number of virtues to DiPaolo's work, but I would especially like to highlight three of them.

First DiPaolo has managed to keep his work focused. Given all the questions connected with these hymns and hymn fragments, one is tempted to deal with all of them. This could have led to a sprawling, undisciplined piece of work. DiPaolo has successfully avoided this. He has limited his attention to six important New Testament texts (Phil 2:5–11; 1 Cor 8:6; Col 1:15–20; John 1:1–18; Heb 1:3–4; 1 Tim 3:16) which most scholars consider hymns or hymn fragments. He has also limited his attention to three distinct and central images in those texts, all of which appear in more than two of the them: the pre-existent Christ (Phil 2:6; Col 1:17; John 1:1-2); Christ the creator (1Cor 8:6; John 1:3, 10; Col 1:16–17, Heb 1:3); and Christ the incarnate divinity (Phil 2:7; John 1:14; 1 Tim 3:16).

A second significant virtue of DiPaolo's study is the care he takes in developing his arguments in a sophisticated and complex way. He begins with the obvious question of whether there are hymns in the New Testament at all and concludes quite reasonably that the texts he is dealing with, while clearly not in meter, do fall into a category of prose hymns quite recognizable in the larger Greco-Roman world. He then looks at each of the texts and analyzes each of the three images of the pre-existent Christ, Christ the creator, and Christ the incarnate divinity in turn. This leads him to a crucial preliminary observation that the first two images seem to be rooted in Hellenistic Jewish wisdom speculation as it appropriated and transformed significant elements in Hellenistic philosophy of both the Stoic and the Middle Platonic sort. The third image, however, that of Christ as the incarnate divinity, seems to find its cultural and intellectual context not in Hellenistic Jewish wisdom speculation or philosophy but in Greco-Roman religion and literature which quite easily talked about the incarnation of various divine figures. The next two chapters develop these initial central observations and show specifically how the first two images of the pre-existent Christ and Christ the creator have their roots in the world of Hellenistic Jewish wisdom speculation and Hellenistic philosophy while the third image appropriates the language and images of divinities become human in form from Greco-Roman religion and literature.

A third virtue of DiPaolo's work is how he consistently combines insight and sound judgment in his analysis of the evidence. This is especially displayed in his analysis of the incarnate divinity in the fourth chapter. In this chapter he examines relevant aspects of Greco-Roman religious thought and literature from Homer and Hesiod through Ovid. He shows how it quite freely thought about divinities in different sorts of human form and how it probably contributed some of the images and language taken over by early Christianity to understand the incarnate Christ. He shows how this is especially the case with the image of "slave" as well as with the rather elastic notions of "form." On the other hand, DiPaolo also shows how the notion of "flesh" which appears in John 1:14 and 1 Tim 3:16 and emphasizes the concrete human reality of Christ finds no real parallels in Greco-Roman religious literature.

The result of DiPaolo's work is, I think, a significant contribution to the study of New Testament hymns and of the thought worlds from which they emerged and of which they were in different ways a part. This is especially the case for the way in which he has shown how early Christians appropriated elements of Hellenistic Judaism, Hellenistic philosophy, and Greco-Roman religious thought and yet transformed them in their efforts to understand their experience of Jesus Christ as the incarnate Logos.

Thomas H. Tobin, S.J.
Professor of Theology
Loyola University Chicago

ACKNOWLEDGEMENTS

I am indebted to numerous friends and family members for the assistance they have given me in the completion of the work contained here. This examination of the Christ hymns was the end result of several years of work, some of it undertaken in Chicago and some undertaken in Camp Lejeune, North Carolina and Iraq where I was stationed as part of Operation Iraqi Freedom in the fall of 2005.

Initially, I would like to thank my dissertation director Fr. Thomas Tobin, S.J., for he withstood a full year of rejected proposals on my part in an attempt to arrive at a topic that was workable. Once we agreed upon an investigation of the Christ hymns, it was Fr. Tobin who shepherded me through the voluminous material pertaining to these hymns as well as the equally voluminous material on Philo. It was Fr. Tobin who engaged in perhaps the greatest "distance learning" experiment in our theology department, exchanges e-mails with me while on active duty with the United States Navy in Al Anbar Province, Iraq.

Secondly, I am indebted to Prof. Wendy Cotter, C.S.J. and Dr. Gregory Dobrov of Loyola University of Chicago. Prof. Cotter gave this work a focus it would not have achieved without her input and Prof. Dobrov lent the well needed eye of a classicist throughout. Mrs. Catherine Wolf of the Department of Theology also deserves a special note of thanks for the tremendous amount of assistance she gave to me throughout the writing of this work as well.

Thirdly, I would like to thank the men and women of the 2nd Marine Logistics Group, Group Chaplains Office, Camp Lejeune, North Carolina, who were so supportive of my work while I served on active duty both here and at Camp Taqqadum, Iraq. In particular I would like to thank Captain Vince Arnold, Captain Ronnie C. King, Lt Col Daniel Elzie, Fr. Timothy Hogan, Fr. Waldemar Kilian, Chaplain Michael Pipkin, 1st Lieutenant Julie Ervin, Master Chief Jay

Stuckey and 1st Sgt James Brown for all their help and friendship in my year away. Also, a word of gratitude must be shown to fellow author and Navy Officer Captain Rocky Miracle who, after I returned from Iraq, constantly reminded me about the need to get this work published.

The faculty, staff and students of The University of St. Thomas School of Theology at St. Mary's Seminary were also instrumental in the completion of this work. My students especially deserve a word of thanks as they were at times my harshest critics as I presented the chapters contained here in our Christ Hymns class. Additionally, the Dean of the School of Theology, Dr. Sandra Magie, was tremendously supportive throughout the completion of this work.

Most importantly, I would like to thank my family. It was they who supported my decision to leave the world of finance for the world of academic theology and who have helped me throughout my theological career. My mother, Marilyn, and my father, Lawrence, have been a constant source of support throughout my entire life and especially through these last eight years. It goes without saying that my wife, Aeris, my son, Lawrence III, and my daughter, Rose Sophia, are both the sources of my greatest joys as well as the reason I do what I do. I am forever in debt to them all.

INTRODUCTION

The search for Christian origins is a decidedly literary affair. As the archaeological record from Palestine in the first century is next to non-existent (the ravages of time, war and natural disasters have left us precious little in regard to material evidence), our reconstructions of the time period rest heavily (indeed almost solely) upon the only record that is readily available to us, namely, the literary record. And indeed, if one looks to the first-half of the first century, even the literary record begins to have its' limitations.

Those of us wishing to describe who the early Christians were, what they believed, how they lived, are left with only a handful of texts to base our reconstructions upon. We must rely, in the end, on what these early Christians said about themselves. An examination of the texts of the New Testament, however, reveals very little about these early Christians. Outside of the Acts of the Apostles and a few references in the Pauline corpus, we are left with barely a handful of names, locations and occupations of these first Christians with which we can piece together anything about who they were. This is, however, understandable. When confronted with the miracle of the Incarnation and the Resurrection the first Christians can be forgiven if they did not devote papyrus after papyrus to talking about themselves.

One way to get around this lack of direct accounts of early Christian life is to examine those places in the New Testament where we believe they were expressing communal belief, namely, the hymnic material devoted to Christ. This material is important for the simple reason that we have every reason to believe that this material was *shared*. It represents, if you will, the collective belief of particular Christian communities and thereby gives us not simply a look into what an individual author thought but what many thought. In addition, if we find images within the hymnic material that are shared *among* different communities, we may be afforded a glimpse into what a larger section of the Christian community believed in the first century.   In addition, this hymnic material can, when compared to contemporaneous literary works, give us some indications of what types of literature these authors and the communities for which they wrote were exposed.

I have chosen in this work to examine one small set of Christian writings as a window upon early Christian authors, namely, the Christ hymns of the New Testament.   The quest for the existence of hymns to Christ in the New Testament has drawn a number of prominent scholars to a close examination of the texts for a sign of such early Christian laudatory creations, or even fragments of them still visible in the texts.   While divergencies of opinion over the full collection is still underway, most scholars agree on a collection of six fragments that may fairly be identified as just such material: Phil 2:6-11, 1 Cor 8:6, Col 1:15-20, John 1:1-18, Heb 1:3-4, and 1 Tim 3:16.   Some of these investigations[1] have focused primarily on the style and grammatical construction of the hymns and their similarities with the general hymnic structures in the larger Greco-Roman world[2] whereas others, adopting a similar approach, looked for similarities to Jewish hymnody, either inside or outside of the Jewish canon.[3]   At the beginning of the last century, many

---

[1] By far the most comprehensive treatment of the hymnic fragments in the New Testament remains Ralph P. Martin, *Carmen Christi*, (Downers Grove, IL: InterVarsity Press, 1999) a work to which I am indebted for its' thorough review of scholarship over the last twenty years. For a concise overview of earlier scholarship from the beginning of the twentieth century until the early 1970s, Jack T. Sanders' *The New Testament Christological Hymns*, (Cambridge: Cambridge University Press, 1971) remains essential reading.

[2] Klaus Berger, *Formgeschichte des Neuen Testaments*, (Heidelberg: Quelle & Meyer, 1984), Joseph Kroll, *Die christliche Hymnodik bis zu Klemens von Alexandreia*, (Königsberg, 1921, Darmstadt, 1968), Markus Lattke, "Hymnische Materialeien zu einer Geschichte der antiken Hymnologie", *NT und Orbis Antiquus 19*, (Freibourg: Universitatsverlag: Gottingen: Vandenhoeck & Ruprecht, 1991), Eduard Norden, *Agnostos Theos: Untersuchungen Zur Formengeschichte Religiöser Rede*,(Darmstadt: Wissenschaftliche Buchgesellschaft, 1956), and *Die Antike Kunstprosa*, (Stuttgart: B.G. Teubner Verlagsgessellschaft, 1958).

[3] James H. Charlesworth, *The Old Testament Pseuedepigrapha and the New Testament*, (Cambridge: Cambridge University Press, 1985), Lorenz Durr, *Die Wertung des göttlichen Wortes im Alten Testament und im Antiken Orient*, (Leipzig, 1938).

entertained Gnostic origins for the Christ hymns, a position largely abandoned since the discoveries at Nag Hammadi.[4] Other investigations, representing the lion's share of the work done on these particular hymnic fragments, investigate parallels with Jewish prophetic materials, most notably Isaiah.[5] As a subset of this group one would categorize those who have endeavored to find parallels to the hymnic fragments among Hellenistic Jewish authors reflecting upon Jewish wisdom literature, most notably in the works of Philo of Alexandria.[6]

The aspect which has still remained insufficiently explored, however, is the cultural contextualization of these images assigned to Jesus. The character of these images, and the associations that accompany these in the first century Mediterranean world must be fully explored if one is to understand the attribution being given to Jesus and its implications for the authors and the communities they represent. This clarification then, reveals the lens of the community and their expectation of Christ. Finally, such a full examination allows one to note

---

[4] Rudolf Carl Bultmann, *The Gospel of John,* (Philadelphia: Westminster/John Knox Press, 1971). One of the few relatively more recent theologians who have maintained Bultmann's position in relation to the Gnostic-Redeemer as source for the Christ hymns is Walter Schmithals, *An Introduction to the Theology of Rudolf Bultmann,* (London: SCM Press, 1968).

[5] Lucien Cerfaux, 'L'hymmne au Christ-Serviteur de Dieu,' *Miscellanea historica in honorem Alberti de Meyer,* (Louvain, 1946), vol. 1, pp. 117-130 and *Christ in the Theology of St. Paul.* English translation by Geoffrey Webb and Adrian Walker, (New York: Herder and Herder, 1959), J. D. G. Dunn, *Christology in the Making,*(Philadelphia: Westminster Press, 1980), Morna D. Hooker, *Jesus and the Servant: The Influence of the Servant Concept of Deutero-Isaiah in the New Testament (*London: SPCK Publishers, 1959), Joachim Jeremias, *The Servant of God,* (London: SCM Press, 1957), Ernst Lohmeyer, Die *Briefe an die Kolosser und an Philemon,*(Göttingen : Vandenhoeck & Ruprecht , 1961), Jerome Murphy-O'Connor, *Paul,* (Oxford: Clarendon Press, 1996), Eduard Schweizer, *The Letter to the Colossians,* (Minneapolis: Augsburg, 1982), David M. Stanley, 'The Theme of the Servant of Yahweh in Primitive Christian Soteriology and its Transposition by St. Paul,' *CBQ,* vol 16, 1954.

[6] C. H. Dodd, *The Interpretation of the Fourth Gospel,* (Cambridge: Cambridge University Press, 1953) although Dodd sees influences on the hymns coming from *both* normative Judaism, the wisdom literature and the works of Philo, Martin Dibelius, *The Pastoral Epistles,* (Philadelphia: Fortress Press, 1972) and *An die Klosser, Epheser, an Philemon,* (Tübingen: Mohr, 1953), Jean Héring, "Kyrios Anthropos,' *RPHR,* vol. VI (1936), pp. 196-209 was one of the first to engage the possible Philonic parallels to the Philippians hymn and is pivotal to the discussion of Hellenistic Jewish origins of the images, and extensive discussion of which can be found in Martin, *Carmen Christi,* p. 162ff, Thomas Tobin, *The Creation of Man,* (Washington, DC: The Catholic Biblical Quarterly Monograph Series, 1983, and 'The Prologue of John and Hellenistic Jewish

4

trajectories where one image appears to be especially popular and re-imerges in first and second century material and popularly incorporated into Christian devotion. Again, this evidence allows a view of these communities in context. This is the endeavor of this work.

The limits on the size of the work forbid a comprehensive investigation of all suggested hymns and hymnic fragments of the New Testament. Rather this examination will focus on six texts agreed upon by scholars, Phil 2:6-11, 1 Cor 8:6, Col 1:15-20, John 1:1-18, Heb 1:3-4, and 1 Tim 3:16[7]. The importance of the images in these texts, as we have stated above are of immense importance to the study of earliest Christianity. Three distinct images will be examined:

The Pre-Existent Christ   Phil 2:6a, Col 1:17, John 1:1-2

Christ the Creator   1 Cor 8:6, John 1:3, 10, Col 1:16a,c, 17, Heb 1:3c

Christ the Incarnate Divinity   Phil 2:7, John 1:14, 1 Tim 3:16

As early as the nineteenth century, scholars have proposed OT allusions for the first two images here, as we shall see in the work. What the reader will soon recognize, however, is that the pool of parallels is normally confined to Jewish texts, either from within the Hebrew scriptures or from outside of the Hebrew canon in the works of Philo. Yet the ordinary world of the first century Mediterranean, and the context in which the ordinary people heard such images attributed, has been left outside, excised from the discussion. Hermann Gunkel

Speculation," *CBQ* Vol. 52, No. 2, April 1990 and "The World of Thought in the Philippians Hymn (Philippians 2:6-11), unpublished, 2006.
[7] All New Testament quotes are taken from *The Greek New Testament,* Fourth Revised Edition, Barbara Aland, Kurt Aland, Johannes Karavidopoulos, Carlo M. Martini, and Bruce Metzger, eds., (Deutsche Bibelgesellschaft/United Bible Societies in cooperation with the Institute for New Testament Textual Research, Münster/Westphalia), 1998.

himself observed that all texts must be seen through the lens of the age in which they were chosen and used. This means that, even when the texts from the Jewish scriptures are intended, the persons who chose these texts understood them in a first century manner, a first century mode of understanding. This critique is of special significance with respect to the third listed image, that of Christ, the Incarnate Divinity. Since this image is not at all an uncontroversial claim within the traditions of Judaism, we must look for the places in the ordinary world of the Mediterranean where it is used readily and exultantly and without shadow of any kind at all. One simply must allow non-Jewish traditions to be examined. Indeed all three images from the hymnic fragments require an unrestricted access to the allusions and association that were common in the Greco-Roman world, contexts both Jewish and non-Jewish and their full implications. From this we will be able to say something about the authors of the hymns, about the communities of which they were a part and, perhaps, even suggest a trajectory of Christian favored attributions to Jesus.

The Appropriated God

A key element in our discussion will be the idea of theological appropriation by which is meant the incorporation of certain theological ideas from one religion by another. This is to be differentiated from syncretism which is more of the idea of fusion whereby various god-names and god-attributes are mingled[8], resulting often times in a hybrid divinity. What we witness in our examination of the images which led up to the depictions of Christ in the hymnic material of the New Testament are specific elements of neighboring religious traditions being appropriated by the religious writings of the Jews and, eventually, the Hellenized Jewish Christians. Never do we see the sublimation of YHWH under a foreign guise nor do we see the accumulation of additional divinities, i.e. the development of a Jewish pantheon. No, what we witness in our examination

[8] "Syncretism", Richard L. Gordon, Oxford Classical Dictionary, Oxford: New York, 1996, 1462-1463.

of images from the Book of Proverbs to the Pauline literature is a very careful borrowing of individual concepts and ideas of a neighboring divinity being used to describe the religious reality of the Jews. The imagery surrounding the Egyptian goddess *Ma'at* can be incorporated into the creative aspect of the YHWH in Proverbs, similar creative attributes can be borrowed from Isis later in works such as the Wisdom of Solomon, all the while maintaining the monotheism of the Jewish faith.

This process continued well into the Hellenistic era, only by this time the theological appropriation came into the Jewish religious tradition from the world of Greek philosophical literature, albeit that subset of Greek philosophical literature which dealt with the actions of the divine in the world and the workings of that which transpired beyond the sensible realm, i.e. metaphysics. As before, most notably in writers like Philo, specific ideas were taken from Greek philosophy and incorporated into depictions of the Lord and his creative aspect, *Sophia*, in the Hellenistic Jewish tradition. It is our contention that the process by which Judaism incorporated images from other religious traditions throughout her history is analogous to what later happened in early Christianity with the images in the Christ hymns. To a great extent the authors of the hymnic material about Christ were the next logical step in the process which began with the development of the character of *Hokmah/Sophia* in the Jewish wisdom tradition. The centuries of theological appropriation that was represented by discussions of *Hokmah/Sophia* in the Book of Proverbs, Sirach and the Wisdom of Solomon paved the way for early Christian depictions of Christ. However, like the writers before them, these early Christian authors reached beyond the images contained in their tradition when confronted with a reality that did not lend itself to the use of traditional images, i.e. the Incarnation. When faced with the challenge of describing the Incarnation, the early Christians could not draw upon any antecedent images in their tradition. Although the images of *Hokmah/Sophia* in Hellenistic Jewish wisdom speculation easily lent themselves to depictions of the

Pre-Existent Christ and Christ the Creator, no such images were available for the idea of Christ the Incarnate God. However, in an analogous fashion to their literary forebears, the early Christian authors borrowed from another religious tradition, this time the numerous images of incarnated divinities found in Greco-Roman religion. It is this process of borrowing and modifying various religious literary traditions in the centuries leading up to the hymnic material devoted to Christ in the New Testament that forms the backbone of this work.

<u>The Aims of the Work</u>

Before embarking upon what I believe the aims of this particular study will be, a few words need to be said about what this study *is not*. It is not a comprehensive examination of every study on the hymns in the New Testament which has been undertaken over the course of the last two centuries. As we are dealing with six separate hymnic fragments from six separate New Testament works (Phil 2:6-11, 1 Cor 8:6, Col 1:15-20, John 1:1-18, Heb 1:3-4, and 1 Tim 3:16), a comprehensive treatment of this secondary literature in the commentaries alone would stretch to volumes. Secondly, this study does not investigate every area of interest concerning the hymns, i.e. questions concerning strophic placement or possible reconstructions of earlier hymns only play into the discussion when they affect questions of provenance. In addition, I will not investigate, at least at the outset, all possible *meanings* for the images contained in the hymnic material as exegetical treatments are beyond the scope of my study. Finally, and most importantly, I will confine my investigation solely to those images contained in the subset of Christological hymns of the New Testament that I put forth at the outset. I have opted to concentrate on this subset of hymns as they offer me the best chance of isolating images not primarily drawn from the Septuagint or earlier Jewish models, such as the hymns found in the Gospel of Luke. It is my aim to explore specifically how traditionally non-Jewish images such as a pre-existent female divinity and an incarnate divinity made inroads into the hymnody of the New Testament, i.e. to concentrate on those images and descriptions in the Christological hymns that would have sounded a bit foreign to those accustomed to the more traditionally Jewish hymns to the Lord found in the Psalms and elsewhere in the Hebrew Bible.

As stated above, my window on this diverse world will be the hymnic fragments found within the New Testament (Phil 2:6-11, 1 Cor 8:6, John 1:1-18, Col 1:1-15, Heb 1:3-4, and 1 Tim 3:16). I have chosen to concentrate my study on this particular aspect of the New Testament for several reasons. First, the above list (as will be shown in the next chapter) represents the general consensus among New Testament scholars as material that can be classified as "hymnic" or contain elements normally associated with accepted definitions of hymnody. Secondly, the images contained in these particular hymnic fragments represent ideas that occur in more than one hymn. For example, the image of the incarnate Christ appears in three hymns (Philippians 2:6-11, John 1:1-18 and 1 Timothy 3:16) and thus offers us a valid area of investigation in that we are clearly dealing with an image common to three somewhat disparate authors. To put it another way, the concentration on hymnic images that appear in more than one place allows us to investigate evidence analogous to the concept of "multiple attestation" in the study of New Testament pericope. Simply put, if we find similar images of Christ[9] in two independent sources we are clearly dealing with an important image. We will thus concentrate our efforts on shared images, images that were important enough to be used by several early Christian authors.

Organization of the Work

The examination will be conducted in five chapters.

---

[9] I am using the term of "Christ" in reference to the hymnic fragments under investigation for several reasons. First, as it is clear that it is the divine manifestation of that is the subject of these hymnic fragments, Christ is the most appropriate title as opposed to Jesus. Second, the hymnic fragments each in their own way deal with Christ as someone who is operative outside of the normal sphere of existence, usually in the period prior to the creation of the world. Finally, in concentrating solely upon those hymns in which Christ is the subject, I leave alone those hymns

Chapter One

    Chapter One will begin with a clarification of the terminology used for identifying the "hymn." Since the separate disciplines of Classical Studies and Biblical exegesis have their own history of scholarly investigation of hymn criteria, both sets of contributions will be presented. Following this clarification, the review of the main research regarding hymn study will be presented, the *status quaestionis*. Normally in a work of this scope the first chapter would be devoted entirely to one *status quaestionis*. In our case, however, the scholarship necessitates the review of not one but several questions. First, can one even find hymns in the New Testament? To answer this question the bulk of my first chapter unsurprisingly wrestles with the question of terminology. As such, a survey of the relevant scholarship from the late nineteenth century onwards from the perspective of both classical studies and theology is undertaken. It is a conversation fraught with difficulty as, unfortunately, these two related disciplines speak vastly different languages so a bit of translation is necessary to get the relevant scholars on the same page. Once these questions of terminology have been answered sufficiently to proceed, we must then examine the scholarship on a general level prior to examining the history of scholarship for the individual hymnic fragments. This is an analytical move imposed upon the author of this work simply by the scholarship itself. In essence you have two types of literature involved when one decides to investigate the provenance of the hymnic fragments of the New Testament, those that deal solely with the hymns (of which Ralph Martin's *Carmen Christi* is perhaps the best and most recent example), and those which deal solely with the work in which the hymnic fragment is imbedded such as the commentaries which were consulted throughout this work.

---

which contain an allegorical representation of Christ as subject, i.e. the hymns to the "Lamb" in Revelation.

Chapter Two

Our second chapter concentrates on those hymnic fragments which the majority of New Testament scholars in the latter half of the twentieth century and the very beginning of the twenty-first have designated as having hymnic elements and which discuss images that appear in more than one work. Thus, the second chapter will concentrate on the isolation of three core images of Christ in the hymnic fragments of the New Testament, namely, the Pre-Existent Christ (Phil 2:6, Col 1:17 and John 1:1-2), Christ the Creator (1 Cor 8:6, John 1:3, 10, Col 1:16-17, and Heb 1.3c) and Christ the Incarnate Divinity (Phil 2:6a, 7b, John 1:14, and 1 Tim 3:16a). In addition, the second chapter will lay out in detail what New Testament scholars have said in regard to the sources for these images in the most recent scholarship.

Each section of chapter two which deals with a specific hymnic fragment will follow the same essential form. First, we will lay out how the image is described in Greek as this is the bedrock for all further speculations because comparisons can only be made to other images on the basis of language. Once we have analyzed the description of the image we will then survey recent New Testament scholars in regard to questions of provenance, arriving at general consensus views where possible and putting forth subsequent areas of investigation when not. The aim of the second chapter is to put forth the best evidence for the source of these images and to lay out the areas where detailed investigation will take place in subsequent chapters.

In chapter two we will first survey all recent New Testament scholarship in relation to the description of the pre-existent Christ in Philippians 2:6, concentrating on the debates surrounding whether or not pre-existence is even a factor in relation to this hymn. Following this discussion we will investigate the scholarship in regards to the description of the images put forth in both John 1:1-2 and Col 1:17 for similarities to the pre-existent Christ in Philippians as well as to each other.

When one speaks of pre-existent divinities in the New Testament, the discussion must begin with the world of Jewish wisdom speculation.[10] Beginning with similar images which are found in Proverbs 8:23-24, 30b-31 and Sirach 24:9, our investigation examines how such Old Testament passages may have formed the backdrop for what we see in our New Testament hymns. As we have previously stated, this section only attempts to "point the way" to subsequent chapters and serves primarily to lay out the lines of argument in the subsequent chapter.

From our discussion of the Pre-Existent Christ we then move to an analysis of how Christ the Creator is described in the New Testament hymnic fragments. Like the discussion which preceded it, our discussion of Christ the Creator centers upon how the images were put forth in Greek as a means of adequately drawing out relevant parallels. 1 Cor 8:6, John 1:3, 10, Col 1:16-17 and Hebrews 1:3c are analyzed in this section which similarly precedes our discussion of the provenance of these images. It is our position that the Greek used to discuss Christ the Creator bears close affinity with the manner by which Middle-Platonic and later Stoic philosophers similarly discussed the *Logos*. In addition, parallels will be seen between the Greek of our New Testament hymns and Sirach 24, leading to a brief discussion of the influence of Middle-Platonic philosophy on that work as well.

The final and most problematic section of chapter two deals with our final image, that of Christ the Incarnate Divinity. Seeing a much more concrete divinity than anything put forth in Hellenistic Jewish wisdom speculation, the images of the divine Christ found in Philippians 2:6-7, John 1:14 and 1 Timothy 3:16 offer up their own set of challenges, not the least of which is the troublesome

---

[10] I have restricted my examination of Jewish Wisdom literature to include only those texts which speak of personified Wisdom, namely Proverbs, Sirach and the Wisdom of Solomon.

use of σάρξ to refer to someone previously designated as divine. It is our contention that the preponderance of evidence for incarnate divinities in the world of Greco-Roman myth offers a far more fruitful area of investigation than anything that could be found in the image worlds of either philosophy or Hellenistic Judaism.

Chapter Three

If chapter two can be seen as an investigation of how images from Hellenistic Judaism, and to some extent the world of Greco-Roman myth, entered the hymnic fragments of the New Testament, chapter three serves as an investigation of how two of these more troubling images (a female divinity as well as a separate divine presence with creative powers) made their way into Judaism in the first place. As such, chapter three traces the origins of the feminine divine presence of Wisdom in the Book of Proverbs, the beginning point of any discussion. The aim of this chapter is to examine how such ideas as a pre-existent divinity with creative powers distinct from the one God of the Jews managed to make its' way into the Jewish and later Christian tradition.

Starting with the Book of Proverbs and making our way to Sirach and the Wisdom of Solomon, we shall demonstrate that at each step along the way the Jews were borrowing images from pagan religious traditions and modifying them to fit their own theological needs. By the time of the writing of Sirach and the Wisdom of Solomon, however, influences from Hellenistic philosophy were making their way into the religious writings of the Jews as well. This is seen most notably in the works of Philo, where the great Alexandrian philosopher discusses the *Logos*, specifically *De Opificio Mundi, Legum Allegoriae* and *Questions and Answers on Genesis*, in which the Middle-Platonic idea of the *Logos* is intertwined with Jewish ideas concerning Wisdom. It is this interplay between *Logos* and *Sophia* in Hellenistic Jewish wisdom speculation that we see as the most probable font for the images we see in the Christ hymns which deal with a pre-existent divinity with creative powers (Phil 2:6, 1 Cor 8:6, John 1:1-2, Col 1:16-17 and Heb 1:3).

Chapter Four

Chapter four examines the remaining images in our selection of Christ hymns, namely those which deal with Christ as an incarnate divinity, Phil 2:7, John 1:14 and 1 Timothy 3:16. This chapter looks at three aspects of these images, specifically, the god in human form, the god as slave and the god as flesh. Our investigation at this point must necessarily leave the world of Hellenistic Judaism, and indeed even the world of Hellenistic philosophy, as enfleshed gods were anathema to both of the aforementioned bodies of knowledge. For the Jews such discussions amounted to blasphemy and for the philosophers, especially those Middle-Platonic and Stoic philosophers of the later Hellenistic/early Roman Empire, such ideas of an incarnate divinity were at best consigned to a far distant and unenlightened mythic past. Thus, we turn to the world of Greco-Roman myth and religion to locate our best sources for the incarnational images we find in the Christ hymns of the New Testament.

Chapter four begins with a discussion of the god in human form in such works as Hesiod and Homer. It is a discussion which, like those that have preceded it, centers upon the specific way such images were put forth in Greek, namely, how did Greek authors describe the transformation from divine to mortal? Drawing upon the aforementioned authors as well as Euripides, Apollodorus, Isidorus, Plutarch and Pausanias we investigate the myriad of ways such transformations were described. This fourth chapter lays out the three basic ways in which such classical writers as the ones mentioned above described a god taking human form: a. by stating that a god was simply *seen* as another, b. by stating that a god *exchanged his or her form* for another or c. by stating that that the god was *manifested* as something else, methods which are all employed in varying degrees by our New Testament authors.

Our discussion of the god as slave takes us as well to the world of

14

Greco-Roman myth: specifically the myths surrounding the god Apollo and the demi-god/hero Herakles. As with the previous section, authors from Homer and Hesiod to Clement of Alexandria are examined for the way in which the god/slave was described. We notice in the cases of both Apollo and Herakles that the specific word for serving as a slave that we find in Phil 2:7 (δοῦλος) is rare in Classical Greek, however, as we enter the later Hellenistic period and enter the time of the Roman Empire it becomes more common. Thus, the descriptions of a god serving as a slave that we find in such authors as Plutarch, Clement of Alexandria and Lucian of Samosata will be shown to bear a close affinity to what we find in Philippians 2:7.

The discussion of the god as flesh concludes our fourth chapter. We initially examine all the ways in which σάρξ was used in the Classical period, exploring works by Plato, Aristotle and Euripides who saw flesh as referring either to the entire human person or simply a part of a body, whether human or animal. In addition, we briefly look at a cross section of usages in the New Testament and find that the use of σάρξ in the Christ hymns bears little affinity to the bulk of uses throughout that corpus. One must indeed look outside the world of the New Testament, to the realm of Greek tragedy, to find anything resembling a similar use to what we have in the Christ hymns. Outside of one scant reference in Euripides,[11] we are left with few contemporary parallels to the manner by which the authors of the hymnic fragments described Christ as God in the flesh.

Chapter Five

The work will conclude with review of the evidence of context for each of the six hymnic fragments under investigation. Any signs of trajectory in meaning will be clarified. A final word will be contributed as to the ways in which these hymns shed light on the lenses of the authors and the communities behind them, and their expectations of the Christ they so honored.

---

[11] Euripides, *Herc. fur.* 1265-1269 (Way, LCL).

Chapter One

Are There Hymns in the New Testament?

As with all investigations, a good portion of the initial discussion, and indeed a tremendous part of the controversy, centers around terminology. The first question in the investigation in which we are about to begin rests upon the question of whether or not one can look for hymns in the New Testament in the first place. This, in term, hinges upon one's definition of what precisely constituted a hymn in the first century. There is, as the reader will undoubtedly suspect, somewhat of an impasse in regards to this question owing to the fact that definitions as to what constitutes a hymn vary widely among scholars. It is imperative prior to any investigation to get one's "cards on the table" in regard to terminology, as precision at the outset will prevent lack of clarity in subsequent chapters. In order to properly answer whether or not hymns exist in the New Testament, a brief examination of the scholarship in regards to the terminology must be undertaken.

The seminal work in the investigation of this question is without a doubt Eduard Norden's *Agnostos Theos.*[1] Relying upon the strict isolation of form, Norden was not inclined to designate any material in the NT as clearly a hymn. For Norden, as with Aristotle, a hymn simply had to have three parts: the invocation or *epiklēsis*, the middle section of praise or *eulogia*, and a final petition or *euchē.*[2] Drawing upon work done in his *Antike Kustprosa,*[3] Norden saw in his

---

[1] Eduard Norden, *Agnostos Theos: Untersuchungen Zur Formengeschichte Religiöser Rede, Darmstadt: Wissenschaftliche Buchgesellschaft,* 1956.
[2] Jan Maarten Bremer and William D. Furley, *Greek Hymns,* Tübingen: Mohr Siebeck, 2001, p.51.

examination of New Testament hymnody either echoes of the Old Testament Psalms (as in Phil 2:6-11)[4], Stoic doxologies (as in 1 Cor 8:6[5], Col 1:1-15[6], and Hebrews 1:1-4[7]), Greek prophetic theological prose (John 1:1-18[8]), or liturgical commitment forms (1 Tim 3:16[9]). The vast majority of scholars since Norden, whether writing from within the fields of either Classical studies or Theology, use his work as a starting point for all discussions, i.e. they have adopted the position that Greek hymns in the formal sense do not exist in the New Testament, however, elements of what we find in Greek hymns may exist in fragmentary form.[10]

As one would expect, the field is fairly split between those who do not see hymns in the New Testament (the vast majority of both Classical scholars and a minority of New Testament scholars) and those who do. Modern authors who fail to see hymns in the New Testament are represented by authors such as Michael Lattke[11] and Klaus Berger[12]who each take similar stands on the issue. Lattke begins his discussion of the New Testament hymns by concentrating almost entirely on terminology, with his underlying assertion being that a good number of New Testament scholars have designated as hymns those areas of the New

---

[3] Eduard Norden, *Die Antike Kunstprosa*, Stuttgart: B.G. Teubner Verlagsgessellschaft, 1958. Norden was one of the first to seriously examine the relationship between Christian literature and that of the Greco-Roman world. The intersection of Hellenism and Christianity greatly interested Norden, who saw the new religion as supplying belief systems grounded in historical and geographic reality, as opposed to a mythic past, as well as the underlying conviction of the individual's powerlessness in the face of an all-powerful divine. It was his work in *Antike Kunstprosa* which formed the basis for his subsequent discussion in *Agnostos Theos*.
[4] Norden, *Agnostos Theos*, p. 284, n.2
[5] Norden, *Agnostos Theos*, p. 241, 253 n.4, p. 347.
[6] Norden, *Agnostos Theos*, p. 241, p. 251-253.
[7] Norden, *Agnostos Theos*, p. 386-387.
[8] Norden, *Agnostos Theos*, p. 1.
[9] Norden, *Agnostos Theos*, p. 254-255, p. 272.
[10] One of the few German authors who find hymns in the New Testament is Klaus Thraede who is not as tethered to rigid formal definitions of hymn as it pertains to the Greek world. Klaus Thraede, *Reallexicon für Antike und Christentums*, C .Lf. 126 (1993) col. 916-946.
[11] Michael Lattke, "Hymnische Materialeien zu einer Geschichte der antiken Hymnologie", *NT und Orbis Antiquus 19*. (Freibourg: Universitatsverlag: Gottingen: Vandenhoeck & Ruprecht, 1991).
[12] Klaus Berger, *Formgeschichte des Neuen Testaments*, (Heidelberg: Quelle & Meyer, 1984), p. 238.

Testament much more suited to doxology or encomium.[13] He bases his argument initially upon an investigation of how earlier translators handled the so called "hymnic material" in the New Testament, citing the predominance of translators as designating such material as either "psalm" or "ode" as opposed to hymn.[14] Most importantly, Lattke emphasizes how rare the word Ὕμνος is in proximity to those passages normally designated as hymns in the New Testament, i.e. if the authors of the New Testament either failed to designate these excerpts as hymns or chose to designate them as something else (ex. ψαλμῶν in Luke 20.42, ψαλμοῖς in Luke 24:44, ᾠδὴν in Rev 14:3 and 15:3) why should later commentators designate them as hymns?[15] At the very best, Lattke can see doxologies (ex. Phil 2:6-11, 1 Cor 8:6, Eph 4:5-6) in the New Testament or in some cases hymnic fragments of rhetorical prose (ex. 1 Tim 3:16, Heb 1:3 and 1 Peter 3:18-22[16]). What he cannot find, however, are complete hymns in the formal sense, i.e. containing the generally agreed upon tripartite structure of the classical Greek hymn.

Those who adhere to strict definitions of form in regards to what constitutes a Greek hymn like Lattke invariably find little in the New Testament to their liking. Authors such as Klaus Berger also fail to find hymns, at least hymns in the formal sense, in the New Testament. As with the preponderance of German authors, Berger sees formal elements that simply have to be found in anything resembling a Greek hymn such as the call of the divinity in the opening lines, a summons usually demarcated by some introduction containing elements of song ("I will sing..."), a recitation of divine attributes, ancestry and deeds, an anaphoric address containing the use of "Thou", a reliance upon subordinate, relative and purpose clauses, and a request for the divinity to appear at a certain specified geographic location as well as a formal closing.[17] Although Berger sees

---

[13] Lattke, "Hymnologie," in *NT und Orbus Antiquus*, p. 227.
[14] Lattke, "Hymnologie," in *NT und Orbus Antiquus*, p. 229-230
[15] Lattke, "Hymnologie," in *NT und Orbus Antiquus*, p. 228.
[16] Lattke, "Hymnologie," in *NT und Orbus Antiquus*, p. 232-233.
[17] Berger, *Formgeschichte*, p. 239.

echoes of Greek hymns in certain New Testament hymns, he sees these more often than not to be patterned on Old Testament psalms such as Acts 4:24b-30, Mark 6:9-13/Lk 11:2-4, 1 Cor 16:22.[18] In the few instances where New Testament hymns seem to overlap somewhat with Greek hymns, Berger sees at best only hymnic elements, and nowhere sees a complete New Testament hymn which could fit his formal definitions.

There are several problems, however, inherent on a strict reliance on form when examining the Christ hymns in the New Testament as outlined by Lattke and Berger, or for applying such formal definitions to Greek hymns in general. First, this approach applies formal definitions to a genre of literature that from the perspective of the extant hymns we possess, either within the New Testament or in the Hellenistic world at large, seemed to lack any similar adherence to rigid forms. For example, if one were to adopt even Aristotle's very general tripartite definition of a hymn, "for all wholes must contain a beginning middle and end,"[19]very few of the agreed upon extant hymns from the Hellenistic period would qualify as hymns, and a good portion of even classical hymns would fall by the wayside as well. Rigorous application of even this very general tripartite definition, which modern scholars such as Norden and others[20] have defined as the *epiklesis, eulogia* and *euche* sections,[21] eliminates a fair number of hymns mainly because of the fragmentary nature of the extant evidence. For example, in Furley and Bremer's recent *Greek Hymns,* of the twelve hymns designated as such from the Hellenistic period under examination only four possessed the requisite tripartite structure.[22] Classicists have created a procrustean bed in which few, if any, hymns fully adhere to the stringent classifications normally employed.

---

[18] Berger, *Formgeschichte,* p. 240-241.

[19] Furley and Bremer, *Greek Hymns,* p. XX

[20] William D. Furley, "Praise and Persuasion in Greek Hymns, "*The Journal of Hellenic Studies,* Vol. 115 (1995), p. 35, brings forth other examples of those who have followed Norden's tripartite classification scheme of a hymn such as Ausfeld (*invocatio, pars epica, precatio*).

[21] Furley and Bremer, *Greek Hymns,* p. 51.

[22] Even the hymn attributed to Aristotle, *The Hymn to Virtue,* seems to be lacking the requisite *euchē* section.

19

In addition, when examining the world of the Greek hymn one is invariably confronted with over seven or eight hundred years of evolution of the form. Thus, if one bases his or her definition of a hymn form upon the Homeric Hymns for example, the general starting point amongst scholars in regards to form, by the time the later Hellenistic era dawns evolutions in the hymn form will have placed any but the most anachronistic hymns outside of the boundaries of what constitutes a hymn. To cite our previous example from Furley and Bremer's *Greek Hymns,* aretalogies such as those to Isis from the Fayyum, although written in Greek to a goddess and arguably fitting the tri-partite schema followed by most authors, fail to pass muster as a hymn and are not investigated.[23] Other authors, most notably Vera F. Vanderlip in her *Hymns of Isidorus* allow for the modification of the hymn form in the Hellenistic era.[24] Vanderlip sees the Hellenistic hymns differing from the Homeric hymns in that they lack the components of either a recitation of the legend of the divinity as well as the reference to a specific cult site.[25]Vanderlip sees Hellenistic hymns comprised of four divisions delineated by the invocation, a section expressing the universal power of the deity, a recitation of the works of the god and ending with a personal request of the poet who names himself at the end of the hymn.[26]

Hymns in the New Testament

When one turns to the fragmentary evidence of hymns in the New Testament, such rigorous application of any definition of a hymn, whether Classical or Hellenistic, eliminates all potential candidates for there are simply no complete Christ hymns in the New Testament. The faults in applying such strict formal definitions to fragments are readily apparent. It is the general consensus that the majority of hymns we possess in the New Testament only exist in fragmentary form and were edited to fit the purpose of the authors who utilized them in their works. Thus, we are at best dealing with hymnic fragments when

[23] Furley and Bremer, *Greek Hymns,* p. 144.
[24] Vera F. Vanderlip, *The Hymns of Isidorus,* Toronto: A.M. Hakkert, Ltd., 1972.
[25] Vanderlip, *Hymns of Isidorus,* p. 89.
[26] Vanderlip, *Hymns of Isidorus,* p. 89-90.

we examine what has commonly been agreed upon as the "hymnic material." Applying rigorous formal definitions to the hymnic fragments we have in the New Testament and pronouncing that no hymns exist is akin to removing seven or eight verses from the *Homeric Hymn to Demeter* and then expecting the resultant small portion of the quintessential Greek Hymn to pass muster.

The second problem one encounters when one uses formal definitions lies in the aforementioned realm of terminology. Modern authors classify hymns, or the component parts of hymns, based upon criteria that were in all probability not used by the original authors of these hymns. To compound the problem of terminology, writers in antiquity used a plethora of terms to describe what we today consider as hymns. Plato in *Laws* iii, 700b differentiates *threnoi, paeans, dithyrambs* and *nomes* from hymns, a confusing classification scheme not made any clearer when Pindar tackled the same subject.[27] In an ongoing attempt to classify the material modern scholars only make matters worse by the proliferation of terms currently in use for this material such as prayer, psalm, poetry, aretalogy, enthymeme, doxology, *hodayoth,* eulogy, creedal statement, and confession to name only the most common.[28]

As a means around the impasse created by rigid formal structures and confusing terminology, several New Testament scholars have tried to simplify matters by delineating both linguistic and literary characteristics shared by hymns and then attempting to fit the various New Testament hymns into this mold. There are numerous pitfalls to this approach as well, not the least of which is the fact that the criteria seem especially geared to solely the hymns in the New Testament and have very little use when one looks at the Greek hymnic world at large. One representative example of a New Testament scholar who attempted such a classification scheme is James Strange who has laid out six criteria that

---

[27] Furley, "Praise and Persuasion in Greek Hymns," p. 31

[28] In addition to the above terms some have opted for a combination of terminologies, i.e. "creedal hymn." For a full discussion on the modern and varied terminology in regard to the Christ hymns consult Jerome D. Quinn and William C. Wacker, *The First and Second Letters to Timothy,* (Grand Rapids, MI: Eerdmans, 2000), p. 319ff.

designate a hymn in the New Testament, although he cautions about using this criteria too rigorously.[29] First, for Strange the hymnic material will normally begin with a relative pronoun and elicit a "participial style." Although this first criterion works well with several of what have been traditionally regarded as New Testament hymns, the problem occurs when one attempts to apply this to the larger collection of hymns from the Classical and Hellenistic period. Few, if any of the Greek hymns from either the Classical or Hellenistic period begin with a relative pronoun. Secondly, Strange believes one should find some elements of parallelism within the material and that evidence of parallelism indicates that you are dealing with something that can be designated as a hymn. The obvious problem with this criterion is that parallelism exists in other literary genres, in the prose of Mark's Gospel as well as in Paul's rhetorical arguments, and does not necessarily indicate the presence of a hymn. Third, Strange notes that there should be some ascertainable rhythm, however Strange admits that this rhythm is not measurable in the quantitative classical meters, making it a somewhat dubious criterion to begin with. Fourth, Strange believes we should expect to find rhetorical devices such as assonance or *paronomasia*, *homoioteleuton* (the use of similar endings) and/or chiasm. As with our second criterion, rhetorical devices such as the repetition of similar sounding words could just as easily indicate a bit of rhetoric as hymn. Strange's fifth criteria, that the third person singular should dominate alongside use of the first person plural, also is problematic as it mirrors what we would expect to find in prose narrative. And finally, the hymnic material should display what Strange calls the "reportorial narrative form" and employ verbs which describe the acts of God,[30] which, in the final analysis, is a somewhat complex way of saying that the hymn should describe the actions of a divinity, a classification which is so broad as to be unhelpful.

---

[29] J. F. Strange, *Critical and Exegetical Study of 1 Timothy 3:16*, (Madison, NJ: Drew University, 1970), pp. 4-27.

[30] Quinn and Wacker, *The First and Second Letters to Timothy*, p. 319.

As formal criteria, even the relaxed formal criteria of Strange, fail to really help us in identifying the hymns in the New Testament, it becomes necessary to place reliance upon form aside and take a somewhat different approach when examining the hymnic fragments we have in the New Testament. In order to avoid the pitfalls of overly rigorous formal definitions as well as the confusion surrounding the terminology that is put forth, a more subtle take on the question of hymns should proceed not from the realm of definition but more from the realm of description. We know that hymns were generally looked upon as formal or semi-formal discourse directed at a god or gods, and that in this discourse a description of the divinities' attributes or myth were expressed. Normally, such descriptions were joined with prayers of petition asking the divinity for assistance. Granted, not all hymns or hymnic fragments contained this final element of petition, but a good many did.[31] In the context of the hymnic fragments found in the New Testament, we can say that we are encountering one when we encounter a break in the prose narrative in which the author digresses from his argument- and this is most readily apparent in Paul's letters - to expound upon the characteristics of Christ or recount some aspect of Christ's life. In short, the hymnic fragments that we find in the New Testament are digressions whose removal would remove none of the force of argument of the author. In terms of content, we must agree with the somewhat liberal definition as put forth by Robert Christopher Townley Parker in the Oxford Classical Dictionary who sees a hymn as basically any song about a God or in honor of a god.[32]

It is my intention to use the description of the hymn outlined above in the subsequent chapters and to concentrate solely upon the common hymnic images

---

[31] The petitionary aspect of a hymn is what normally separates it from pure praise, i.e. aretalogy. This can be found in Limenios' *Paian and Prosodiion to Apollo* (128 BCE), Isyllos' *Paian to Apollo and Asklepios* (325-300 BCE), *A Prayer to Asklepios in Herodas* (200 BCE), Makedonikos' *Paian to Apollo and Asklepios* (1st BCE – 1st CE), *A Morning Song for Asklepios* (Roman Period), *A Hymnic Temple Dedication from Paros* (2nd C BCE), translations of which can be found in Furley and Bremer.
[32] R. C. T. Parker, *"Greek Hymns"*, Oxford Classical Dictionary, Oxford: Oxford University Press, 2003.

found in the Christological hymns of the New Testament. In short, when we encounter a section of prose which is differentiated from its surroundings by a description of the attributes or actions of a divinity, in our case Christ, we will examine the description of the images contained in therein. We will consign our investigation solely to those fragments which describe Christ, leaving out those which refer to other persons in the New Testament, the Lukan canticles for example, or those which deal with Christ in an allegorical way, such as the hymns to the Lamb in Revelation.

Prose Hymns: A Brief Word on Aelius Aristides

One incontrovertible fact arises when one examines those hymnic fragments which permeate the New Testament, namely, that we are never dealing with metrical hymns. The one characteristic that all hymns share in both the Classical and Hellenistic period is that we are dealing with works written with a clearly discernable meter. From the *Homeric Hymns* and the works of Callimachus written in hexameter to Cleanthes' *Hymn to Zeus* and later in the works of Ovid and Virgil, we are clearly dealing with authors who were striving to maintain some sense of meter. When we encounter hymns such as the Christ hymn in Philippians that is clearly not the case as we are definitively in the realm of prose. Yet, even here, a few examples exist of Greco-Roman authors who wrote prose hymns in honor of a god or goddess. In terms of content these hymns are clearly in line with the aforementioned definition of a hymn in that they praise a god or goddess, recount the deeds of the divinity and on occasion ask or petition the god or goddess for some benefaction.

The best example we have of an author who composed prose hymns roughly contemporaneous to the New Testament writings are those of Aelius Aristides (AD 117 – 181). Regarded as one of the best orators of the 2nd century,[33] Aristides composed orations on numerous topics ranging from defenses of Plato to political orations aimed at defending both sides in the conflict between

---

[33] Charles A. Behr, *P. Aelius Aristides: The Complete Works*, Leiden: E. J. Brill, 1986, p. 1-4.

the Lacedaemonians and the Thebans.[34]   In addition, however, Aristides composed prose orations in honor of numerous divinities to which he owed allegiance such as Athena,[35] Asclepius,[36] Herakles,[37] Dionysus,[38] Zeus[39] and Serapis.[40] In addition, Aristides alludes on occasion to the practice of others composing prose hymns:

> *But, O dearest Herakles, it is the most pleasant sort of labor to praise you. In every way you are much hymned. For there are many who sing your deeds in prose, and the poets have hymned you much in every fashion, but most important there is the daily praise of all men which ever arises at every occasion that befalls.*
>
> (Aristides, *Herakles*, XL, 1)[41]

It is important to note that in this author we have at least one fairly prominent example of an author who turned to prose, and indeed made reference to others who did the same, in his attempts to praise a god.   Thus, in our discussions concerning the hymnic fragments contained in the New Testament, we can at least demonstrate that authors of Phil 2:6-11, 1 Cor 8:6, John 1:1-18, Col 1:1-15, Heb 1:3-4, and 1 Tim 3:16 were in fairly good literary company.

The One Source of the Christ Hymns: Scholarship until Nag Hammadi

The second question that arises once we have agreed that it is indeed fruitful to look for hymns in the New Testament is the question of provenance. From the beginning of the twentieth century the hymns of the New Testament have elicited much scholarly interest, but the earliest full treatments of all the hymns tended to spend the majority of the time wrestling with the same issues of classification alluded to above. The study which formed the basis for all subsequent works, either in the realm of Christian theology or Antiquities, was the previously cited Eduard Norden's *Agnostos Theos* which was concerned primarily

---

[34] Behr, *Aristides,* Orations II, III, IX – XVI.
[35] Behr, *Aristides*, XXXVII, p. 230 – 234.
[36] Behr, *Aristides*, XXXVIII, XXXIX, pp. 230-238 and XLII, pp. 247-250.
[37] Behr, *Aristides*, XL, pp. 239-243.
[38] Behr, *Aristides*, XLI, pp. 244-246.
[39] Behr, *Aristides*, XLIII, pp. 251-256.
[40] Behr, *Aristides*, XLV, pp. 261-268.
[41] Behr, *Aristides,* pp. 239.

with the formal classification of the hymns of antiquity, of which the chapters on Christian hymnody formed a small part.[42] Building upon the philological work of Norden, Kroll's *Die christliche Hymnodik bis zu Klemens von Alexandreia* in 1921,[43] sought to classify the hymns of the New Testament as distinct from confessions or prayers.[44] Kroll's work, like Norden's which preceded it, was mainly concerned with classification and, as most of the hymns in Kroll's study centered upon the idea of the New Testament hymns as "psalms of praise," discussion began, and ultimately ended, with the Septuagint psalms as a source for these particular hymns.

However, as individual treatments of the hymns began to surface in the numerous commentaries that began in the late twenties of the last century, questions of provenance beyond the Septuagint began to be entertained in earnest.[45] In general these treatments dealt with the hymns of the New Testament that bore little affinity with the hymns of the LXX (such as the Lucan canticles) and concentrated instead upon the Johannine prologue, Phil 2:6-11, Col 1:15-20, Eph 2:14-16, Heb 1:3, 1 Tim 3:16, and 1 Peter 3:18-22. Scholarship in regard to the hymns after the First World War tended to look to two interrelated sources for the images contained in these hymns, namely, early Gnosticism with a small

---

[42] Norden, Eduard, *Agnostos Theos. Untersuchungen zur Formengeschichte religiöser Rede,* (Leipzig/Berlin, 1913). Of special interest is the first section of Norden's third chapter, "Eine stoische Doxologie bei Paulus. Gesichte ener Allmachtsformel."

[43] Joseph Kroll, *Die christliche Hymnodik bis zu Klemens von Alexandreia, Verzeichnis der Vorlesungen an der Akademie zu Braunsberg im Sommer 1921,* (Königsberg, 1921; reprinted in Darmstadt, 1968).

[44] Jack T. Sanders, *The New Testament Christological Hymns,* (Cambridge: Cambridge University Press, 1971), p. 2.

[45] A small representative sample of these treatments would include: Rudolph Bultman, "Der religionsgeschichtlilche Hintergrund des Prologs zum Johannes-Evangelium," *Eucharisteriion, Festschrift für Hermann Gunkel,* ed. Hans Schmidt, vol. II (Göttingen, 1923), Martin Dibelius, *An die Kolosser, Epheser an Philemon* (HNT, 12) (Tübingen, 1953) and *Die Pastoralbriefe,* HNT, (Tübingen, 1955), Ernst Käsemann, *Das wandernde Gottesvolk: Eine Untersuchung zum Hebräerbrief,* Forschungen zur Religion und Literatur des Alten und Neuen Testaments, (Göttingen, 1961), Ernst Lohmeyer, *Kyrios Jesus: Eine Untersuchung zu Phil. 2, 5-11. Sitzungsberichte der Heidelberger Akademie der Wissenschaften,* (Jahrgang 1927/8, 4. Abhandlung; reprinted Darmstadt, 1961), Heinrich Schlier, *Christus und die Kirche im Epheserbrief,* Beiträge zur Kontroverstheologie, (Münster-Westphalen, 1930), Eduard Schweizer, *Erniedrigung und Erhöhung bein Jesus und seinen Nachfolgern.* Abhandlungen zur Theologie des Alten nd Neuen Testaments, 28 (Zurich, 1962).

minority of scholars entertaining the Wisdom tradition of Hellenistic Judaism as a potential source for these images. The lion's share of the discussion, however, centered on Gnostic origins of the hymnic material.

The chief proponent of Gnosticism as the source for New Testament hymnody, specifically a "Gnostic Redeemer Myth", was Rudolph Bultmann who saw an incarnate redeemer as one part of early Gnosticism that was taken over quite early by Christianity.[46] After initially positing Jewish *Sophia* as the source for the images described in the Johannine prologue and elsewhere, Bultmann later expanded upon this by positing a still earlier source for these images, namely the Gnostic-Redeemer myth[47] which he saw as the wellspring for both Hellenistic and Gnostic wisdom speculation.[48] In this myth, the redeemer, who possesses a unity or equality with God and who serves as a mediator of creation, descends and dies only to be made alive again and effect a reconciliation with humanity prior to his eventual exaltation and enthronement.[49]

However, from the beginning voices were heard which contradicted this majority view, chief among these was C. H. Dodd who asserted, "there is no Gnostic document known to us which can with any show of probability be dated ...before the period of the New Testament."[50] Dodd, reacting against Bultmann's earlier position, saw such images as the *Logos* and images of an incarnate divine being as stemming from normative Judaism with some ideas from the Wisdom literature and from Philo brought in.[51] However, most scholars followed Bultmann's lead against Dodd and the majority of the works up to the late 1960's

---

[46] Rudolph Bultmann, "Die Bedeutung der neuerschlossenen mandäischen und manichischen Quellen für das Verständnis des Johannesevangeliums," ZNW, vol. XXIV (1925), p. 100-146.

[47] Bultmann constructed this myth by examining the works of Plotinus, Valentinus, Poimandres, the Odes of Solomon as well as mentions of the doctrine of the Sethians and others in the works of Hippolytus.

[48] Rudolph Bultmann, "Johanneische Schriften und Gnosis," *OLZ* 43 (1940), pp. 150-175.

[49] Sanders, *New Testament Christological Hymns*, p. 24-25.

[50] C.H. Dodd, *The Interpretation of the Fourth Gospel,* (Cambridge: Cambridge University Press, 1953), p. 98.

[51] Sanders, *The New Testament Christological Hymns*, p. 41.

dealt with the New Testament hymns from the perspective of how they were representative of this particular aspect of Gnosticism.[52]

Texts discovered from excavations at Nag Hammadi began to slowly whittle away at the agreed upon consensus that had been built upon since Bultmann.[53] Works by Carsten Colpe[54] and H.M. Schenke[55] severely weakened conceptions of a fully formed Gnostic-Redeemer myth prior to Christianity in favor of a more nuanced view which saw disparate elements of the Redeemer myth in existence prior to Christianity and only reaching full form with the advent of Manicheism in the third century after Christ. These disparate elements, such as the image of the "heavenly man," could be traced to numerous sources somewhat removed from Gnosticism such as Jewish speculation on Genesis 1:26.[56] In place of Bultmann's fully formed Redeemer came discussions of "proto-Gnosticism" or "pre-Gnostic ideas" that filtered into early-Christianity from numerous sources ranging from Platonism to pagan myths surrounding deities such as Osiris. The discussion concerning the origins of New Testament hymnody shifted as well with the majority of scholars[57]abandoning the Gnostic–Redeemer myth in favor of

[52] James A. Charlesworth, "A Prolegomenon to a New Study of the Jewish Background of the Hymns and Prayers in the New Testament," *Journal of Jewish Studies 33,* Spring/Autumn, 1982, list the following synthetic studies as indicative of the 1960's-1970's: Schille, *Frühchristliche Hymnen* (Berlin, 1965), Schattenmann, *Studien zum neutestementlichen Prosahymnus* (Munich, 1965), Deichgräber, *Gotteshymnus und Christushymnus in der frühen Christenheit: Untersuchungen zu Form, Sprache und Stil der Frühchristlichen Hymnen* (SUNT 5, Göttingen, 1967), Sanders, *The New Testament Christological Hymns: Their Historical Background* (JSNTS Monograph Series 15; Cambridge, 1971); Wengst, *Christologische Formeln und Lieder des Urschristentums* (SNT 7; Gutersloh, 1972).
[53] The first books discussing the comprehensive findings at Nag Hammadi began to appear in the early 1960's. A representative sample includes: Alexander Böhlig, *Koptissch-gnostiche Apokalypsen aus Codex V von Nag Hammadi,* (Halle-Wittenberg, 1963), Jean Daniélou, "Judéo-christianisme et gnose," in *Aspects du Judéo-christianisme,* (Paris, 1965) as well as his *Théologie du judéo-christianisme,* (Tournai, 1958), Jean Doresse, *The Secret Books of the Egyptian Gnostics,* (New York: Viking Press, 1960), and Hans Jonas, *The Gnostic Religion,* (Boston: Beacon Press, 1963).
[54] Carsten Colpe, *Die religionsgeschichtliche Schule: Darstellung und Kritik ihres Bildes vom gnostischen Erlösermythus,* FRLANT 78, (Göttingen, 1961).
[55] H. M. Schenke, *Der Gott 'Mensch' in der Gnosis,* (Göttingen, 1962).
[56] R. Wilson, *Gnosis and the New Testament,* (Philadelphia: Fortress Press, 1968), p. 28.

Hellenistic Jewish wisdom speculation as the source for the hymns and hymnic fragments in the New Testament. It was a retrenchment which, coincidentally, marked a shift back to Bultmann's original position. Since the late 1960's to the present, Hellenistic Jewish wisdom speculation has formed the basis for much of the discussion concerning the non-septuagintal hymns and hymn fragments in the New Testament. Thus, a great portion of my initial discussion of this material in the next chapter will trace the evolutions in this line of reasoning as it pertains to the hymnic material normally associated with the Christological hymns of New Testament.[58] The change from a Gnostic-Redeemer to the world of Hellenistic Jewish wisdom speculation that was ushered in by the discoveries at Nag Hammadi ushered in a sea-change for all discussions concerning the provenance of the images contained in the Christ Hymns which deal with a pre-existent/creator deity.

We have endeavored in this first chapter to lay out the basic lines of argument and tackle, at least initially, the thorny problem of terminology as it applies to the hymnic fragments found in the New Testament. We have arrived, albeit in a round about way, at a definition of a hymn which allows us to treat any language which discusses a god as hymnic. This has resulted in a movement away from formal classification schemes, and hence away from Greek hymns in the strict sense, to a discussion of material in the New Testament that can be classified as hymnic in that it pertains to seeks to describe a divine entity, in our case Christ. In addition, we have begun to trace the scholarship as it pertains to the origin of the images found in our hymnic fragments and have followed the

---

[57] One of the main proponents of Bultmann's view to this day is Walter Schmithals who has maintained a belief in the fully formed Gnostic-Redeemer myth as the source of Gnostic antagonism to Paul the Apostle.

[58] James A. Charlesworth, "A Prolegomenon", pp. 264-285. Although some scholars have followed the pendulum swing from the gnostic-redeemer myth beyond the realm of Hellenistic Wisdom Jewish speculation and back into the world of inter-testamental Jewish prayer and liturgical practices. One such author is James Charlesworth who sees the hymnic material contained in the New Testament as borrowed and redefined mostly from early Jewish hymns and prayers, most notably the Hellenistic Synagogal prayers which he believes are contained in the *Apostolic Constitutions*. It is Charlesworth's contention that these prayers formed the basis for what later became the hymns of the New Testament.

progression of thought from the now largely abandoned Gnostic-redeemer myth to the beginnings of the investigation of Hellenistic Jewish wisdom speculation as the more probably font for these images.   It is the exploration of this line of thought which will form the basis for the second and, to some extent, the third chapter.

Chapter Two

Hymnic Elements in the New Testament

<u>The Hymnic Fragments</u>

When we examine the material in the New Testament normally designated as hymnic we are confronted with numerous images which attempt to describe Christ. This material (Phil 2:6-11, 1 Cor 8:6, Col 1:15-20, John 1:1-18, Heb 1:3-4, 1 Tim 3:16) offers up numerous images. This chapter, however, seeks to examine solely those that occur incontrovertibly in more than one hymn. For example, as intriguing the image of Christ as the "firstborn of the dead" may be, especially in relation to the numerous Philonic parallels that can be drawn,[1] it occurs solely in Col. 1:15-20, and is, therefore, representative of only one viewpoint. Given the fragmentary character of some of these passages, we have have chosen to concentrate on those images that appear more than once.

This is done for several reasons. First, the images that appear in numerous hymns offer us insights into multiple early Christian authors. In the case of image of the Pre-Existent Christ found in Phil 2:6, Col 1:17 and John 1:1-2, for example, we are getting the viewpoints of three separate authors, and to some extent the communities they wrote for. Second, concentrating solely on those images which appear in multiple passages allows us limit our area of investigation to the main images connected with Jesus in the hymnic fragments, i.e. those images important enough to be used by several authors. This chapter, therefore, will concentrate on those three images which tend to permeate the material normally designated as Christological hymns, namely, the image of the Pre-Existent Christ, the image of Christ the Creator, and the image of Christ the Incarnate Divinity. We shall examine the following passages:

The Pre-Existent Christ	Phil 2:6a, Col 1:17, John 1:1-2
Christ the Creator	1 Cor 8:6, John 1:3, 10, Col 1:16a,c, 17, Heb 1:3c
Christ the Incarnate Divinity	Phil 2:7, John 1:14, 1 Tim 3:16

The end result of this investigation will be not only to trace the literary trajectory of these images but also to try to begin to explain why these images spread over these hymnic fragments were so important to the Christian communities of the first and early second centuries. Why would the authors of these hymns concentrate on these images and why would these three in particular be so warmly received by their communities? The answer to this question lies in the centuries which lead up to our Christ hymns.

The organizational structure of this chapter is fairly simple. First, the Greek of each hymnic fragment shall be described, examining both vocabulary and syntax. After laying out the Greek text and giving a brief description of the image contained in the hymn, I will then examine any major debates among contemporary theologians concerning the terminology used in the hymnic fragments, specifically as they relate to provenance. Second, I will lay out the general consensus positions among New Testament scholars where they exist concerning the provenance of these images. It is the aim of this chapter to give the general lay of the land of the scholarly debates concerning where all of these images come from. Once the general lines of debate are laid out in this second chapter we can then examine in subsequent chapters specific areas of provenance and explore the possible range of meanings of these images, both to the authors and the communities that first received them. Thus, this chapter serves as a pointer to the in depth investigations that will follow in chapters three and four.

---

[1] Philo, *Cher.* 54.

The Pre-Existent Christ

The first image, that of Christ as pre-existent, appears in three places in the New Testament, Phil 2:6, Col 1:17, and John 1:1-2[2]. Before proceeding any further, however, a word must be said about the term "pre-existent." Ideas of Christ's pre-existence differ considerably among the three hymns. As the subsequent discussion will show, I interpret Phil 2:6 as indicating pre-existence for Christ, although Christ's activity as a pre-existent divinity is limited to his contemplation of his relationship to God. This is not to be confused with a similar image, that of a pre-existent *and* pre-temporal Christ, existing with God prior to the moment of creation such as we find in John 1:1-2 and Col 1:17 and being actively involved in creation. Although it is clear in all three images that we are dealing with some divine entity existing alongside God, the image we find in Phil 2:6 lacks the connection to the creative act that is present in the Johannine prologue or in the Colossians hymn. The image encountered in Phil 2:6 makes no claims on whether or not Christ was involved in the divine work of creating nor does it indicate when this activity takes place. In the Christological hymn found in Philippians only the most fleeting glimpse of his actions is given in that celestial sphere which are attributed to his being cognizant of God and the choices before him. When temporal or perhaps pre-temporal markers are added to this idea such as are found in John 1:1-2 and Colossians 1:17 appear they shall be examined in turn.

---

[2] There is considerable debate as to whether the image of the pre-existent Christ in 1 Pet 1:20 (*He was known before the foundation of the world*) occurs in a hymnic fragment. As there is no general consensus as to the hymnic nature of 1 Pet 1:20-21 it will not be treated here. For a discussion of the various positions regarding its' possible hymnic nature consult John H. Elliot, 1 Peter, (New York: Doubleday, 2000), J. Ramsey Michaels, *1 Peter*, (Waco, TX: Word Books,

The Image Described: *Philippians 2:6*

ὃς ἐν μορφῇ θεοῦ
ὑπάρχων οὐχ ἁρπαγμὸν ἡγήσατο τὸ εἶναι ἴσα θεῷ,
ἀλλὰ ἑατὸν ἐκένωσεν...

Who, though he was in the form of God, did not regard equality with God something to be grasped, but he emptied himself...

Any discussion of the pre-existent nature of Christ in the Christological hymns is replete with theological difficulties. The study must begin with the evidence as put forth in the long held position represented by scholars such as J. D. G. Dunn who holds that no such pre-existence can be found in Phil 2:6.[3] Drawing upon Jerome Murphy-O'Connor[4] and others, Dunn maintains that "the common belief that Phil 2:6-11 starts by speaking of Christ's pre-existent state and status and then his incarnation is, in almost every case, a presupposition rather than a conclusion."[5] In an effort to free this discussion from what he sees as theologically motivated presuppositions, a worthy endeavor indeed, Dunn concludes from the literary and cultural evidence the most probable background is the first-century Adam theology common to both Philo and Paul which shall be examined shortly. Dunn holds that as Adam theology requires no recourse to ideas of pre-existence, the Philippians hymn, in borrowing language from this Adamic theology, also does not speak to the pre-existence of Christ. According to Dunn, Christian writers like Paul must certainly have been drawing on these ideas

---

1988), Donald Senior, *1 Peter*, (Collegeville, MN: Liturgical Press, 2003), and Sanders, *Christological Hymns*, p. 18, n.2.
[3] Ralph P. Martin, *Carmen Christi*, (Downers Grove, IL: Intervarsity Press, 1997), p. 163, details this line of reasoning as originating with H. J. Holtzmann, *Lehrbuch der N.T. Theologie, II,* (1911), who suggested that in Paul's anthropology Adam was thought of as created in the image of the pre-existent, "ideal man."
[4] Jerome Murphy-O' Connor, "Christological Anthropology in Phil 2.6-11," RB 83 (1976): pp. 25-50.
[5] J. D. G. Dunn, *Christology in the Making,*(Philadelphia: Westminster Press, 1980), p. 114.

in the hymnic material such as Phil 2:6 and thus there is no claim for Christ's pre-existence.

Dunn proves that Adam theology was actively discussed in the first half of the first century, pointing to Philo's contrast of the heavenly man and the earthly man (Adam) in such works as *Legum allegoriae* I.31-53, *De opificio mundi* 134, *Quaestiones et solutions in Exodum* I.4. Moreover, he makes the point that Philo made the connection between the *Logos* and the figure of the "heavenly man" as a direct contrast to Adam.[6] It is when Dunn shifts the discussion to Adam Christology in the works of Paul,[7] however, that weaknesses in the application to Phil 2:6-11 are exhibited, as shall be shown.

Dunn examines the numerous places in the Pauline letters where Paul discusses the dichotomy between Christ and Adam or makes allusions to the text of Genesis 1-2 (Gal 4:4, 1 Cor 15:45-49, 2 Cor 4:4, Rom 1:18-25, 3:23, 5:12-19, 7:7-11, 8:19-22) and thus concludes that Phil 2:6-11 is best understood as an expression of this Adam Christology.[8] Further, Dunn concludes that since Christ walks in Adam's footsteps then Christ need be no more pre-existent than Adam.[9] There are several problems with Dunn's argument.

First, one cannot place the mold of Paul's Adam Christology so easily upon the images contained in Phil 2:6-11 since Paul's writings say precious little about the birth or creation of Adam. Rather Phil 2:6-11, by contrast, seems to go out of its way to emphasize a transition, by Christ, from one state to another. Put more simply, there is a temporal element in Phil 2:6 at which point Christ, cognizant of his relationship to God, makes the decision to enter the world, an element lacking in any first century speculations on Adam.

---

[6] Dunn, *Christology,* p. 100.
[7] Dunn does not tackle the problems inherent in such a comparison if Paul is seen *not* to have penned the hymn in Philippians 2.6-11, i.e. making a comparison between Adamic theology in Paul and Phil 2.6-11 even more problematic.
[8] Dunn, *Christology,* p. 115.
[9] Dunn, *Christology,* p. 119.

Second, Dunn attempts, like so many of the authors to be explored in this chapter, to find one source for *all* the images in this particular hymn. For him, Adam theology is *the* source for the multiple images contained in the hymn. He does not allow that the author of the Philippians hymn may have been working in a cumulative fashion and "casting his net wide," culling from numerous sources and not solely confined to the images of Gen 1 and 2. One must note for example the allusions to Isa 45:23 suggested by Phil 2:10 ("that at the name of Jesus every knee should bend").[10] Even if the allusion is not precisely to Isa 45:23, the image is clearly one which comes from outside any Adamic theology. The name "Adam" clearly is never given such exalted status. The author of this hymn was clearly comfortable with drawing upon distinct tradition here which suggests a readiness to accumulate rather than strictly confine his images to Genesis and Adam in his composition and was not tethered to any one biblical model. If the author was comfortable with drawing from different sources, we should not try to impose one overarching source on the images contained in the hymn.[11]

Third, parallels to the Adam/Christ discussion in Paul are not that easily apparent. The creation of Adam, his being formed in the image of God as recounted in Genesis 1-2, is at best a minor aspect of Paul's discussion of Adam. Dunn points out the primary examples of Paul's thought on Adam in Rom 5:12-21 and 1 Cor 15:21-25, all of which deal expressly with the actions of Adam as contrasted with the actions of Christ, i.e. the actions of the former bringing sin and death and the actions of the latter bringing grace and life. The one passages where Paul introduces thoughts on the creation of Adam, 1 Cor 15:47 ("The first man was from the earth, earthly; the second man from heaven.") he concentrates

---

[10] The arguments both for and against the allusion to Is 45 are laid out in detail in Dunn, *Christology,* pp. 268-271.

[11] If Paul did not include Phil 2:6-11 in his *Letter to the Philippians* because of its' links with his Adam Christology, why then did he use it? A more probable answer lies in the use of the idea of being obedient in the hymn (ὑπήκοος), a theme Paul uses in the section immediately following in

on the contrast between the two states of being, i.e. an earthly existence versus a heavenly one. If a parallel were to be found comparable to what we see in Phil 2:6, clearly the example of the "man from heaven" is more applicable than the man "from the earth."

The final weakness in Dunn's argument lies with the connections he makes between the creation account in Genesis 1 and Philippians 2:6 in the use of μορφή, which he sees as a cognate for εἰκων in the LXX.[12] Thus, according to Dunn, the use of μορφή in Phil 2:6 is a clear parallel to the use of εἰκων in Genesis 1:27ff[13], and hence a clear allusion to Adam. However, if one takes the presence of μορφή as a pointer to the use of εἰκων in the LXX, why would one necessarily only examine its' use in the book of Genesis?[14] Thus the author of the Philippians hymn may have used μορφή as an allusion to Genesis 1:27ff, or the author may have been alluding to numerous other passages in the LXX which use εἰκων, or the author may not have been alluding to the LXX at all. The link to *only* Genesis 1 is far from certain.[15] When one examines the subsequent verses where μορφή is used in Phil 2:6ff, to be discussed in our description of the incarnational images contained in the hymn, this link to Genesis is weaker still.

---

which Paul praises the Philippian community for being obedient (ὑπηκούσατε) in Paul's absence, Phil 2:12-18.

[12] Dunn, *Christology*, p. 115 citing R.P. Martin, 'Μορφή in Philippians 2.6,' *ExpT* 70, 1958-1959, pp. 183ff as well as *Carmen Christi*, pp. 102-119.

[13] There are instances from inscriptions in which the two terms εἰκων and μορφή are contrasted such as the one cited by Ceslas Spicq, *Theological Lexicon of the New Testament*, Vol. 2, translated and edited by J. D. Ernest, (Peabody, Mass: Hendrickson, 1994). It reads: "I bear the bodily form (μορφῆς) of Doctitius, but the image (εἰκόνα) of his divine virtue is carried on the lips of each person."

[14] Other instances of εἰκων in the LXX include Deut 4:16, IV Kgdms 11:18, 2 Chr 33:7, Ps 38(39):6, 72(73):20, Wis 2:23, 7:26, 13:13, 16, 14:15, 17, 15:5, 17:21, Sir 17:3, Hos 13:2, Is 40:19, 20, Ez 7:20, 8:5, 16:17, 23:14, Dan 2:31, 34, 35, 3:1, 2, 3, 5, 7, 10, 12, 14, 15, 18.

[15] Martin, *Carmen Christi*, pp. 109-110.

In addition, an insistence on an examination of εἰκων as a synonym for μορφή fails to examine the other uses of μορφή in the New Testament.[16]

If the writer signals that images beyond those of Adam are employed for Jesus, the character of Jesus' special existence is open to ideas of a pre-existence or an existence elevated above simple creation as Adam was created.[17] It is clear from passages like 1 Cor 15:48 ("As was the earthly one, so are also the earthly, and as is the heavenly one, so are also the heavenly.") the Pauline Christology contrasts the two modes of being, the first for Adam the second for Christ. It is equally clear that Phil 2:6 has much more in common with Paul's description of the "heavenly" Christ than the "earthly" Adam. We shall discuss this contrast subsequently in our discussion of the provenance of this image.

The Image Described: *John 1:1-2*

Ἐν ἀρχῇ ἦν ὁ λόγος, καὶ ὁ λόγος ἦν πρὸς τὸν θεόν, καὶ θεὸς ἦν ὁ λόγος. οὗτος ἦν ἐν ἀρχῇ πρὸς τὸν θεόν.

In the beginning was the Word, and the Word was with God, and the Word was God. He was in the beginning with God.

The second image under consideration in regards to the hymnic representation of a pre-incarnational Christ occurs in the opening line of the Johannine prologue. This hymn which begins the Gospel of John states the pre-existent nature of Christ in a more unambiguous manner than Phil 2:6. Two phrases contribute to clarity concerning the claim of pre-existence for Christ: namely, the indication that Christ's activity took place Ἐν ἀρχῇ, in the beginning, and the identifying of Christ with the *Logos,* a concept which we will discuss in greater detail when we examine the image of Christ the Creator. For

---

[16] For example, one cannot find allusions to Adam in Mk 9:2 or Mk 16:12 where the evangelist is clearly describing Christ in a state of being other than mortal.

[17] As such I am in line with such authors as J.B. Lightfoot, H. Schumacher, E.H. Gifford, H.R. Mackintosh, H.C.G. Moule, E. Käseman, G. Bornkamm and M.R. Vincent. For a fuller treatment

now, however, the *Logos* will enter our discussion only insofar as it speaks to pre-existence.

The Image Described: *Colossians 1:17a*

> καὶ αὐτός ἐστιν πρὸ πάντων...
>
> *He himself is before all things...*

The crux of the problem with determining whether the image of Christ in Colossians 1:17 is indicative of pre-existences rests upon the meaning one ascribes to the Greek preposition πρό, (before). Dunn has laid out three possibilities in the exegesis of this phrase. It may be taken as implying a temporal marker, i.e. indicating pre-existence, it may be taken as implying priority, i.e. in terms of Christ's status before all beings, or it may be taken as a deliberate ambiguity on the part of the author.[18] Since Dunn is convinced from his interpretation of Phil 2:6 that Adam Christology predominates in reference to Jesus' status, he sees a coherence in the second of these possible interpretations.[19] But it must be noted that for this interpretation to hold, Dunn separates Col. 1:17a from the first verse of the hymn, "he is the firstborn of all creation." When allowed to be connected to the rest of the hymn, an attestation of something more than a greater dignity for Jesus seems to be intended by the author, namely pre-existence. The pre-existence of Christ in Col 1.17a is the view shared by the majority of scholars,[20] i.e. Dunn's first possibility.

---

of the arguments both for and against the pre-existence of Christ in Phil 2.6-1 consult R. P. Martin's *Carmen Christi,* pp. 99-133.

[18] Dunn, *Christology,* p. 191.

[19] Dunn, *Christology,* p. 91.

[20]David E. Garland, *Colossians,* (Grand Rapids, MI: Zondervan, 1998), p. 88, Margaret J. Harris, *Colossians and Philemon,* (Grand Rapids, Mi.: Eerdmans, 1990), pp. 46-57, Eduard Lohse, *Colossians and Philemon: A Commentary on the Epistles to Colossians and Philemon,* (Philadelphia: Fortress Press, 1971), p. 52, Margaret Y. MacDonald, *Colossians and Ephesians,* (Collegeville, Minn.: Liturgical Press, 2000), p. 61, Ralph P. Martin, *Colossians and Philemon,* (London: Oliphants, 1974), p. 47, Richard R. Melick, *Philippians, Colossians, Philemon,* (Nashville, Tenn.: Broadville Press, 1991). p. 220., C. F. D. Moule, *Colossians and Philemon,* (Cambridge: Cambridge University Press, 1957), p. 66, Jack T. Sanders, *The New Testament Christological Hymns,* (Cambridge: Cambridge University Press, 1971), p. 78, Eduard Schweizer,

The Pre-Existent Christ and the Question of Provenance

The question of possible antecedents for the image of a pre-existent Christ that we find in John 1:1-2, Col 1:17, and Phil 2:7, is a difficult one. Notions of a being other than the one and only God existing in the heavens before becoming human are for the most part foreign to Jewish tradition. It seems clear that the idea of such expressions of divinity must be located in the non-Jewish traditions in the Hellenistic world that have been incorporated into Jewish thought. One obvious example of this integration of Hellenistic ideas with Jewish thought is found in Hellenistic Jewish wisdom speculation[21] as this is the only location in Jewish literature where one dares discuss any other divine entities occupying the same dimension, the same celestial area as the Lord.[22] In addition, the image world of Hellenistic Jewish wisdom speculation would seem to be the best place to find comparisons between Hellenistic Jewish wisdom, *Sophia*, and the Greek philosophical concept of the *Logos.*[23] As we have previously discussed in our first chapter, the middle of the last century saw the abandonment of the theory of

---

The Letter to the Colossians, (Minneapollis, Minn.: Augsburg Publishing House, 1976), p. 71. The minority position that the phrase "firstborn of creation" refers rank rather than to any pre-existence is exemplified by Markus Barth and Helmut Blanke, *Colossians,* (New York: Doubleday, 1994), p. 247ff, and Marianne Maye Thompson, *Colossians and Philemon,* (Grand Rapids, MI: Eerdmans, 2005), pp. 31-32.

[21] Thomas H. Tobin, "The Prologue of John and Hellenistic Jewish Speculation," *Catholic Biblical Quarterly,* vol. 52, no. 2, April 1990, p. 256.

[22] It is this notion of a divine entity in existence in some way along side God which distances John 1.1-2 from any exact parallels with the account of creation found in Genesis 1. Although the author of the prologue is clearly making some connection to the creation account, he quickly adds to the complexity of the image through the introduction of the *Logos.* Although the majority of modern commentators see more connections to Greek philosophy as interpreted through the lens of Hellenistic Judaism than to O.T. parallels in John 1.1-2, others such as David J. McLeod, "The Eternality and Deity of the Word: John 1:1-2," *Biblioteca Sacra,* 160, January-March 2003, pp. 48-64, seem to find very little in John 1 which can be linked to Greek philosophical systems.

[23] Sanders, *Christological Hymns,* p. 70-74, cites Dieter Georgi, "Der vorpaulinische Hymnus Phil. 2.6-11, *Zeit und Geschichte. Dankesgabe an Rudolf Bultmann zum 80. Geburstag,* pp. 263-93, who sees the figure of the Righteous One in Wisdom as being influenced by the Servant Song of Isaiah 52.12. This hybrid Righteous One/Wisdom character which Georgi sees as behind the image of Christ in Phil 2.6-11 is portrayed as a servant who assumes human form, suffers and is eventually exalted. As Georgi notes, however, ideas about pre-existence are ascribed to Wisdom

the "Gnostic Redeemer" myth as the sole basis for these images of the pre-existent Christ.[24]   Since that time commentators have looked primarily at Hellenistic Jewish wisdom speculation as the main source for the images of the pre-existent Christ that we find in the hymnic fragments under investigation.[25] Yet, before we too posit a "one source" approach to the pre-existent images we see in the above examples, great care must be taken to differentiate the images. The pre-existent Christ that is portrayed in Philippians 2:6 is quite different from that of the Christ in the Johannine prologue and each in turn are different from Col 1:17, each portraying this pre-existence differently in Greek. The differences can be summarized in the following way: Phil 2:6 emphasizes the thought processes of Christ through the use of ἡγήσατο τὸ εἶναι and relegates his role prior to his own birth solely to the decision to become a mortal.   The image in John 1:1-2, by contrast, clearly emphasizes the pre-temporal/pre-creation aspects of Christ via the reference to the *Logos* and the use of the temporal marker of "εν ἀρχῇ," bringing with it as well possible allusions to the Book of Genesis. In a similar but not identical way, Colossians 1:17a uses a temporal marker, albeit a

---

herself in the Book of Wisdom and not the Righteous One making this parallel somewhat problematic.

[24] Lohmeyer, *Kyrios Jesus*, p.23ff went the farthest in linking the image of the pre-existent Christ in Phil 2:6 with pre-Christian redeemer imagery taken from, among other sources, the Iranian Gayōmart.

[25] Within the schools of thought that see Hellenistic Jewish thought as the source of the images of the pre-existent Christ in the hymnic fragments found in the New Testament there are two camps. The first sees Hellenistic speculation on Adam as the source for these pre-existent images. C. H. Dodd, *The Bible and the Greeks*, (London: Hodder and Stoughton, 1935 along with Jean Héring, 'Kyrios Anthropos,' *RPHR*, xvi (1936), pp. 196-209, were among the first to seriously entertain the idea that Hellenistic Jewish speculation on Adam may have formed the basis for the images in Phil 2:6ff. This speculation on Adam as the basis for the images in Philippians has continued in the work of W. D. Davies, *Paul and Rabbinic Judaism*, (London: SPCK Publishers, 1970). The second camp, and the one where the current author falls, sees Hellenistic Jewish speculation on Wisdom as the basis for the images. One of the first to put forth this position was Lorenz Dürr, *Die Wertung des göttlichen Wortes im Alten Testament und im Antiken Orient* as cited in Sanders, *New Testament Christological Hymns*, 43 ff. Although Dürr saw this development as naturally growing out of Old Testament literature and not influenced by Hellenistic philosophy, later authors, to be discussed below, nuanced Dürr's position precisely with this influence from Hellenistic philosophy, specifically philosophy as seen through the eyes of Hellenistic Jews.

different one, which places Christ "before all things"(πρὸ πάντων). Keeping these distinctions at the forefront, we must now look at the specific language whereby wisdom was described in the works that may have formed the basis for the images of the pre-existent Christ that we see in the New Testament.

Proverbs 8:23-24, 30b-31[26]

The images of the pre-existent power somehow distinct from God no doubt have their origin at least in part in similar speculations contained in Proverbs 8:23-24, 30-31.[27] This image of Wisdom in Prov 8, as well as a similar depiction in Sirach 24, sees Wisdom as somehow active with God in a period prior to the creative acts of the Lord. Both depict this pre-existence similarly, however, the depiction in Proverbs offers us up a bit more detail concerning the "persona" of Wisdom, looking on as creation takes place.[28] It is necessary here to examine the language used to describe Divine Wisdom in the Book of Proverbs, because this image is really starting point for all subsequent images.

Prov 8:23-24

מֵעוֹלָם , נִסַּכְתִּי מֵרֹאשׁ-- מִקַּדְמֵי-אָרֶץ

בְּאֵין-תְּהֹמוֹת חוֹלָלְתִּי ; בְּאֵין

מַעְיָנוֹת , נִכְבַּדֵּי-מָיִם .

In the distant past I was fashioned, at the beginning, at the origin of the earth. There was still no deep water when I was brought forth, no springs rich in water.[29]

πρὸ τοῦ αἰῶνος ἐθεμελίωσέ με,
ἐν ἀρχῇ πρὸ τοῦ τὴν γῆν ποιῆσαι, καὶ πρὸ τοῦ τὰς ἀβύσσους ποιῆσαι, πρὸ τοῦ προελθεῖν τὰς πηγὰς τῶν ὑδάτων.

---

[26] The Greek is given in addition to the original Hebrew at this juncture to help draw out any parallels that later authors, making use of the LXX, may have incorporated into their works.
[27] Gerard Rochais, "La formation du prologue," *Science et Esprit*, 37 My-S 1985, p.173-82
[28] Werner Kelber, "The Birth of the Beginning: John 1: 1-18," *Semeia* no 52 1990, p 121-144.
[29] English translation from the Jewish Publication Society,Tanakh Translation.

*He established me before time was in the beginning, before he made the
earth: Even before he made the depths; before the fountains of water
came forth.[30].*

Prov 8:30b-31[31]

וָאֶהְיֶה אֶצְלוֹ , אָמוֹן : וָאֶהְיֶה שַׁעֲשֻׁעִים ,
יוֹם יוֹם; מְשַׂחֶקֶת לְפָנָיו בְּכָל-עֵת.
מְשַׂחֶקֶת , בְּתֵבֵל אַרְצוֹ; וְשַׁעֲשֻׁעַי , אֶת-בְּנֵי
אָדָם.

*I was with him as his confidant, a source of delight every day, rejoicing
before him at all times, rejoicing in his inhabited world, finding delight
with mankind.*

...ἤμην παρ᾽ αὐτῷ ἁρμόζουσα.
ἐγὼ ἤμην ᾗ προσέχαιρε. καθ᾽ ἡμέραν, δὲ εὐφραινόμην ἐν προσώπῳ
αὐτοῦ ἐν παντὶ καιρῷ, ὅτι ἐνευφραίνετο τὴν
οἰκουμένην συντελέσας,καὶ ἐνευφραίνετο ἐν υἱοῖς ἀνθρώπων

*I was by him, suiting myself to him, I was that wherein he took delight;
and daily I rejoiced in his presence continually. For he rejoiced when he
had completed the world, and rejoiced among the children of men.[32]*

Proverbs uses the same wording as Genesis, and in turn John 1:1, in
describing the time period in which Wisdom is active with the Lord, i.e. in the
beginning (בְּרֵאשִׁית / ἐν ἀρχῇ) a period clearly before any acts of creation,
before the creation of the earth itself. In the speech given by personified Wisdom

[30] English translation from Sir Lancelot C. L. Brenton, *The Septuagint with Apocrypha: Greek and
English*, (Peabody, Mass.: Hendrickson, 1986).
[31] The MT differs here versus the LXX in regards to verse numbers. The all important line
discussing Wisdom as either "artificer" or "nurseling" occurs in verse 30 in the MT and at the end
of verse 29 in the LXX. I have maintained the verse numbering of the MT.
[32] A full discussion of the various meanings attached to אָמוֹן/ἁρμόζουσα will be found
below in the section of Christ the Creator as well as in Appendix A.

it is clear that *Hokmah* is seen as feminine, delighting in creation and supplying the feminine force in a vivid way. *Hokmah* is feminine and thus Wisdom is invited to be seen as a feminine principle not giving all power to God. In Greek too, Sophia maintains the feminine and, in a similar way to Phil 2:6, we have the idea of a pre-existent relationship, although this time masculine, in place. Here we also have a clear indication that we are dealing with an entity which conducts thought processes, i.e. the act of delighting in and rejoicing in the culmination of God's creation lends something of a personality to this decidedly playful witness to the work of the Lord. Thus, like Philippians 2:6, we have a divine entity engaging in cognitive processes prior to existence. However, the character of Wisdom engages in this activity prior to all of creation whereas Jesus in Phil 2:6 engages his cognitive processes solely prior to his own creation.

Sirach 24:9a

A direct connection to Proverbs 8:23-24 and *Hokmah* is seen in Sirach's depiction of Divine Wisdom, *Sophia*:

Πρὸ τοῦ αἰῶνος ἀπ᾽ ἀρχῆς ἔκτισέ με...

Before all ages, in the beginning he created me...

As with Proverbs 8:23 in the LXX, ἀρχῆς is used to describe the period prior to creation in which Wisdom is active. Yet, here the depictions of Wisdom as somehow active in this state are far from clear.

In the case of Sir 24:9ff the actions of Wisdom are consigned to post-creation activity ("Over waves of the sea, over all the land, over every people and nation I held sway") leaving any activity she might have undertaken in the period prior to the creation of the world as conjecture. There are echoes of Prov 8 in Sir 24. Clearly we have the same subject matter of Divine Wisdom and the same first

---

[32] A full discussion of the various meanings attached to 1 אני/ἁρμοόζουσα will be found below in the section of Christ the Creator as well as in Appendix A.

person descriptions. Yet, the actions of Wisdom when she and God alone dwelled "in the vault of heaven" (Sir 24:5), are nowhere near as clear to the reader as they are in Prov 8.

These speculations among Jewish authors on the nature of Wisdom continue into the Hellenistic period. However, these depictions of Divine Wisdom appear to be accentuated at this time by the incorporation of the Greek philosophical concept of the *Logos* alongside Divine Wisdom. Hellenistic Jewish writers such as the author of *The Wisdom of Solomon* were the first Jewish writers to somehow equate the Greek idea of the *Logos,* the ordering principle of the universe often equated with Zeus, and *Sophia/Wisdom*[33]:

Θεὲ πατέρων καὶ Κύριε τοῦ ἐλέους,
ὁ ποιήσας τὰ πάντα ἐν λόγῳ σου, καὶ τῇ σοφίᾳ σου
κατεσκεύασας ἄνθρωπον.

God of my fathers, Lord of mercy, you who have made all things by your word, and in your wisdom have established man. (Wis. 9:1-2)

These integrations of Greek philosophical thought and traditional Jewish religious thought reach their fullest development amongst Jewish authors in the writings of Philo of Alexandria (20 B.C.E. – 50 C.E.), who sought primarily to interpret the Mosaic law in light of Middle Platonic philosophy in works such as *De confusione linguarum.*[34] In addition to such philosophical speculations Philo also examined the Greek concepts as virtue, most notably in *De virtutibus.* It is in his discussion on the virtue of courage in which he recounts the choice of Joshua by Moses to lead Israel where Philo extols the benefits of employing Divine

---

[33] This link will be further examined in the section on the image of Christ the Creator as well as in the final section on the image of Christ as a distinct divine entity.
[34] Thomas Tobin, "The Prologue of John and Hellenistic Jewish Speculation," *The Catholic Biblical Quarterly,* Vol. 52, No. 2, p. 256.

Wisdom in making such a decision.   In Moses' speech extolling Wisdom's

benefits we hear echoes of Proverbs 8[35]:

Σοφίαν δὲ πρεσβυτέραν οὐ μόνον τῆς ἐμῆς γενέσεως
ἀλλὰ καὶ τῆς τοῦ κόσμου παντὸς-οὖσαν
οὔτε θέμις οὔτε δυνατὸν ἄλλῳ τῳ κρίνειν ἀλλ᾽ ἢ τῷ θεῷ καὶ
τοῖς ἀδόλως καὶ καθαρῶς καὶ γνησίως αὐτῆς ἐρωσιν.[36]

*Now Wisdom's years are from of old, ere not only I, but the whole
universe was born. And it is not lawful or possible that any other should
judge her save God, and those who love her with a love that is guileless
and pure and genuine.[37]*

Philo, in *Legum allegoriae* explicitly links the character of *Sophia* with the

concept of the *Logos* in his discussion of the word river (ποταμός) in Genesis

2:10-14 as an allegory for virtue (ἀρετή):

αὔτη ἐκπορεύεται ἐκ τῆς ᾽Εδέμ, τῆς τοῦ θεοῦ σοφίας.
ἡ δέ ἐστιν θεοῦ λόγος.[38]

*This issues forth out of Eden, the wisdom of God, and this is the Reason of
God.*

Philo, like the author of Sirach, easily accommodated ideas surrounding

Hokmah, the Jewish concept of Divine Wisdom, alongside similar ideas from the

Greek *Sophia*. However, in addition to drawing upon Jewish concepts of *Hokmah*

as found in works such as Proverbs and Sirach, Philo also integrated the Greek

philosophical concept of the *Logos* into his discussions. Although the complexity

of the *Logos* as laid out by Philo is beyond the scope of this chapter,[39] we can

broadly describe it in the works of Philo as something which he sees as both an

---

[35] Jean LaPorte, "Philo in the Tradition of Wisdom," *Aspects of Wisdom in Judaism and Early Christianity,* Robert L. Wilken ed., (Notre Dame/London: University of Notre Dame Press, 1975), p. 114.
[36] Philo, *Virt.* 62.
[37] All quotes from Philo are taken from *The Loeb Classical Library,* G.P. Gould ed., (Cambridge: Harvard University Press, 1991).
[38] Philo, *Leg.* 1.165.

intermediary figure instrumental in the formation of the world and an intermediate metaphysical reality through which the universe was originally ordered.[40] The *Logos* in Hellenistic Jewish wisdom speculation combined aspects of Heavenly Wisdom with the Platonic idea of the thought of God which was perceived as the transcendent design of the universe.[41]

As we shall see subsequently, the language used to describe the images of an intermediate divine entity combining aspects both from traditional Jewish ideas of Divine Wisdom/*Hokmah* and the philosophical concept of the *Logos* that we see in Hellenistic Jewish wisdom speculation form one of the most probable backgrounds for both of the pre-incarnational images found in John 1:1 and Col 1:17a. and, to a lesser extent, the image found in Phil 2:6. With the exception of Phil 2:6, the other Christological hymns which describe a pre-existent Christ echo the language found in both Prov 8:23-24, 30b-31 and Sir 24:9. The New Testament authors, like the Hellenistic Jewish writers who preceded them, all seem to have drawn upon the same images taken from opening lines of Genesis, to describe the moments prior to creation in which Wisdom was active. Philo as well looks back to similar images of Wisdom, yet concentrates on the meaning of Jewish wisdom in relation to the Greek *Logos,* and does not speculate upon the actions of Divine Wisdom in that period prior to the creation of the world. In only one place do we find Philo referring to the pre-creative activities of Wisdom, and that is in his reference to Proverbs 8 that we find in *De ebrietate.* In his discussion of Genesis 9:20-29, Philo expounds upon how drunkenness may cause one to dishonor those around him, such as wife and mother:

εἰσάγεται γοῦν πρά τινι τῶν ἐκ τοῦ θείου χοροῦ ἡ
σοφία περὶ αὐτῆς λέγουσα τὸν
τρόπον τοῦτον "ὁ θεὸς ἐκτήσατό με

---

[39] How such as ideas as the Stoic *Logos* made their way into Hellenistic Jewish wisdom speculation will be discussed in Chapter 3.
[40] Tobin, "Prologue," p. 266.
[41] C. H. Dodd, *The Fourth Gospel,* (Cambridge: Cambridge University Press, 1963), p. 295.

ἐθεμελίωσέ με." ἦν γὰρ ἀναγκαῖον τῆς μητρὸς
καὶ τιθήνης τῶν ὅλων πάνθ᾽ ὅσα εἰς γένεσιν ἦλθεν
εἶναι νεώτερα.

Thus in the pages of one inspired company, wisdom is speaking of herself after this manner: "God represented as obtained me first of all his works and founded me before the ages." (Prov. 8:23) True, for it was necessary that all that came to the birth of creation should be younger than the mother and nurse of all.[42]

As with the previous examples from *De virtutibus* and *Legum allegoriae*, we see Philo referring to Wisdom but failing to expand upon her activities. It is clear that the relationship between Wisdom and Greek philosophical thought is of far more importance to Philo than speculations of Wisdom's activities with God prior to creation.

In one other place do we find Philo discussing a pre-existent entity in a manner analogous to what we find in the hymnic fragments under consideration, specifically as it applies to the image of the pre-existent Christ described in Phil 2:6. In *Leg* 2.4 Philo describes the "heavenly man" which he had previously contrasted to the "earthly man," Adam:

It is not good that any man should be alone. For there are two kinds of men, the one made after the image, and the one molded out of the earth. For the man made after the image it is not good to be alone, because he yearns (ἐφίεται) after the image. For the image of God is a pattern of which copies are made, and every copy longs after that which it is a copy, and its station is at its side.[43]

This example from Philo is important for several reasons. First, it shows that a Hellenistic Jewish author was comfortable in describing a celestial entity engaging in thought process, in this case the act of yearning (ἐφίεται), much in the same way the Wisdom herself engages in independent thought processes at the side of the Lord (Prov 8:30-31). Secondly, this passage from Philo shows that it

---

[42] Philo, *Ebr.* 8.31.
[43] Philo, *Leg.* 2.4

was not Hellenistic speculation on Adam which has the clearest parallel to what we see in the hymnic fragments under investigation but speculation upon the "heavenly man", the image of God, in that these speculations incorporate both pre-existence and a thinking entity similar to what we find in Prov 8:30-31.

It must be noted, however, that although the bulk of scholarship sees the closest parallels between Hellenistic Jewish wisdom speculation and descriptions of the pre-existent Christ in the hymnic fragments under investigation, the lines of influence are not terribly clear. One cannot draw a straight line from the Middle-Platonic discussions on the *Logos* found in Philo to the images of the pre-existent Christ under investigation. Or, to put it a little more specifically, one cannot only draw that line, as the *Logos* as a concept was not the sole property of Hellenized Jews in the first century. Granted, the language used to describe the time this pre-temporal divinity was active bears strong similarities to what we see in Proverbs, Sirach and the Wisdom of Solomon, and the functions of this entity, now designated as *Logos* in Philo, are very similar to what we see in our hymnic fragments. Nevertheless, we must be open to other voices from the Greek philosophical and mythic world, voices which we shall explore in our next chapter.

As we explained in the beginning of this section, the image of the pre-existent Christ is intimately tied to the image of Christ the Creator in many of our hymnic fragments. This is to be expected, for in both Hellenistic Jewish wisdom speculation and Greek discussions of the *Logos* it is precisely this pre-creation entity that is active, in some ambiguous way, in the creation and maintenance of the physical realm. We must now examine more closely the connection to creation that we find in our next core image, that of Christ the creator found in 1 Cor 8:6, John 1:3, Col 1:16-17, and Heb 1:3.

Christ the Creator

The image of Christ the Creator is the most prevalent image in our examination of the Christological hymns in the New Testament being found in four places, 1 Corinthians 8:6, John 1:3, Colossians 1:15-17 as well as in Hebrews 1:3. As with our discussion concerning the image of a pre-existent Christ, the image of Christ the creator is also intimately linked to similar ideas found in Hellenistic Wisdom speculation, most notably Wisdom 7:22-24, as well as in several of the works of Philo. However, Divine Wisdom as specifically a creative divine presence is an idea that entered into Jewish thought from elsewhere.

I have chosen to use the title "Christ the Creator" here out of simplicity, although in fact Christ's role relative to creation is decidedly ambiguous in most of the hymnic fragments under discussion below. He is at times the source of existence (1 Cor 8:6, John 1: 3,10), the being "in which" all things are created (Col 1:16) as well as the supporter of creation (Heb 1:3). That Christ has some role to play in creation is certain. What specifically this entails differs subtly in each hymn.

The Image Described: *1 Corinthians 8:6*

ἀλλ᾽ ἡμῖν εἷς θεὸς ὁ πατὴρ ἐξ οὗ τὰ πάντα
καὶ ἡμεῖς εἰς αὐτόν, καὶ εἰς
κύριος Ἰησοῦς Χριστὸς δι᾽ οὗ τὰ πάντα καὶ ἡμεῖς δι᾽ αὐτοῦ

Yet for us there is one God, the Father, from whom all things are and for whom we exist and one Lord, Jesus Christ, through whom all things are and through whom we exist.

The creative attributes of Christ are expressed somewhat indirectly[44] in this passage from the hymnic fragment in Corinthians through the use of parallel prepositions, used to describe the activity of both God and Christ. In the case of God, his creative activity is expressed via the preposition ἐξ (from) whereas in the case of Christ the author uses δία (through). Christ is taken as somehow

---

[44] Hans Conzelmann, *1 Corinthians,* (Philadelphia: Fortress Press, 1975), p. 145.

51

connected to all creation (πάντα) as a mediator[45] or agent.[46] The role of Christ in relation to creation is admittedly ambiguous because the particular actions of Christ relative to creation are left unclarified. All we can say from this hymnic fragment is that the One God is perceived by the author as the source for creation and the One Lord Jesus Christ, existing in a subordinate role to the One God, is also active in relation to creation in some undefined way. It is precisely this ambiguity which will allow us to draw parallels to both Jewish religious thought and Greek philosophical speculations subsequently.

The Image Described: *John 1:3, 10*

πάντα δι' αὐτοῦ ἐγένετο, καὶ χωρὶς αὐτοῦ ἐγένετο οὐδὲ ἕν

All things came to be through him and without him nothing came to be.

ἐν τῷ κόσμῳ ἦν, καὶ ὁ κόσμος δι' αὐτοῦ ἐγένετο, καὶ ὁ κόσμος αὐτὸν οὐκ ἔγνω.

He was in the world, and the world came to be through him, but the world did not know him.

As with 1 Cor 8:6, Christ's mediating role in creation is seen via the use of the same participial formations (δι' οὗ, δι' αὐτοῦ). However, in the case of John 1:3, 10 we have the presence of ἐγένετο in place of implied verbs. Whether this was used as a means of emphasizing the creative action of Christ or was simply a different way of saying what was implied in 1 Cor 8:6 is unclear. When one couples the use of ἐγένετο with the use of the *Logos* to describe Christ, there does seem to be a somewhat greater emphasis on the actions of Christ than we have seen previously.[47]

---

[45] Rudolph Bultmann, *The Theology of the New Testament*, (New York: Scribner, 1965), saw in this formula a combination of Christ's soteriological and cosmological roles, p. 30-35.
[46] Raymond F. Collins , *1 Corinthians,*(Collegeville: Liturgical Press, 1999), p. 315.
[47] Dodd accurately points out that the φῶς is formally the subject of v.10. I have adopted the first of Dodd's two ways of interpreting this passage, i.e. that φῶς can be seen as an aspect of the

The Image Described: *Colossians 1:16a,c, 17*

ὅτι ἐν αὐτῷ ἐκτίσθη τὰ πάντα ἐν τοῖς οὐρανοῖς καὶ ἐπὶ τῆς γ
ῆς...τὰ πάντα δι᾽ αὐτοῦ καὶ εἰς αὐτὸν ἔκτισται.

For in him were created all things in heaven and on earth; all things were created through him and for him.

καὶαὐτός ἐστιν πρὸ πάντων καὶ τὰ πάντα ἐν αὐτῷ συνέστηκεν.

He is before all things, and in him all things hold together.

Colossians 1.16a, c and v. 17 offer similar participial usages as those we have already seen in our first two examples.[48] We have again the in him/through him language (ἐν αὐτῷ/δι᾽ αὐτοῦ) and, like our example from John 1:3, 10 the use of a distinct verb to describe the action of Christ, namely that he acted somehow as mediator of God's creation (ἐκτίσθη, ἔκτισται). In addition, as with the example from John and 1 Corinthians, the entirety of the creative act is emphasized through the use of "all things" (τὰ πάντα). Yet, Colossians 1:17 goes a step further than our other examples in that it proceeds from the act of creation to the act of sustaining or holding together (συνέστηκεν) all things (τὰ πάντα).

The Image Described: Hebrews 1:3c

φέρων τε τα πάντα τῷ ῥήματι τῆς δυνάμεως αὐτοῦ

λόγος, and as such as referring to Christ. C. H. Dodd, *The Fourth Gospel*, (Cambridge: Cambridge University Press, 1953).

[48] Contemporary authors who have seen the link between Hellenistic Jewish Wisdom speculation and the Colossians hymn include L. Helyer, "Arius Revisted: The Firstborn over All Creation (Col. 1:15)," *JETS 31* (1988), p.161, Elisabeth Schüssler-Fiorenza, "Wisdom Mythology and the Christological Hymns of the New Testament," *Aspects of Wisdom in Judaism and Early Christianity* (ed. R.L. Wilken; Notre Dame: University of Notre Dame, 1975), p. 17-42, E. J. Schnabel, *Law and Wisdom from Ben Sira to Paul*, (WUNT: Tübingen: J.C.B. Mohr, 1985), pp. 252-253, T. E. Pollard, "Colossians 1:12-20: A Reconsideration," *NTS* 27 (July 1981), 575-575.

And who supports[49] all things through the word of his power.

Our final example describes Christ's role in a similar fashion as Colossians 1:17, although using somewhat different terminology. In the hymnic fragment under investigation the author describes Christ's post-creational activity[50] with a synonym of συνίστημι, φέρω. As with all previous examples, the subject of the sustaining/bearing refers to all creation (τὰ πάντα). In addition, the choice of ῥήματι (word, saying) differs from all previous examples in that the personified word or speech of God is not Christ, but the mode by which Christ sustains all creation.[51]

In summary then our hymnic fragments describe the image of Christ in three distinct ways. First, the authors emphasized the direct link of Christ to the creative act via the use of prepositions which solidify, if only somewhat ambiguously, Christ's role in the process (δι᾽ οὗ, δι᾽ αὐτοῦ, ἐν αὐτῷ, εἰς αὐτὸν). Second, the subject of Christ's creative actions are directed towards all of creation (τὰ πάντα, τὰ πάντα ἐν τοῖς οὐρανοῖς καὶ ἐπὶ τῆς γῆς). Finally, in our last two examples we see Christ referred to as one who holds together or supports this creation once it has been brought into existence (συνέστηκεν, φέρων) by God.

As with our previous image of the pre-existent Christ, the image of Christ the Creator that we find in the hymnic fragments of the New Testament can be shown to be borrowing many ideas from Hellenistic Jewish wisdom speculation which had long been in conversation with the philosophical traditions of the

---

[49] I have opted to differ from the NAB translation concerning φέρων so as to distinguish it from συνέστηκεν.

[50] As with the other hymnic fragments under investigation, where one decides to locate the end of prose and the beginning of a hymn is rather problematic, no more so than in the case of Hebrews 1.3. Although the general consensus is that the hymnic fragment starts at v.3 with the occurrence of the relative pronoun ὅν, it is far from certain that the fragment may have started with the first instance of the relative pronoun ("Whom he made heir of all things and through whom he created the universe..."). If indeed this is the case, Hebrews 1:2-4 would offer us still more evidence for the use of the metaphysics of prepositions in the hymnic fragments of the New Testament.

Greek speaking world. Two possible literary antecedents for the image of Christ the Creator present themselves, the image of Divine Wisdom in the Wisdom of Solomon as well the concept of the *Logos* in Greek philosophy. The literary development of both Divine Wisdom and the *Logos* in the centuries leading up to the time of the writing of the hymnic fragments under investigation will form the basis of our next chapter. Although we will be investigating in detail how Hellenistic philosophy was adopted by Hellenized Jews in the subsequent chapter, a few words need to be said about the language adopted by the authors of the hymnic fragments investigated above.

Christ the Creator and Language: Contemporary Parallels

Although we will be investigating the development in Greek philosophical thought in the Hellenistic period in the following chapter, a few words need to be said about the language adopted by the authors of the hymnic fragments investigated above. As has been shown, the prepositional usage in the Christological hymns under investigation bear a close affinity with similar usages found in both Middle Platonism as well as later Stoic philosophy. The first three images of Christ the Creator under investigation, 1 Cor 8:6, John 1:3, 10 and Col 1:16a,c, 17 all exhibit prepositional usage closest to what we see in Middle Platonic thought of the period where the phrase δι᾽ οὗ was often used to describe an intermediate figure through whom the world was formed.[52] This "metaphysics of prepositions" was prevalent in Middle Platonic discussions and was adopted by Hellenistic Jewish philosophy appearing numerous times in Philo but most clearly in his treatise *On The Cherubim.*:

πρὸς γὰρ τήν τινος γένεσιν πολλὰ δεῖ συνελθεῖν, τὸ ὑφ᾽ οὗ, τὸ ἐξ οὗ, τὸ δι οὗ, τὸ δι ὅ. καὶ ἔστι τὸ μεν ὑφ᾽ οὗ, τὸ αἴτιον, ἐξ οὗ δὲ ἡ ὕλη, δι οὗ δε τὸ ἐργαλεῖον, δι᾽ ὅ δὲ ἡ αἰτία.[53]

---

[51] Harold W. Attridge, *Hebrews,* (Philadelphia: Fortress Press, 1989), p. 45.
[52] Tobin, "Prologue", p. 259.
[53] *Cher.* 125-126.

For to bring anything into being needs all these conjointly, the "by which", the "from which," the "through which," the "for which," and the first of these is the cause, the second the material, the third the tool or instrument, and the fourth the end or object."

Clearly the creative aspect of this "metaphysics of prepositions" is at work in Philo, tied as it is to bringing things into "being." However, all of our hymns which exhibit this Middle Platonic predilection for the δι ού also link this usage to τὰ πάντα (the all) as the object, a common element in what we see in later Stoic thought. The one hymnic image that does not make use of the δι ού construction, Hebrews 1:3c, nevertheless makes full use of τὰ πάντα as the object of the sustaining power of Christ's word as well.

This connection between Stoic discussions of "the all" (τὰ πάντα) and the image of Christ the Creator has long been seen,[54] and has formed the basis for many of the debates concerning the philosophical underpinnings of the images contained in the Christological hymns. The evidence for this link is fairly strong, drawing upon both authors contemporary to the NT writings such as Seneca[55] as well as somewhat later followers of Stoicism such as Marcus Aurelius. Seneca, in describing the activities of God relates how "the highest and most powerful of beings, carries all things *(omnia)* on his shoulders."(*Epist. Moral.* 31:10).[56] Marcus Aurelius, writing in the latter half of the second century, employs a similar usage too in his use of "the all" [57] when he discusses the attributes of Nature[58]:

---

[54] Eduard Norden, *Agnostos Theos,* (Darmstadt: Wissenschaftlliche Buchgesellschaft, 1956), p. 249ff.
[55] Conzelmann, 1st *Corinthians,* p. 144.
[56] James Moffatt, *Hebrews,* (New York: Scribner's Sons, 1924), p. 7.
[57] In *Spec. Leg* 1.208 Philo speaks of "the all" but this usages bears only very tangentially upon the creative act :
ἡ δὲ εἰς μέλη τοῦ διανομὴ, ἤτοι ὡς ἓν τὰ πάντα ἢ ὅτι ἐξ ἑνός εἰς ἕν...
The division of the animal into its limbs indicates either that all things are one or that they come from one and return to one.
[58] Conzelmann, *1st Corinthians,* p. 144.

56

πᾶν μοι καρπός, ὃ φέρουσιν αἱ σαὶ ὧραι, ὦ φύσις. ἐκ σοῦ
πάντα, ἐν σοὶ πάντα, εἰς σὲ πάντα.

*All that thy season's bring, O Nature, is fruit for me! All things come from
thee, subsist in thee, go back to thee. (Medit. 4:23)*[59]

When we turn from the metaphysics of prepositions to the image of Christ
as the sustainer or bearer of creation, the general consensus is that these images
from Colossians and Hebrews[60] have extremely close parallels to Hellenistic
Jewish wisdom speculation,[61] although to be fair the evidence in favor of seeing
Wisdom as "sustainer" or "bearer" of creation in Hellenistic Jewish literature is a
bit paltry. Perhaps the best example we have of a similar usage occurs in Sir 43:26
where the word of the Lord is given the attribute of the sustainer of all creation:[62]

Δι' αὐτὸν εὐοδία τέλος αὐτοῦ, καὶ ἐν λόγῳ αὐτοῦ
σύγκειται πάντα.

Through him all things prosper, and by his word all things hold together.

We see a somewhat analogous usage in Philo where he describes the "the four
first principles and principalities from which the world has been framed
(συνέστεκεν)," (*Her.* 281), as well as in his interpretation of Ex. 17:6 where he
recounts how God "established (ἔστηκα) the being of all things."(*Somn. 1.241*),[63]
yet in both cases, no reference is made to Wisdom.

---

[59] For a complete list of modern commentators making the parallel to Stoicism see Anthony C.
Thiselton , *The First Epistle to the Corinthians*,(Grand Rapids: Eerdmans, 2000), p. 635.
[60] Thomas G. Smothers, "A Superior Model: Hebrews 1.1-4.13," *Review & Expositor* 82.3,
Summer 1985, p. 334.
[61] Attridge, *Hebrews*, p. 45, Dunn, *Christology*, p. 190 ff., William L. Lane, *Hebrews*, (Waco,
Texas: Word Books, 1991), p. 14, E. Lohse, *Colossians and Philippians*, p. 52, James Moffatt,
Hebrews,(Edinburgh: T&T Clark, 1924), p. 7, Sanders, *New Testament Christological Hymns*,
p.51.
[62] The lexical connections, however, are much stronger for the use of "sustains" (συνέστηκεν) in
Col. 1:17 than the similar usage of "bearing" (φέρων) that we find in Hebrews 1.3. Most modern
commentators have drawn their comparisons based upon the similar meanings as opposed to a
direct lexical connection.
[63] Attridge, *Hebrews*, p. 44, note. 124.

In conclusion, two distinct yet often related literary traditions seem to be influencing the description of Christ the Creator in our hymnic fragments, namely, the depictions of Divine Wisdom in Hellenistic Jewish wisdom writings like the Wisdom of Solomon and both Stoic and Middle Platonic philosophical thought. Yet, uncovering these two most probable literary sources for the images under discussion raises several more questions. First, in regard to Hellenistic Jewish wisdom speculation in the Wisdom of Solomon, how did the Jews arrive at a place where they were comfortable with discussions of a divine entity somehow distinct from God? Also, once this Divine Wisdom found her place in the literature in Proverbs and Sirach, how did the Jews then ascribe to her creative attributes? Secondly, Philo represents the end result of centuries of philosophical speculation, both Stoic and Middle Platonic. The "metaphysics of prepositions" that he used, and that we see in our hymnic fragments, were themselves the end result of centuries of philosophical speculation. Finally, the concept of the *Logos* that we see in our hymnic fragments also had a decidedly long literary history, one that has to be explored before we can even begin to appreciate its use in the hymnic fragments. Chapter three will attempt to answer these questions. For now we must turn to the final image under investigation, that of Christ the Incarnate Divinity.

The Image of Christ the Incarnate Divinity

In our first two images under consideration, that of the pre-existent Christ and that of Christ the Creator, we drew some initial parallels to the images of *Sophia/Hokmah* found in Hellenistic Wisdom speculation and Hellenistic philosophy. However, our final image of Christ the Incarnate Divinity is of a noticeably different character than the aforementioned images of the pre-existent Christ and Christ the Creator. In these first two images, the authors all dealt with Christ as in some manner existing with God, in the same celestial sphere as it were. Similar to the depictions of Divine Wisdom on which they were based, the descriptions of Christ in these hymnic fragments maintained what can only be described as a theological distance between that which is divine (One God, One Lord, Jesus Christ) and that which is the object of their activity, i.e. creation.

In the last set of images, that of Christ the Incarnate Divinity, the divide between celestial and earthly is breached, Christ is underscored as an individual being, a person. The chief manner in which this is undertaken in the Christological hymnic fragments under investigation is through incarnational language which we see most clearly in Phil 2:6-11, John 1:1-18 as well as one other hymnic fragment found in 1 Tim 3:16. The incarnational language in these hymnic fragments is the chief mode by which Christ is differentiated from God, and in doing so, is differentiated from being perfectly correlated with either Divine Wisdom/*Sophia* or the *Logos*. Whereas writers in the Hellenistic period could describe both Divine Wisdom/*Sophia* and the *Logos* as distinct from God, these entities were never described as a person. The introduction of a distinct divine entity taking human form ushers us into a world vastly removed from the world of Judaism.

The Image Described: Philippians 2:6a, 7b

ὃς ἐν μορφῇ θεοῦ ὑπάρχων...μορφὴν δούλου λαβων,
ἐν ὁμοιώματι ἀνθρώπον γενόμενος και σχήματι εὑρεθεὶς ὡς ἀνθρώπος

Who, though he was in the form of God...taking the form of a slave, coming in human likeness and found human in appearance.

There are two central terms in the above image, namely, the idea of Christ "taking the form of a slave" and "coming in human likeness." Each poses its own set of difficulties. Both phrases describe a transition from one state to the other, as witnessed by the choice of verbs λαβών (taking) and γενόμενος (becoming)- Christ cannot "take" the form of something unless he existed prior and cannot "become" man unless he existed in some non-human   state   before   the transformation. The manner by which this transformation is described is crucial to the investigation of where this terminology may have arisen. Similarly, the end result of this transformation, the form (μορφῇ) of a slave and the likeness (ὁμοιώματι) of man also are of paramount importance in understanding the background of the image being described here. Unfortunately, we have few parallels to guide us within the NT, as μορφή appears only here and in Mark 9:2 and 16:12, and only slightly more often in the LXX (Jdg 8:18, Jb 4:16, Is 44:13, Dn 3:19, Tob 1:13, Wis 18:1).[64] The term "in the likeness" (ὁμοιώματι) is likewise quite rare appearing only twice in the NT, 1 Cor 7:31 and Rom 8:3, and once in the LXX, Is 3:17.[65] Unlike our previous depictions of Christ in reference to the pre-existent divinity and Christ the creator, the depiction of Christ the incarnate divinity that we find in Phil 2:6a-7 seems to offer no easy parallels.

The Image Described: John 1:14

Καὶ ὁ λόγος σάρξ ἐγένετο κάι ἐσκήνωσεν ἐν ἡμῖν

And the word became flesh and made his dwelling among us.

The association of the word "flesh" (σάρξ) seems to have been associated with the incarnation from the earliest days of Christian theological expression as seen in Paul's frequent use of the word to describe both the lineage of Jesus, "descended from David according to the flesh (κατὰ σάρκα)", Rom 1:3, as well as the scandal of this occurrence "sending his own Son in the sinful flesh (ὁμοιώματι σαρκὸς)", Rom 8:3.[66] The use of the phrase here in the Johannine prologue evokes, as Rudolph Bultmann accurately pointed out, the language of mythology[67] to describe the moment of the incarnation. Although the second part of the verse steers the listener back into the comfortable world of the Old

---

[64] Peter Thomas O'Brien, *Commentary on the Philippians,* (Grand Rapids, MI: Eerdmans, 1991), p. 206.
[65] O'Brien, *Commentary on the Philippians,* p. 208
[66] Raymond Edward Brown, *The Gospel of John,* (New York: Doubleday, 2003), p. 31.

Testament through its use of σκηνόω, evoking images of the tent of meeting,[68] this first image of the *Logos* taking the form of a lowly human also deviates from the previously examined images we have associated with Hellenistic wisdom speculation. As with the above image, we are also dealing with something that is decidedly transformational, i.e., the *Logos* is becoming (ἐγένετο) flesh (σάρξ), similarly implying that we are witnessing the movement from one state to another. Although we have the above two instances in Paul where Christ is in the flesh, we do not find instances within either the NT or OT which similarly describe the *transition* to flesh.

The Image Described: 1 Timothy 3:16a

> Ὅς ἐφανερώθη ἐν σαρκί...

> *Who was manifested in the flesh...*

The most difficult aspect of 1 Timothy 3:16a is determining whether the phrase speaks of the incarnation of Christ or the resurrection of Christ. This is made even more difficult, when this particular hymnic fragment is described by many as the heart of the "Christology of the Pastorals" [69] thereby raising the theological stakes considerably. Good arguments have been presented on each side of the debate.[70] However, when one accepts the poetic character of the hymn, i.e. accepts that the hymnic fragment need not be a *chronological* list of the facts of salvation, the idea that the phrase refers to the incarnation makes the most sense. The chief argument in favor of this interpretation is that the phrase "manifested in the flesh" appears to be a parallel to the following verse

---

[67] Rudolph Bultmann, *The Gospel of John,* (Philadelphia: Westminster Press, 1971), p. 61.

[68] George Raymond Beasley-Murray, *John,* (Waco, Texas: Word Books, 1987), p. 14.

[69] Luke Timothy Johnson, *The First and Second Letters to Timothy,* (New York: Doubleday, 2001), p. 232

[70] Raymond F. Collins, *I and II Timothy and Titus,* (Louisville: Westminster John Knox Press, 2002), p. 109 for arguments in favor of the phrase referring to the Resurrection. A more recent article which defends the incarnational language of the hymn: David J. McLeod, "Christology in Six Lines: An Exposition of 1 Timothy 3.16", *Biblica Sacra* 159 (July-September 2002), p. 339.

"vindicated in the Spirit," which can only refer to the resurrected Christ. Thus, unless our author chose to present two verses back to back which describe the resurrection, our first verse must speak to some other event in the life of Christ, namely the incarnation.

Once we have accepted the phrase "who was manifested in the flesh" (Ὃς ἐφανερώθη ἐν σαρκί) as referring to the incarnation of Christ, we can more clearly see the parallels with our previous image, specifically in the use of "flesh" (σάρξ) to again emphasize the humanity of Jesus. As we also saw in the image from John, Christ is undergoing a transition from one state of being to another as exemplified by the use of "was manifested" (ἐφανερώθη), similar to the use of "became" (ἐγένετο) in John 1:14.

The Image of Christ the Incarnate Divinity and the Question of Provenance

Unlike our previous discussions concerning the provenance of the images of the pre-existent Christ and Christ the Creator, there is no consensus among biblical scholars as to the best place to look for literary antecedents. Although the images of the pre-existent Christ and Christ the Creator fit comfortably into Hellenistic Jewish thought, the image of Christ the Incarnate Divinity does not. Thus, the general consensus among New Testament scholars concerning the literary antecedents of the first two images evaporates when we examine the third. When one examines Hellenistic Jewish literature for probable antecedents to the images we find in the New Testament of Christ Incarnate, nothing seems to be an exact, or even a very close parallel, to the images of the divine Christ taking human form that we see here. Our examination of the current state of the question concerning provenance, therefore, leaves us with more questions than answers. In order to make the cacophony of competing voices a bit more orderly, we shall look at each image individually and lay out the various theories as to where the images of Christ the Incarnate Divinity may have originated.

Philippians 2:6a, 7b

The first troublesome image in Philippians 2:6a is that of Christ, "being in the form of God" (ὃς ἐν μορφῇ θεοῦ ὑπάρχων). This image is notoriously difficult to understand owing in no small extent to the failure by many commentators to take the entire phrase into account, i.e. choosing to concentrate upon the etymological aspects of either μορφῇ θεοῦ or ὑπάρχων.[71] Thus, when one consults the secondary literature the majority of commentaries isolate one aspect of the image in their exegesis. Peter T. O'Brien lists the five current lines of debate concerning the possible meaning of the phrase ἐν μορφῇ θεοῦ.[72] What is notable about these respective theories outlined below is that none have managed to examine the entirety of the phrase. The first theory holds that the author of the hymn could have been drawing upon the language of Greek philosophy, namely the works of Aristotle in his numerous discussions on μορφή.[73] However, little evidence has been martialled in favor of this position first espoused by Lightfoot.[74] A second position holds that μορφή could be understood as a synonym for δόξα, thereby linking Phil 2:6a with numerous OT texts. This position as well has attracted criticism, owing to, among other things, the problem with interpreting μορφή to mean "glory" in the subsequent usage of the word in 7b, "taking the form of a slave," which seems quite improbable. A third interpretation, popularized by Käsemann, reads the phrase of "in the form of God" against the backdrop of the Gnostic myth of the "heavenly-man" as exhibited in the *Sibylline Oracles* and the *Corpus Hermeticum.*[75] As we have

---

[71] Connections between Hellenistic literature concerning gods taking various forms will be the subject of Ch. 4.
[72] O'Brien, Peter T., *The Epistle to the Philippians*, (Grand Rapids: Eerdmans, 1991), pp. 207-210.
[73] An examination of the Greek philosophical tradition in regards to μορφή will take place in chapter four.
[74] O'Brien, *The Epistle to the Philippians*, p. 207
[75] O'Brien, *Philippians*, p. 209.

discussed the improbability of the "Gnostic Redeemer" as the source for these images at length in our first chapter, this third interpretation also appears to be fairly improbable.

The fourth position recognizes the link between the phrase ἐν μορφῇ θεοῦ with similar images from the world of Hellenistic Judaism, namely speculations on the first man, Adam. This position, championed by Dunn and others, makes much of the parallels between the term μορφή and εἰκών. As this position and the one which will be discussed subsequently are the two major lines of debate in regards to the phrase ἐν μορφῇ θεοῦ found in Phil 2:6a, a brief word needs to be said about the origins of these respective arguments.

The idea that the author of Philippians 2:6-11 was drawing upon similar Adamic speculation in Hellenistic Jewish thought was developed in 1936 by Jean Héring,[76] who saw Philonic speculation on Adam to be the key to understanding Philippians 2:6a. The strength of this argument rests upon both the contemporaneous character of Philo's discussion of Genesis 2:7 in *Leg.* 1. 31, *Opif.* 134, as well as similar references to Adam in other Pauline letters such as Rom 5:12-17 and 1 Cor 15:20-49. The chief weakness to this position, however, is the fact that in the two texts normally cited from Philo in support of Adamic speculation μορφή is not used. Appeals to the synonymous nature of μορφή and εἰκών in the literature of the Hellenistic period, although strong especially in regard to the usage in the LXX, falter when one attempts to make sense of the somewhat opaque parallel phrase "the image of a slave" in Phil 2:7b. Simply put, if μορφή is to be seen as a cognate of εἰκών, and hence a direct reference to Genesis 2 as "image," then one must do the same with the subsequent reference of taking the form of a slave, reading it instead as taking the "image" of a slave. As the phrase "image of a slave" makes little sense, appeals to the use of "image" as a synonym for "form" in Philippians would appear to falter.

The final theory draws upon parallels between the phrase "form of God" and Hellenistic Jewish Wisdom speculation and has been championed by Dieter Georgi[77]. Georgi sees the figure of the Righteous One in Wisdom as being influenced by the Servant Song of Isaiah 52:12. Thus, when one gives the attributes of this hybrid Righteous One/Wisdom character to Christ, as Georgi believes the author of Phil 2:6-11 has done, we are left with a servant who assumes human form, suffers and is eventually exalted. As Georgi notes, however, ideas about pre-existence are ascribed to Wisdom herself in the Book of Wisdom and not the Righteous One in Isaiah 52:12, making all parallels to the figure of the Righteous One and Christ in Phil 2:6a highly problematic. Thus, each of the five reigning theories as to the provenance of the phrase "being in the form of God" is found lacking.

Argumentation on the provenance of this image has tended to fall along only three basic lines, namely, the Gnostic Redeemer of Gnosticism, the Suffering Servant of Isa 52-53 and the Righteous Sufferers of post-biblical Judaism exemplified in such works as *2 Maccabees* and *IV Ezra* and *The Similitudes of the Ethiopic Enoch.*[78] Only the last two possibilities need be examined here.

First, if we have accepted the basic tri-partite structure of the hymnic fragment found in Philippians, namely that it recounts pre-existent, incarnate and exalted states of Christ, this central panel of the triptych deals with the life of Christ, i.e. that time prior to Christ's death upon the cross, prior to his resurrection. This accepted structure, however, causes problems for anyone who would ascribe the image of Christ emptying himself and taking the form of a slave to Isaiah 53:12, for the surrender recounted in Isaiah clearly refer to the Servant's

---

[76] O'Brien, Philippians, p. 207ff.

[77] Dieter Georgi, "Der vorpaulinische Hymnus Phil. 2.6-11, pp. 263-293 as cited in Sanders, p. 70.

death and not to some incarnational moment. Thus, if the image of Phil 2:7 was based upon Isaiah 53:12 we would have a double recounting of Christ's death in 2:7a and 2:7b which greatly disturbs the parallelism. Arguments that this is an example of a parenthetical aside are not convincing.[79]

E. Schweizer has championed the belief that Phil 2:7b refers to the righteous sufferer of post-biblical Judaism,[80] noting the parallels with the Righteous Sufferers who endure torment only to be later exalted in such works as *2 Maccabees*, *IV Ezra* and *The Similitudes of the Ethiopic Enoch*. As G. Bornkamm has rightly pointed out, however, the suffering servant of these works exercised obedience during their lifetimes and not in any pre-existent state, as the hymn clearly suggests.[81] As with the image of Christ taking the form of God, this image as well defies any easy classification in terms of provenance.

John 1:14

The search for the provenance of the image of Christ the divine in John 1:14 has a long and distinguished lineage. Augustine, after reading the Platonists and neo-Platonists of which he was so fond of, found many parallels with the Johannine prologue yet remarked, "that the Word was made flesh, and dwelt among us, I read not there." (*Confessions* 9:13-14).[82] Other philosophical schools in the Hellenistic period which dealt in the concept of the *Logos,* also failed to provide anything close to the incarnation.[83] Indeed, even if we posit a proto-Gnostic movement at the time of the writing of the Johannine prologue, a dicey proposition, they too would have recoiled at the thought of the *Logos* becoming flesh.

[78] Sanders, p. 62
[79] O' Brien, *Philippians,* p. 220, n. 98.
[80] Sanders, *New Testament Christological Hymns,* p. 61ff.
[81] Bornkamm, *Studien,* p. 181-182 as cited in O'Brien, p. 221-222.
[82] Beasley-Murray, *John,* p.6.
[83] Brown, *The Gospel of John,* p. 22.

After exhausting parallels with the major Hellenistic philosophical movements, we naturally must turn to the chief source of our other images, namely Hellenistic Jewish wisdom speculation. However, here too, we come up short for all our biblical sources (Proverbs, The Wisdom of Solomon, Sirach) and our mainstay Philo fail to provide us with any clear parallels. Hellenistic Jewish wisdom speculation goes a long way in providing a background for the incarnation of the *Logos* yet understandably never crosses that particular threshold.

Lorenz Dürr was one of the first exegetes to see this image in John 1:14 as the end process of the hypostatization of the *Logos* that began in Genesis 1 and continued through Proverbs, Isaiah and the Wisdom of Solomon.[84] At each step in the process, *Hokmah/Sophia* takes on more and more characteristics of a separate divine entity (the ability to go out and return, Is 55:10ff, the ability to dwell, walk, be begotten, Prov. 8, the ability to accomplish the will of God, Wisdom 14,16, 18.)[85] Yet, in each example, the full hypostatization or incarnation of the *Logos* does not occur. Philo as well stops short of the full hypostatization of the *Logos*. There seems to be an intermediary step in Philo's thought whereby those not ready to be called "sons of God" may first be called sons of the *Logos*,[86] but no direct incarnation of the *Logos* seems to be implied. In addition, in John 1:14 the *Logos* takes on human form and becomes an individual where in Philo the nomenclature of "sons of God" or "sons of the logos" is decidedly communal. In short, there is a specificity attached to the *Logos* in John, a distillation into one incarnate entity, that is noticeably absent from Philo.

1 Timothy 3:16a

Few commentators have posited a provenance for the image of the divine incarnate Christ that we see in 1 Timothy 3:16a, seeing this hymnic fragment as

---

[84] Sanders, *Christological Hymns*, p. 49-50.
[85] Sanders, *Christological Hymns*, p. 48
[86] Philo, *Conf.* 40-41, 62-63, 146-147.

stemming from early Christian kerygma in which the fundamental story of Jesus was proclaimed, and leaving the discussion there.[87] Many see the language employed in this image to be influenced not by sources from Hellenistic Jewish Wisdom speculation or Hellenistic philosophy, but by the Pauline corpus.[88] Others concentrate on the image of the exalted Christ and see his incarnation as simply a precursor to this later exaltation.[89] As with our other examples, the image of Christ the Incarnate Divinity being manifested in the flesh seems to have few antecedents.

Conclusion

As the above discussion has shown, the first two images under consideration, that of the pre-existent Christ and Christ the Creator, seem to be stemming from often intertwined thought worlds of Hellenistic Jewish wisdom speculation and Hellenistic philosophy, of both the Stoic and Middle Platonic variety. Yet, comparisons to either Hellenistic Jewish wisdom speculation or Greek philosophical thought in the Hellenistic period fall short when we examine the third and perhaps overriding image of the Christological hymns, that of Christ the Incarnate Divine. This images had to have originated in the one area where such images dominated the hymnic landscape, namely, Greco-Roman religion and literature which celebrated the incarnation of divine beings, albeit in forms in addition to human ones. The religious literature of the Greco-Roman world will offer up numerous parallels to what we see in our hymnic fragments which deal with Christ the Incarnate Divinity. However, these parallels which we will examine in our fourth chapter will only take us so far as an incarnate god is one thing, the incarnate *Logos* is something all together different.

---

[87] L. Ann Jervis, "Paul the Poet in First Timothy 1:11-17, 2:3b-7; 3.14-16," *Catholic Biblical Quarterly* 61.4 (Oct 1999), notes "this hymn is based on the fundamental story of Jesus", p. 711.
[88] Collins, *I and II Timothy*, p. 108, Johnson, *The First and Second Letters to Timothy*, 222ff.
[89] Martin Dibelius, Hans Conzelmann trans. , *The Pastoral Epistles*, (Philadelphia: Fortress Press, 1972), p. 62-63, Joachim Jeremias *Die Briefe an Timotheus und Titus* (NTD, 9) (Göttingen, 1947), p. 21 as cited in Sanders, p. 94

However, before we examine how incarnate divine entities may have made their way into Christian hymnody from the pagan world we must first examine how the Jew's wall of monotheism was breached in the first place. We must explore how a people thoroughly comfortable with singing the praises of Yahweh and Yahweh alone incorporated another presence to first rejoice in the creation of the Lord (Proverbs, Sirach) and then eventually aid in the work of creation (Wisdom of Solomon). Some accommodation was reached with the polytheistic surrounding cultures to the extent that aspects of images, even troublesome ones like feminine divinities, infiltrated the sacred literature of the Jews. We must investigate these earlier examples of the theological appropriation of the religious images of one culture by another as it will illuminate what ultimately happens in the writing of the Christ hymns. Just as aspects of *Ma'at* and eventually Isis made their respective way into Jewish and later Hellenistic Jewish depictions of Divine Wisdom/*Sophia*, images akin to what we see in the myths of Apollo and Herakles similarly made their way into New Testament depictions of Christ in human form.

Chapter Three

Jewish Wisdom Speculation and the Christological Hymns

In the last chapter we examined the Christological hymnic fragments found in the New Testament as well as the general consensus views as to where the images contained in these fragments originated. In this chapter we will explore in greater detail how such images made their way into both the religious literature of the Jews as well as the philosophical literature of the Greeks. It is an investigation that necessitates taking two disparate, if occasionally parallel, paths. On one hand we will explore the origins of the Jewish concept of Wisdom, starting with the Book of Proverbs and working our way forwards through such books as Sirach and the Wisdom of Solomon, for the development of the character of Wisdom undoubtedly had a profound impact on the images of Christ we find in our hymnic fragments. On the other hand we will spend considerable time tracing the evolution of both Platonic and Middle Platonic tradition, specifically in regards to the development of the *Logos* in the centuries prior to the Christian era, for Middle Platonism, especially as it relates to cosmology, contributed a great deal to the images of Christ that we see in the New Testament hymnic fragments as well. This investigation is of paramount importance because it is only through an examination of the development of these parallel traditions, Wisdom and *Logos,* through the centuries that we can get a full appreciation for the form these images take in the New Testament.

In the first part of this chapter we will examine how the images of the pre-existent or pre-creation divinity existing alongside the monotheistic God of the Jews made its' way into Hellenistic Judaism. One would not naturally expect Jewish monotheism to reach such an easy accommodation with the tendrils of Hellenism ushered in by Alexander in so tender a theological spot as the basic

tenets of monotheism or the creation of the world but find it we do. This
accommodation, however, was not reached instantaneously when Alexander's
armies conquered the various cities throughout the Mediterranean region where
the Jews found themselves, for the inroads of other religious traditions had been
felt in Israel's religious literature before Alexander. The origins of Jewish
speculation on the feminine character of Wisdom are to be found in a work which,
even adopting the latest potential dating, existed several centuries prior to the
Hellenistic period, namely, the Book of Proverbs. It is in Proverbs where we first
see an ostensibly monotheistic Jewish author describe another entity alongside
Yahweh, Divine Wisdom. Although the exact functions of Divine Wisdom in
Proverbs are the subject of much debate, what is patently clear is that we are
dealing with an entity which is qualitatively different from God in the period both
directly prior to and during the actions of creation. The character of Divine
Wisdom in Proverbs forms the basis for subsequent characterizations of Wisdom
in all the other works. Sirach, who writes seemingly to counteract the separateness
of Divine Wisdom from God, draws upon the images found in Proverbs and
reinforces her identification with Torah. The Wisdom of Solomon, on the other
hand, greatly expands upon the imagery that we find in Proverbs, seeing Wisdom
as both "artificer" (Wis 7:22) as well as "all pervading" (Wis 7:24), ideas which
may have been derived from similar images in Isis theology.

The second part of this chapter will investigate the question of language,
specifically the language of Hellenistic philosophy, and the role it played in our
two core images under investigation, the pre-creative Christ and Christ the
Creator. This discussion will center upon two main lines of argument. First, we
shall argue that the parallels between the use of prepositions in Middle Platonic
philosophy and similar usage in the Christological hymnic fragments show a clear
link to Hellenistic Jewish wisdom speculation, specifically those examples that
we find in Philo of Alexandria. Second, also drawing upon Philo and other

Middle Platonists such as Alcinoous, we shall argue that discussion of the *Logos* that we find in these authors also show a strong connection to similar language found in the hymnic fragments under investigation.

I must be clear at the outset that the two streams of argumentation that I intend to pursue did not follow one another in anything even approximating historical sequence, i.e. the development of Divine Wisdom in the religious literature of the Jews did not give way to the more philosophic, Hellenistic speculation of Philo. There is, as can be expected in any such investigation that spans centuries, a considerable amount of overlap between the two. The inroads of Isis theology that influence the author of the Wisdom of Solomon, for example, may have already been influenced by both Stoic and Platonic philosophical discourse prior to being incorporated into that work. I have laid out my argumentation not to show any genetic relationships, but simply to lay out the general developments in these two bodies of literature and to trace to some extent the paths they took before being incorporated into the Christological hymnic fragments under discussion.

Origins of Divine Wisdom in the Book of Proverbs

We are first introduced to the character of Wisdom personified as a woman in Jewish literature in the eighth chapter of Proverbs. After she takes her stand at the approaches to the city gate she begins to instruct the men of Israel in her ways, assuring them that they will be rewarded for a sympathetic ear and an adherence to her dictates. As a means of demonstrating her credentials, Divine Wisdom embarks upon a speech in Prov 8:22ff in which she recounts her origins and her good standing with God:

> *The Lord begot me, the first-born of his ways, the forerunner of his prodigies of long ago; From before the ages He established me, in the beginning before He made the earth, And before He made the depths, before the fountains of waters came forth. Before the mountains were settled into place, before the hills, I was brought forth; While as yet the earth and the fields were not made, nor the first clods of the world. When*

he established the heavens I was there, when he marked out the vault over the face of the deep; When he made firm the skies above, when he fixed fast the foundations of the earth; When he set for the sea its limit, so that the waters should not transgress his command; I was by him growing up. I was before him every day, and I took delight before him at all times, for I took delight in the completion of mankind, and took delight in the sons of men.

(Wis 8:22-31)

There are two distinct difficulties when one engages in any discussion concerning the origins of the character of Divine Wisdom in the Book of Proverbs namely, the date of the work and, linked to this dating, the possible influences upon Proverbs from neighboring religions. For example, if one posits a very early date for Proverbs, say in the time of the Israelite monarchy, certain potential later religious influences, such as from the cults of Isis, are eliminated. The same goes for a later date, i.e. if we assume an early Hellenistic date for the composition of Proverbs appeals to Akkadian or Syro-Palestinian Canaanite influences become much less tenable.

Since the latter half of the nineteenth century there has been consensus among scholars that Proverbs 1-9 come from a later date than the remainder of the work and were most probably placed at the beginning of the earlier collection.[1] When this was done is a matter of considerable debate. P.W. Skehan saw the final shape of the whole of Proverbs coming together no earlier than the second century B.C.E, and bases this upon his observation that the chapters of the work are delineated by initial Hebrew consonants, whose use to separate material was not attested before the second century B.C.E.[2] Unfortunately, however, this only gives us an indication of the date of the final editing, and not the date of the collection which composed Prov 1-9. Attempts to date Prov 1-9 via thematic parallels to other works, most notably the books of Ezra and Nehemiah have also

---

[1] R. N. Whybray, *The Book of Proverbs: A Survey of Modern Study,* (New York: E.J. Brill, 1995), p. 62.
[2] Whybray, *Proverbs,* pp. 62-66.

proven unsuccessful.[3] The general consensus that has emerged in relation to Proverbs 1-9, and it is a shaky consensus indeed, is that it probably took shape at roughly the same time as the much of Israel's other sacred literature, namely, between 600 and 300 B.C.E.[4]

Echoes of Divine Wisdom in Other Religious Traditions

Deciphering the origins of the character of Divine Wisdom encountered in Proverbs is also one of the thornier problems in Old Testament scholarship, and poses even more problems than the problem of date. Why would a monotheistic religion such as Judaism produce a text in which there is a clear distinction between the one God and another divine entity, Divine Wisdom, existing alongside God at the time of creation? Numerous theories have been put forth about how this seemingly foreign idea of a female divine presence made their way into Judaism, but there is no consensus from the numerous competing theories. The field of potential influences stretches from pre-Israelite Syro-Palestinian deities like Astarte, to Akkadian sages and eventually to Egyptian Isis. Each of these theories, while creative, seems to lack the requisite evidence required for a firm connection to any of these divinities.

In the mid-twentieth century J. N. Albright posited a connection between Divine Wisdom and the Canaanite-Phoenician goddess *hokmót.*[5] This theory, however, has failed to gain many adherents because as of now we have no examples of Canaanite Wisdom literature.[6] One of the more recent proponents of the theory that Proverbs 1-9 owes its origins to a Syro-Palestinian goddess is Bernhard Lang.[7] Lang posited that early Israel worshipped a daughter of El,

[3] Clifford, Richard, J., *Proverbs,* (Louisville, KY: Westminster John Knox Press, 1999) pp. 3-5.
[4] Clifford, *Proverbs*, p. 6, Fox, p. 6, Scott, R.B.Y, *Proverbs,* New York: Doubleday, 1966, p. X, Whybray, R.N., *Proverbs*, p. 27-30, remains unconvinced of the post-exilic dating but posits no alternative.
[5] J. N. Albright, "Some Canaanite-Phoenician Sources of Hebrew Wisdom," *VT* Suppl. 3., 1955, pp. 16-25.
[6] Whybray, *Proverbs*, p. 18.
[7] Bernhard Lang, *Wisdom and the Book of Proverbs,* (New York : Pilgrim Press, 1986), p. 4-6

Astarte, as the patroness of its schools until the Yahweh alone movement forced a reading of her as a mere personification.[8] Unfortunately, Lang's theory is based upon scant archaeological evidence for the linking of Astarte with any school of Wisdom and a knowledge of Israelite education that we do not possess.[9] A third position is that of Richard Clifford who sees a connection between the Akkadian *ummānu,* the post flood sages and bringers of culture to the human race,[10] and the character of Divine Wisdom. Clifford's theory centers upon reading the word āmôn in Prov 8.30 as ummānu and then linking this to the Mesopotamian sages in the Armenian text of the *Babyloniaca* from Eusebius' *Chronicle* as well as the van Dijk list of kings from Uruk dated to 164 B.C.E in which the ummānu figure prominently.[11] The weakness of this theory is that one has to accept not only this vocalization but also the link to an Armenian text taken from Eusebius as well as to a text from the second century B.C.E., a position that seems highly tenuous.

Perhaps the best theory about the connection between the character of Divine Wisdom in Proverbs and another deity comes from C. Kayatz who did the most to establish a link to the Egyptian goddess of order, *Ma'at.*[12] The connections between Proverbs and Egyptian literature were first made with the publication of the *Teachings of Amenope* in 1923. This papyrus document dating from around 1100 BCE had been part of the British Museum collection since 1888 and contained instructions from a father to a son on such various topics as the forgiveness of debt and the proper treatment of elders. As such, *Amenope* was hailed as having a direct relationship to many aspects of the Book of Proverbs, most notably Prov 22:17-24:22.[13] This relationship to Egyptian literature was

---

[8] Clifford, *Proverbs*, p. 23.
[9] Whybray, *Proverbs*, p.45.
[10] Clifford, *Proverbs*, p. 99-101.
[11] Clifford, *Proverbs*, p. 25-26.
[12] C. Kayatz,, *Studien zu Proverbien 1-9: Eine Form-und Motivgeschichtliche Untersuchung unter Einbeziehung ägyptischen Vergleichsmaterial* (WMANT 22), Neukirchen-Vluyn: Neukirchener Verlag, 1966.
[13] Whybray, *Proverbs*, p.6.

expanded upon greatly by Kayatz who, taking her cues from *Amenope*, investigated further this connection to Egyptian instructional literature specifically as it related to the first nine chapters of the Book of Proverbs. Kayatz demonstrated that *Ma'at* is described very similarly to Divine Wisdom, namely as a child embraced by her father who "set her at his nose."[14] Such childlike depictions of *Ma'at* seem to be echoed in similar depictions of Divine Wisdom's origins, specifically her actions at the side of God ("I was with him as his confidant, a source of delight every day, rejoicing before him at all times, rejoicing in his inhabited world, finding delight with mankind," Prov 8:30-31). This parallel is made all the more stronger when one reads of precisely when *Ma'at* came down to men, namely "at the beginning of time as the right order of things.[15]" This can be compared to Prov 8:23-24 "From before the ages He established me, in the beginning before He made the earth, And before He made the depths, before the fountains of waters came forth." As with our other potential candidates, however, this connection to *Ma'at* is not without its' problems, not the least being that nowhere in the extant Egyptian literature do we have *Ma'at* giving a speech in the first person as we do in Prov 8. However, even if the form of the depiction of Wisdom, i.e. in first person speech, differs from the way in which *Ma'at* is described, third-person narrative, there seems to be at least some similarity between the two.

The most nuanced discussion concerning the provenance of the character of Divine Wisdom in Prov 8 comes from G. von Rad[16] and others,[17] who see

---

[14] Kayatz, *Studien zu Proverbien 1-9*, p. 76.

[15] H. Brunner, 'Agyptologie,' *Handbuch der Orientalistik*, Vol 1-2, p. 93, cited on p. 153 of G. Von Rad, *Wisdom in Israel*, Nashville: Abingdon Press, 1972.

[16] Gerhard Von Rad, *Wisdom in Israel*, (Nashville: Abingdon Press, 1972), p. 153.

[17] Michael V. Fox, *Proverbs 1-9*, New York: Doubleday, 2000, Roland Murphy, "Wisdom and Eros in Proverbs 1-9," *CBQ*, 50.4, 1988, pp. 600-603, Jane S. Webster, "Sophia: Engendering Wisdom in Proverbs, Ben Sira and the Wisdom of Solomon," *JSOT*, 43.1, Feb 1998, pp. 63-79, Gail Yee, "I Have Perfumed My Body with Myrrh: The Foreign Woman in Proverbs 1-9," *JSOT*, Feb 1989, pp. 53-68, Cecilia M. Deutch, *Lady Wisdom, Jesus and the Sages*, (Valley Forge, PA: Trinity Press International, 1996), pp. 9-41.

Divine Wisdom as primarily a literary construct, arising from the theological reflection of the author of Proverbs alone and not dependent upon whole-scale borrowing or direct influence from other religious traditions:

> "For in the process of transference of foreign ideas to the Hebrew thought-world, many of them have become completely different. What is described in Proverbs 8 as 'wisdom', as world order, can be compared only with difficulty with the Egyptian concept *Ma'at*. (Wisdom) has no divine status, nor is it a hypostasized attribute of Yahweh; it is, rather, something created by Yahweh and assigned to its proper function. Although it is clearly differentiated from the whole of creation, it is an entity which belongs in the world, event if it is the first of the works of creation, the creature above all creatures."[18]

Thus for von Rad and the others who see Divine Wisdom primarily as a literary construct, any borrowings from Egyptian *Ma'at* language have been integrated and completely sublimated to the primary literary aim of the author of Proverbs, namely, the firm belief in Wisdom as subordinate to God. Any divinity that may have been attached to *Ma'at* in the Egyptian religious context has been stripped away in this Jewish context. Although we would agree that appeals to linking the world order as represented by *Ma'at* to Divine Wisdom is tenuous, the fact remains that prior to the writing of Proverbs no separate divine presence in any form was described in Jewish scripture. That such a figure would show up in Proverbs, at the beginning of creation, in the guise of a female with childlike attributes, is too coincidental to allow for a complete dismissal of *Ma'at* as a source. The fact remains that whatever the author of Proverbs chose to do with the image of *Ma'at* it seems clear that there must be some connection, however faint, to this earlier female Egyptian divinity. What we cannot say incontrovertibly in regard to the image of Wisdom in Proverbs is whether she exhibited any creative function. It would seem that the bulk of the evidence

---

[18] Von Rad, *Wisdom,* p. 155.

points against her having any such role, however, the original Hebrew text is decidedly ambiguous.[19]

Divine Wisdom Domesticated in Sirach

The Wisdom of Ben Sira, Sirach or Ecclesiasticus (the Latin title which means "the ecclesial or church book"), although originally written in Hebrew, was put into its final Greek form around 180 BCE.[20] There is considerable debate about the extent of borrowing from Hellenistic sources. Authors such as T. Middendorp see roughly one hundred verses[21] in Sirach that shows the influence from outside sources. On the other side of the debate, J. T. Sanders takes a far more conservative view seeing only a handful of works that could have influenced Sirach, most notably *Theognis,*[22] a collection of some 1,400 lines of elegiac poetry some of which is concerned with Greek wisdom sayings. Although a good number of the parallels to Hellenistic literature found in Sirach seem to pertain more to collections of folk wisdom or descriptions of Egyptian divine kings,[23]there is general agreement that no convincing Hellenistic parallels exist in those sections pertaining to Divine Wisdom, specifically Sir 24.[24] Although Ben

---

[19] For a detailed discussion of the ambiguity of the Hebrew, Appendix A is provided.

[20] Unfortunately, none of the existing fragments of Sirach in Hebrew unearthed at Qumran, Masada or in Geniza contain chapter 24 of Sirach. Thus a direct comparison to the way Wisdom is depicted in Hebrew in Prov 8 is impossible. The fragments found at Qumran contain only Sir 6.14-31 (2Q18) and Sir 51.13-18 (11QPs^a). The Masada fragments contain a very partial Sir 39.27-44.17. The Geniza fragments, although containing the largest portion of Sirach (Sir 3.6-16, 4.23, 30, 31, 5.4-7, 9-13, 6.18-19, 28, 35, 7.1, 2, 4, 6, 17.20-21, 23-25, 18.31-19.3, 20.5-7, 13, 25.8, 13, 17-24, 26.1-2, 30.11-33.3, 32.12-33.18, 32.24-32.7, 35.22-38.27, 36.29-38.1, 37.19, 22, 24, 26, 39.15-51.30), also lack Sir 24 . For an overview of the finds at Qumran, Masada and Geniza see Alexander Di Lella, *The Hebrew Text of Sirach*, London, The Hague, Paris: Mouton & Co., 1966, Corrado Martone, "Ben Sira Manuscripts from Qumran and Masada," *The Book of Ben Sira in Modern Research: Proceedings of the First International Ben Sira Conference*, 28-31 July 1996, Pancratius C. Beentges, Ed., Yigael Yadin, *The Ben Sira Scroll from Masada* (Jerusalem: Israel Exploration Society, 1965), Patrick W. Skehan, *The Wisdom of Ben Sira,*(New York: Doubleday, 1987).

[21] Theophilus Middendorp, *Die Stellung Jesu Ben Siras zwischen Judentum und Hellenismus,* (Leiden: Brill, 1973), pp. 8-24.

[22] Jack T. Sanders, *Ben Sira and Demotic Wisdom*, Chico: Scholars Press, 1983, pp. 55-59.

[23] Sanders, *Demotic Wisdom*, p. 65.

[24] For a discussion of the position which sees Isis aretalogy behind Sir 24 see Middendorp, *Stellung*, p.20, Hans Conzelmann, "The Mother of Wisdom," *The Future of Our Religious Past,*

Sira has accentuated the role of Divine Wisdom by identifying her with Torah (Sir 19:17) and hence expanded upon the image that we found in Proverbs, in most other regards he has remained true to earlier characterizations. Divine Wisdom is clearly an entity that was created in a subordinate position to the Lord (Sir 1:7, 1:13). As with Prov 8, when Divine Wisdom is given center stage and allowed to give a speech the words she uses clearly echoes the earlier work:

> *Wisdom sings her own praises, before her own people she proclaims her glory; in the assembly of the Most High she opens her mouth, In the presence of his hosts she declares her worth: "From the mouth of the Most High I came forth, and mistlike covered the earth. In the highest heavens did I dwell, my throne on a pillar of cloud. The vault of heaven I compassed alone, through the deep abyss I wandered* (καὶ ἐν βάθει ἀβύσσων περιεπάτησα).
> *Over waves of the sea, over all the land, over every people I held sway. Among all these I sought a resting place; in whose inheritance should I abide? Then the Creator of all gave me his command, and he who formed me chose the spot for my tent, saying, 'In Jacob make your dwelling, in Israel your inheritance.' Before all ages in the beginning* (Πρὸ τοῦ αἰῶνος ἀπ᾽ ἀρχῆς) *he created me, and through all ages I shall not cease to be. In the holy tent I ministered before him, and in Zion I fixed my abode.* (Sir 24:1-10)

As with Prov 8:22-31, Divine Wisdom is clearly a heavenly entity which exists during the earliest moments of creation, here even being designated "before all ages" (Πρὸ τοῦ αἰῶνος). Yet, it is significant that in this section in which Sirach discusses Divine Wisdom, no creative acts are mentioned whatsoever, save for the genesis of Wisdom from the mouth of God. Any ideas the reader may have had concerning Divine Wisdom's role in creation are also clarified in Sirach, most notably in Sir 43 where the litany of God's creations are brought forth such as God's creation of the "orb of the sun" (Sir 43:2), "the rainbow" (Sir 43:11-12), "the quake of the mountains" (Sir 43:16), "his creatures" (Sir 43:26). Divine

(New York: Harper & Row, 1971). Sanders critique of this position is correct in that one cannot posit the first person speech of Wisdom in Sir 24 as non-Jewish by appealing to the "non-Jewish" character of the same speech in Prov 8.23ff.

Wisdom is never mentioned in this passage which instead is summed up with "It is the Lord who has made all things, and to those who fear him he gives wisdom." (Sir 43:35). It is clear that the author of Sirach does not entertain notions of another feminine divine entity having a role, however slight, in the creation of the world.

The Wisdom of Solomon

A later work, however, was not as tethered to the more conservative images of Divine Wisdom that we find in Sirach. This work reached beyond the confines of Jewish monotheism and colored its images of Divine Wisdom with similar ideas found in the decidedly non-Jewish cult of Isis. The work was the Wisdom of Solomon. From the time of Origin, Jerome and Augustine, Solomonic authorship of the Wisdom of Solomon has been questioned.[25] Today there is the almost universal consensus that Solomonic authorship is untenable, owing to the lack of an original Hebrew text as well as the preponderance of terms known only to Hellenistic philosophy which permeate the text. The Book of Wisdom or the Wisdom of Solomon was in all probability written in Alexexandria, Egypt, sometime between the second century B.C.E. and the first century C.E., although a more definitive date than that is impossible to come by.[26] The *terminus a quo* of 200 B.C.E. stems from the Wisdom of Solomon's use of the Greek translations of Isaiah, Job and Proverbs which were probably only available sometime after 200 B.C.E. The *terminus ante quem* is placed sometime in the first century C.E. owing to the use of the Wisdom of Solomon by several New Testament authors.[27] Two factors in particular point to the early Imperial period as the most probably time of composition. First, the description of the development of the ruler cult in Wis 14:16-20 best fits with the perceptions of the rule of Augustus, the first ruler of

[25] J. Alberto Soggin, *Introduction to the Old Testament,* London: SCM Publishers, 1989, p. 444.
[26] John M. G. Barclay, *Jews in the Mediterranean Diaspora: From Alexander to Trajan (323 BCE – 117 CE),* (Berkeley: University of California Press, 1996), p. 181, Daniel J. Harrington, *Invitation to the Apocrypha,* (Grand Rapids, MI: W.B. Eerdmans, 1999), p. 55-56.
[27] David Winston, *The Wisdom of Solomon,* (Garden City, NY: Doubleday, 1979), p. 22-23.

Egypt who exhibited his control from outside the country.[28]   Second, the author uses some thirty-five Greek words or phrases unattested before the first century C.E.[29]

John M. G. Barclay sees the predominant theme in the Wisdom of Solomon to be the social conflict and cultural antagonism between the Jews and non-Jews of Alexandria,[30]a position echoed by J. J. Collins.[31]   It was an attempt by the author to employ Hellenistic language and rhetoric in defense of the Jews of Alexandria who felt themselves surrounded by pagan influences which threatened their community.   However, unlike her depictions in Sirach, Divine Wisdom in the Wisdom of Solomon is never identified with the Torah or with the Jewish people.[32] The language used to describe her is far more universal in tone and owes much to both the Stoic *Logos*[33] discussions in Hellenistic philosophy as well as to depictions of Isis in Egyptian aretalogy to which we now turn.   She is subtly but significantly different from her previous manifestations in Proverbs where she was a child-like observer to the Lord's works ("I was by him growing up. I was before him every day, and I took delight before him at all times," Prov 8:30-31a) or as a distinct subordinate to the Lord ("he created me," Sir 24:9) linked to Torah ("All wisdom is fear of the lord, perfect wisdom is the fulfillment of the law." Sir 19:17).   The character of Divine Wisdom in the Wisdom of Solomon for the first time takes on an unambiguous role of artificer (τεχνίτις). It is not surprising that ideas from both Isis worship and Hellenistic philosophy found their way into the Wisdom of Solomon as Alexandria was both one of the

---

[28] John J. Collins, *Between Athens and Jerusalem,* (Grand Rapids, MI: W.B. Eerdmans, 2000), p. 195, W. O. E. Oesterley, *An Introduction to the Books of the Apocrypha,* (London: The Society for the Promotion of Christian Knowledge, 1935), p. 207, Winston, *Wisdom of Solomon,* p. 21-22.
[29] Winston, *Wisdom of Solomon,* p.23.
[30] Barclay, *Jews in the Mediterranean Diaspora,* p. 183.
[31] Collins, *Between Athens and Jerusalem,* p. 182 and *Jewish Wisdom in the Hellenistic Age,* (Louisville, KY: Westminster John Knox Press, 1997), p. 179.
[32] Barclay, *Jews in the Mediterranean,* p. 183.
[33] Collins, *Between Athens and Jerusalem,* p. 182.

chief places where Isis was worshipped in the century before the Christian era as well as the seat of Middle Platonic philosophy.[34]

The Image of Divine Wisdom in *The Wisdom of Solomon*

Two sets of images seem to permeate the descriptions of Divine Wisdom in the Wisdom of Solomon. The first set of images seem to be borrowing directly from images normally associated with the goddess Isis with the second owing much to Stoic and Middle Platonic philosophical concepts of wisdom. We shall first examine the images from Isis.

In the seventh chapter of the Wisdom of Solomon the author has Solomon sing the praises of Wisdom who, although clearly being directed by God, still has an impressive list of attributes herself:

> *For He is the guide of Wisdom and the director of the wise. For both we and our words are in his hand, as well as all prudence and knowledge of crafts. For he gave me sound knowledge of existing things, that I might know the organization of the universe* (εἰδέαι σύστασιν κόσμου) *and the force of its elements* (ἐνέργειαν στοιχείων) *the beginning and the end and the midpoint of times,*
> (ἀρχὴν καὶ τέλος καὶ μεσότετα χρόνων) *the changes in the sun's course* (τροπῶν ἀλλαγὰς) *and the variations of the seasons* (μεταβολὰς καιρῶν). *Cycles of years* (ἐνιαυτῶν κύκλους), *positions of the stars* ἀστέρων θέσεις) *natures of animals, tempers of beasts, powers of the winds and thoughts of men, uses of plants and virtues of roots-such things as are hidden I learned and such as are plain for Wisdom, the artificer of all taught me*
> ('Η γὰρ πάντων τεχνίτις ἐδίδαξε με σοφία.) (Wis 7.15b-22)
>
> *For Wisdom is mobile beyond all motion, and she penetrates and pervades through all things by reason of her purity.*
> (Πάσης γὰρ κινήσεως κινητικώτερον σοφία διήκει δὲ καὶ χωρεῖ διὰ πάντων διὰ τὴν καθρότηα)
> (Wis 7.24)

---

[34] John S. Kloppenborg, "Isis and Sophia in the Book of Wisdom," *Harvard Theological Review*, 75.1, p. 62.

*And she, who is one, can do all things, and renews everything while
herself perduring.*

(Διατείνει δὲ ἀπὸ πέρατος εἰς πέρας εὐρώστως καὶ διοικεῖ
τὰ πάντα χρηστῶς)

(Wis 7:27a)

John S. Kloppenborg, drawing chiefly upon the work of Richard
Rietzenstein,[35] W. L. Knox[36] and Burton L. Mack,[37] has isolated numerous
important parallels between the depictions of Divine Wisdom in the Book of
Wisdom and corresponding images in Isis theology. Both Divine Wisdom and
Isis are seen as protecting navigators, as consort of both God and King, and as a
divine agent by whom the king first attains kingship and rules.[38] Perhaps the most
striking parallel to Isis theology comes when specific creative actions are ascribed
to Divine Wisdom in the Wisdom of Solomon. We see here a significant
expansion of the creative role of Sophia who had been relegated to merely
observing God's creative acts (Prov 8:22-31) or who had been removed from the
creative process all together when the role of God the lone creator was
emphasized (Sir 43:1-35). However, in the Wisdom of Solomon Divine Wisdom
is ascribed specific roles, given specific actions, which she then teaches to
mankind - roles and creative functions which are paralleled in contemporary
inscriptions of Isis where she is described as creator, regulator of the cosmos,
controller of stars, crops and the weather.[39] We see a similar listing of attributes in
the numerous Isis aretalogies from the Hellenistic period, most notably in the 2nd
century inscription[40] at Kyme:[41]

---

[35] Richard Reitzenstein, *Zwei religionsgeschichtliche Fragen,* Strassburg: Trübner, 1901, pp. 104-112.

[36] W. L. Knox, "Divine Wisdom," *Journal of Theological Studies,* 38, 1937, pp. 230-237.

[37] Burton L. Mack, *Logos und Sophia,* (Göttingen: Vandenhoeck & Ruprecht, 1973).

[38] Kloppenborg, "Isis and Sophia," p. 70-74.

[39] Kloppenborg, "Isis and Sophia," p. 69.

[40] Greek text of Kyme inscription taken from Jan Bergman, *Ich Bin Isis: Studien Zum
Memphitischen Hintergrund Der Griechischen Isisaretalogien,* (Uppsala: Almqvist und Wiksell, 1969), p 301.

Ἐμοὶ Βουβαστος πόλις ὡ(ι)κοδομήθη.
Ἐγὼ ἐχώρισα γῆν ἀπ' οὐρανοῦ.
Ἐγὼ ἄστρων ὀδοὺς ἔδειξα.
Ἐγὼ ἡλίου καὶ σελήνη[ς] πορε(ί)αν συνεταξάμην.

For me the city of Babastis was built.
I divided the earth from heaven.
I showed the paths of the stars.
I ordered the course of the sun and the moon.[42]

In this inscription we see if not a direct mention of Isis' actions at creation at least an intimation that she was active in the phrase "Ἐγὼ ἐχώρισα γῆν ἀπ'οὐρανοῦ," an action which could not have been done at any other time. We also see cosmic powers assigned to her in her ordering of the celestial bodies (Ἐγὼ ἡλίου καὶ σελήνη[ς]

πορε(ί)αν συνεταξάμην). Latin authors as well could recount the many attributes of Isis. Apuleius of Madaura (123 C.E. – 180 C.E.) recounts her many attributes when the great goddess makes her speech prior to Lucius' transformation back into a human being:

"En adsum tuis commota, Luci, precibus, rerum naturae parens, elementorum omnium domina, saeculorum progenies initialis, summa numinum, regina manium, prima caelitum, deorum dearumque facies uniformis, quae caeli luminosa culmina, maris salubria flamina, inferum deplorata silentia nutibus meis dispenso; cuius numen unicum multiformi specie, ritu vario, nomine multiiugo totus venerator orbis.

[41] There is considerable debate as to whether the aretalogy to Isis at Kyme from the second century is indeed a copy of an older aretalogy from Memphis. A similar aretalogy related by Diodorus Siculus (*Library of History*, 1.27), which he places at Nysa in Arabia was in existence no later than 30 B.C.E., the death of Diodorus. It reads: " I am Isis, the queen of every land, she who was instructed of Hermes, and whatsoever laws I have established, these can no man make void. I am the eldest daughter of the youngest god Cronus. I am the wife and sister of the king Osiris. I am she who first discovered fruits for mankind; I am the mother of Horus the king. I am she who riseth in the star that is in the Constellation of the Dog; by me was the city of Bubastus built. Farewell, farewell, O Egypt that nurtured me."
[42] Frederick C. Grant, *Hellenistic Religions and the Age of Syncretism,* (Indianapolis: Bobbs-Merrill/Liberal Arts Press, 1953), p. 131.

"Behold, Lucius. moved by your prayer I have come, I the mother of the universe, mistress of all the elements, and first offspring of the ages; mightiest of deities, queen of the dead, and foremost of heavenly beings; my one person manifests the aspect of all gods and goddesses. With my nod I rule the starry nights of heaven, the health-giving breezes of the sea, and the plaintive silences of the underworld. My divinity is one, worshipped by all the world under different forms, with various rites, and by manifold names." [43]

Similarly to the way she is depicted in the inscription from Kyme, Isis governs the heavens, the elements, as well as natural bodies on the earth. Thus, in his recounting of the many attributes of Divine Wisdom, the author of the Wisdom of Solomon seems to be, if not borrowing directly from Isis theology, than at least quite familiar with it - one cannot look within the corpus of Jewish literature to find a similar listing of the attributes of a goddess. However, it is when one moves beyond the listing of attributes and examines the second set of images used by the author of the Wisdom of Solomon to describe the all pervasive nature of Divine Wisdom, that we begin to see Hellenistic philosophical influences at work in the text.

The Intersection of Hellenistic Philosophy and Religion

At the outset of this chapter was expressed a caution pertaining to the perceived genetic relationships between Hellenistic Jewish wisdom speculation and Greek philosophy. This was done, in part, because at times in the literary tradition the lines between both bodies of literature become somewhat blurred. However, this does not only happen with Hellenistic Jewish literature; the lines between philosophical and religious discourse among the Greeks as well were not so clearly drawn. This should not be terribly surprising as one of the most important aspects of Greek philosophy was the discussion of cosmology or how the powers in the heavens moved objects and people on our plain of existence.

---

[43] Apuleius, *Metamorphoses*, J. Arthur Hanson trans.,(Cambridge: Harvard University Press, 1989), XI, 5.

What we begin to see for the first time in the Wisdom of Solomon is a blending of Greek philosophical discourse with Hellenistic Jewish wisdom speculation, specifically as it pertains to the character of Divine Wisdom. It was a blending that had taken place already in Greek philosophical discourse on Isis, who seems to be the model upon which similar depictions of Divine Wisdom in the Wisdom of Solomon were based. This overlap between with Greek philosophical tradition is seen most readily in three locations in the Wisdom of Solomon where the creative functions of Divine Wisdom are described, Wis 7:22, 7:24 and Wis 8:1:

Ἡ γὰρ πάντων τεχνῖτις ἐδίδαξε με σοφία.

Wisdom, the artificer of all taught me. (Wis 7:22)

Πάσης γὰρ κινήσεως κινητικώτερον σοφία διήκει δὲ καὶ χωρ εῖ διὰ πάντων διὰ τὴν καθρότηα

For Wisdom is mobile beyond all motion and she penetrates and pervades through all things by reason of her purity. (Wis 7:24)

Διατείνει δὲ ἀπὸ πέρατος εἰς πέρας εὐρώστως καὶ διοικεῖ τὰ πάντα χρηστῶς

Indeed, she reaches from end to end and governs all things well.
(Wis 8:1).

What we see in the above depictions of the creative aspect of Divine Wisdom from the Wisdom of Solomon appears to be being drawn from Stoic philosophy. David Winston sees the closest parallels between Stoic philosophy and Divine Wisdom in similar depictions found in Stoic definitions of nature.[44] For the Stoics, the concept of nature, at least as defined by Zeno, was seen as "an artistically working fire (πῦρι τεχνικόν)."[45] Cicero saw the nature of the world,

---

[44] Winston, *The Wisdom of Solomon*, p.176, n. 22.
[45] Diogenes Laertius, *Lives of the Eminent Philosophers*, Zeno, 7.156.

as styled by Zeno, as not merely 'craftsmanlike' but actually 'a craftsman' (*artifex*).[46]

When we turn to the second two verses of the Wisdom of Solomon under investigation (Wis 7:24; 8:1) we also see images that have been drawn from the Stoic philosophical system. The idea of Divine Wisdom as one who penetrates and pervades (διήκει) all things (διὰ πάντων) is very close to what we find in Galen where for the Stoics[47] Nature is described as that which penetrates through all life (τὸ διῆκον διὰ πάντων πνεῦμα).[48]

The Middle Platonist Plutarch of Chaeronia (45 – 125 C.E.), writing roughly contemporaneous to the authors of the Christological hymnic fragments, offers us one of the closest parallels to the depiction of Divine Wisdom in the Wisdom of Solomon in his discussion of the doctrines surrounding the worship of Isis in *De Iside et Osiride*. Largely regarded as one of our best sources for Greco-Roman religious practices in Egypt,[49] Plutarch also gives us a view of Stoic cosmology specifically as it relates to Demeter:

'Αλλὰ ταῦτα μὲν ὅμοια τοῖς ὑπὸ τῶν Στωικῶν θεολογουμένος
ἐστί:καὶ γὰρ ἐκεῖνοι τὸ
μὲν γόνιμον πνεῦμα καὶ τρόφιμον Διόνυσον
εἶναι λέγουσι, τὸ πληκτικὸν δὲ καὶ διαιρετικόν 'Ηρκλέα, τὸ
δὲ δεκτικὸν "Αμμωνα,
Δήμητα δὲ καὶ Κόρην τό διὰ τῆς γῆς καὶ
τῶν καρπῶν διῆκον, Ποσειδῶνα δὲ τὸ διὰ τῆς θαλάττης.

The fact is that all this is somewhat like the doctrines promulgated by the Stoics about the gods; for they say that the creative and fostering spirit is Dionysis, the truculent and destructive is Herakles, the receptive is Ammon, that which pervades the Earth and its products is Demeter and

[46] Cicero, *De natura deorum*, 2.58, as cited in Winston, *Wisdom*, p. 176.
[47] Collins, J., *Jewish Wisdom in the Hellenistic Age*, pp. 197-198.
[48] *Stoicorum Veterum Fragmenta*, Joannes Arnim, trans. (Leipzig: Teubner, 1923), p. 137, as cited in Winston, *Wisdom*, p.182
[49] Daniel S. Richter, "Plutarch on Isis and Osiris: Text, Cult, and Cultural Appropriation," *Transactions of the American Philological Associations*, 131, 2001, p. 191.

the Daughter, and that which pervades the sea is Poseidon. (*De Iside et Osiride*, 367)

In his description of the gods worshipped in Egypt, Plutarch depicts both Demeter and Poseidon as pervading (διῆκον) their respective realms of influence, the earth and the sea, a depiction which is paralleled in the Wisdom of Solomon's depiction of Divine Wisdom in Wis 7:24 as somehow penetrating (διήκει) all things. The most direct parallel to Middle Platonic ideas occurs in Wis 7:25-26:

'Ατμὶς γάρ ἐστι τῆς τοῦ Θεοῦ δυνάμεως.
καὶ ἀπόρροια τῆς τοῦ
παντοκράτορος δόξης εἰλικρινής. διὰ τοῦτο οὐδὲν
μεμιαμμένον εἰς αὐτὴν παρεμπίπτει.
'Απαύγασμα γάρ ἐστι φωτὸς ἀιδίου, καὶ ἔσοπτρον ἀκηλίδωτον
τῆς τοῦ Θεοῦ ἐνεγείας, καὶ εἰκὼν τῆς ἀγαθότητος αὐτοῦ.

For she is the breath of the power of God, and a pure influence flowing from the glory of the Almighty: therefore can no defiled thing fall into her. For she is the brightness of the everlasting light, the unspotted mirror of the power of God, and the image of his goodness.

We see this Middle Platonic influence both in the idea that the God we are dealing with here is beyond this world[50] and the statement that Wisdom is the "brightness" of God, an idea also found in Philo.[51] Although the image of Wisdom as the "brightness" or "effulgence" of God is not encountered more than one place in the hymnic fragments under investigation (Heb 1:3), and hence does not play into our subsequent discussion, it is clear that influences from Middle Platonic thought are entering into depictions of Wisdom in the Wisdom of Solomon, depictions that will later be used by the Christian authors of the New Testament hymnic fragments.

---

[50] Collins, J., *Jewish Wisdom in the Hellenistic Age,* p. 199.
[51] Philo, *De Opif.* 146.

It is really only with the characterizations of Divine Wisdom in the Wisdom of Solomon that we see an unambiguous creative aspect. Unlike Proverbs and Sirach, who went through great pains to cement God's role as sole creator, the author of the Wisdom of Solomon began to entertain a diversification of the creative role normally relegated to God. This is not to say the author of the Wisdom of Solomon began to perceive of female divinities existing alongside the Lord, only that he was more open than previous interpreters of the tradition to give a feminine face to God's creative role. Until the writing of the Christological hymnic fragments found in the New Testament, the depictions of Divine Wisdom in the Book of Wisdom represented the high water mark for the sharing of celestial creative power.

We are left, therefore, with a depiction of Divine Wisdom in the Wisdom of Solomon which seems to be borrowing from both Isis aretalogies as well as Hellenistic philosophical discussions on the pervasiveness or penetrating power of nature and the gods which seems to have its clearest parallels in Stoic thought. In addition, the overall thrust of the Wisdom of Solomon's discussion of Wisdom seems to be concerned with that which is beyond the material. This emphasis seems to be pointing the way to ideas also found in Middle Platonism. Also, the list of attributes of the powers of Divine Wisdom that we see in Wis 7:15-22 have ready parallels in Isis theology. Thus, by the time of the writing of the Wisdom of Solomon (200 B.C.E. – 30 C.E.), Hellenistic philosophy had made inroads into Hellenistic Jewish ideas concerning *Sophia.*

The next logical step might be to examine our Christological hymnic fragments to discern similarities between this philosophical depiction of Divine Wisdom/*Sophia* and Christ. However, such a jump would be premature. In the previous few examples we have seen how both Stoic and Platonic philosophers described both nature and the gods, yet these few examples only illustrate those areas where these two philosophical schools used either nature or one of the gods to represent the creative force which pervades all things. However, philosophical discourse, especially that of the Middle Platonic philosophers, had by the time of the Hellenistic era shied away from designating either nature or one of the gods as the force behind the universe, opting instead to expand upon the creative functions of the *Logos*, a concept which had its genesis in both Stoic and Platonic thought. The language by which Middle Platonic philosophers conveyed descriptions of the *Logos*, the "metaphysics of prepositions," offers us perhaps our best parallels with what we see in the Christological hymnic fragments. The move to describe an all pervasive entity that we only begin to see in the depictions of Divine Wisdom in the Wisdom of Solomon changes with the influence of the Middle Platonic philosophers, specifically in their discussions of the *Logos*.

Middle Platonism and the Metaphysics of Prepositions

Before examining the basic tenets of Middle Platonic philosophy (80 B.C.E. – 220 C.E.), a few words need to be said about Platonism in general. Plato at his death (347 B.C.E.) left a body of work that would be mined by his students and detractors for centuries. We cannot, in the limited space provided, trace all aspects of both Platonic and Middle Platonic thought in the almost four centuries leading up to the Christian era. However, one aspect of this particular philosophical school must be examined more closely as it played a direct role in shaping the images which permeated the Christological hymnic fragments under investigation, namely, the physics of Middle Platonism and the language through which it was discussed, the metaphysics of prepositions.

Physics, for the Middle Platonists, encompassed not only the movement of bodies and the composition of the universe but was also intimately connected to cosmology or how one understood the divine. The language by which these celestial relationships were discussed, often described as the "metaphysics of prepositions," is of pivotal importance to our investigation since it offers us perhaps our clearest link to many of the Christological hymnic fragments which discuss both the Pre-existent Christ as well as Christ the Creator. The "metaphysics of prepositions was a manner of describing the relationships between, among other things God or Zeus and the *Logos*. The phrase "metaphysics of prepositions" was first used by Willy Theiler[52]and by it he meant the expression of metaphysical relationships by means of prepositional phrases. Before we examine these all important prepositions, we must briefly examine a few important aspects of Platonic and eventually Middle Platonic physics which bear upon our investigation.

As John Dillon has so aptly demonstrated in *The Middle Platonists*,[53]piecing together Platonic physics is a difficult affair, relying as it does on the limited and somewhat confusing material contained in the *Timaeus* as well as Plato's "unwritten doctrines" as passed on to us by later authors.[54] What we can surmise is that initially Plato saw the universe as being directed by the supreme principle, initially termed the Demiurge. However, after his death under Neopythagorean influence, this Demiurge was eventually subordinated to the totally transcendent first principle, with the Demiurge then seen as either the intellect (νοῦς) or the agent or *Logos* of the Supreme God.[55] The process by which this dichotomy became firmly established in Platonism and eventually Middle Platonism took several hundred years.

Xenocrates (396 – 314 B.C.) was one of the first philosophers to expand upon the dichotomy hinted at in Plato by differentiating between the Monad, the Supreme God or Zeus, and the Dyad, the ruler of the physical realm, known alternately as the Soul of the Universe or the Mother of the Gods.[56] Xenocrates

---

[52] Willy Theiler, *Die Vorbeitung des Neuplatonismus,* Berlin, 1930, p. 20, as quoted in John Dillon, *Alcinous: The Handbook of Platonism,* Oxford: Oxford University Press, 1993, p. 62.
[53] John Dillon, *The Middle Platonists: 80 B.C. to A.D. 220,* (Ithaca, NY: Cornell University Press, 1996), p.62ff.
[54] Dillon, *Middle Platonists,* p. 2, sees Aristotle's critique of Platonic physics, especially *Met.,* 16,987a29 ff., as illuminative.
[55] Dillon, The *Middle Platonists,* p.27.

was one of the first Platonists to assign gender to the supreme principle and the Demiurge/*Logos* with the unsurprising choice of male for the former and female for the latter.[57] Although it is not terribly clear what connection Xenocrates made between the supreme first principle and the Demiurge/*Logos,* i.e. he did not explain whether the Demiurge/*Logos* existed in a sympathetic or antithetical relationship to the supreme first principle, it is clear that at least by the beginning of the Hellenistic period, Platonic philosophy had developed a view of the cosmos in which two forces existed, one clearly in a subordinate position to the other.

With Eudorus of Alexandria (64 B.C.E. – 19 C.E.) we see further changes to Platonic metaphysics. The change was due mostly to the incorporation of Pythagorean ideas into what had already become, at least by the time of Eudorus, a Platonism which was already borrowing heavily from Stoicism. One of the main changes wrought by the incorporation of Pythagorean ideas into the Platonism of Eudorus was the postulation of a supreme, utterly transcendent first principle, which was also known as God, existing in a superior relationship to both the Monad and Dyad of earlier Platonic systems.[58] It was this development, the idea of a supreme first principle and hence the need for an intermediate being which was to prove so important for Philo of Alexandria as we shall see shortly.

Sometime in the first century B.C.E. as well we also begin to see the use of the aforementioned "metaphysics of prepositions."[59] This use of prepositional phrases, drawing upon Platonic and Aristotelian categories, was prominent in the works of Varro (116 B.C.E. – 27 B.C.E.), Aëtius (c.a. 100 C.E.) and most importantly Seneca (3 B.C.E. – 65 C.E.).[60] Although Seneca details Peripatetic,

---

[56] Dillon, *The Middle Platonists,* p. 25.
[57] Aëtius, in *Doxographi Graeci,* Hermann Diels, ed., 1958, Fr. 15, as cited in Dillon, *Middle Platonists,* p. 25.
[58] Dillon, The Middle Platonists, pp. 127-128.
[59] Theiler, *Die Vorbereitung,* pp. 29-31.

Stoic and Platonic usage of prepositions, it is specifically his discussion of Platonic usage of these prepositions which is the most illuminative. The most systematic and developed description is found in *Epistulae* 65 in which he describes the five causes of Plato:

> Accordingly, there are five causes, as Plato says: the material (id ex quo), the agent (*id a quo*), the make-up (*id in quo*), the model (*in ad quod*), and the end in view (*id propter quod*)...The agent (*faciens*) is God; the source (*id ex quo*), matter; the forms (*forma*), the shape and the arrangement of the visible world. The pattern (*exemplar*) is doubtless the model according to which (*ad quod*) God has made this great and most beautiful creation. The purpose is his object in so doing. Do you ask what God's purpose is? It is goodness.   (Seneca, *Ep.* 65.8-10)

Some Middle-Platonists modified these strict Platonic categories somewhat with the introduction of the preposition διά (through) to describe the instrument of agency or means. One in particular, Alcinous, writing some time in the first century,[61] makes use of διά in this way in his discussion of epistemiology:

> Therefore, as there is a faculty of judgment as well as an object of judgment, so too there is that which is the result of these, that which is called judgment itself. This should properly be called the criterion of judgment, although it is commonly referred to as the faculty of judgment. This criterion is twofold: first, it is that by which (τὸ ὑφ' οὗ) the object is judged, second it is that through which (τὸ δι' οὗ) the object is judged. The former is our mind, the latter is the instrument working through nature used in judging primarily things that are true and secondarily things that are false. The second is nothing other than that reasoning activity working through nature.
>
>   (Alcinous, *Didaskilikos*, IV, p. 154, 8ff)[62]

Thus by the time of the first century we had two ideas in Middle Platonic philosophy which are of utmost importance to our investigation, namely, the idea

---

[60] Thomas Tobin, *The Creation of Man: Philo and the Interpretation of History,* The Catholic Biblical Monograph Series, 14, (Washington: Catholic Biblical Association of America, 1983), p. 68

[61] Dillon, in his *Alcinous: The Handbook of Platonism,* breaks from his earlier identification of this work with Albinus, also writing in the first century, p. XI.

[62] As quoted in Tobin, *The Creation of Man,* p.68-69.

of a supreme first principle (and the corresponding intermediate reality) as well as the use of the preposition διά to designate the instrument of God in this intermediate reality. We see both of these at work in the writer that sheds much light on similar usage in our Christological hymnic fragments, Philo of Alexandria.

Philo of Alexandria and the *Logos*

Philo of Alexandria (10 B.C.E. – 50 C.E.) sought to do for Moses what other Middle Platonic philosophers, most notably Eudorus, had done for Pythagoras, namely, to push back the origins of philosophy to an ever more distant founder. For Philo, this led inevitably to Moses and the Pentateuch. Seeing what had already been done by the Stoics as well as the Middle Platonists in their allegorical interpretation of Homer, Philo sought to interpret the five books of Moses in the same fashion, attempting to demonstrate how Moses was a philosopher on a par with Plato, Socrates and Aristotle and that the writings of Moses, as represented by the Pentateuch, were replete with philosophical content.[63]

Two concepts seem to dominate Philo's metaphysics. First is the idea of identifying the supreme principle, alternately referred to as the One, the Monad, the Really Existent, with the God of the Jews. Second is the idea that the *Logos* acted as the instrument of God in the creation of the world, a *Logos* which is also referred to as the "through which" (τὸ δι᾽ οὗ).[64] Before we begin our examination of these two ideas in Philo, however, we must remember that the great Alexandrian author was not attempting to compose philosophical works, such as creating his own commentary on the *Timaeus* or attempting to put forth an original systematic treatise on the physics of Middle Platonism. His main focus was to interpret Jewish scripture through his own lens of Alexandrian Middle

---

[63] Dillon, *The Middle Platonists*, p. 143.
[64] Dillon, *The Middle Platonists*, p. 160.

Platonism. This is witnessed by the fact that twenty seven of his thirty three extant works deal with the Hebrew scriptures. In addition, Philo was writing during a period, the middle half of the first century of the common era, where rigid lines separating philosophical schools were not all that clearly drawn. Thus, if we fail to see a rigid consistency in Philo, or a clear indication of which idea stems from the Stoa and which from the Academy, we must be forgiving.

Platonic tradition had taken several centuries to arrive at a belief in a supreme, transcendent God beyond the basic principles of existed things.[65] Philo, on the other hand, as a Jew, began all philosophical speculations from this point and accepted a supreme transcendent God as a matter of course. Thus, when Philo comments on the Book of Genesis in *De opificio mundi, Legum allegoriae,* and *Quaestiones et solutions in Genesim,* he is *beginning* from the standpoint of a supreme deity and supporting this central tenet of his theology with ideas taken from Middle Platonism. The end result is, however, somewhat complicated, as biblical texts do not fit all that easily into some of the more systematic aspects of Middle Platonism.

We see the complicated nature of the enterprise Philo has undertaken when we examine how he incorporated Middle Platonic ideas of the *Logos,* as well as some Stoic notions in regard to the divine spark, to explain the creation accounts in the first two chapters of Genesis. The creation of man in Genesis was discussed in eleven of Philo's works,[66] with each work describing this creation in subtly different ways. In *De Opificio Mundi,* to cite one example, Philo interprets the two separate creation accounts in Genesis as referring to two separate aspects of man's creation with Gen 1:26-27 corresponding to the creation of man's mind (the heavenly man) in the image of God and Gen 2:7 corresponding to the earthly

[65] Tobin, *The Creation of Man,* p.15.
[66] *Op.* 24-25, 69-75, 134-135, 139, 145-146, *Conf.* 41, 62-63, 146, 168-182, *Mut.* 27-32, 223, *L.A.* 1.31-32, 1.36-40, 1.42, 1.53-55, 1.88-96, 2.4, 3.95-96, 3.161, *Fug.* 68-72, *Her.* 55-57, 230-231, 281-283, *Spec.* 1.171, 1.80-81, 3.83, 3.207, 4.123, *Somn.* 1.33-34, *Q. G.* 1.4, 1.8, 2.56, 2.59, 2.62, *Det.* 80-90, *Plant.* 14-27, 44-46.

or sense perceptible man.[67] However in some of Philo's interpretations of Genesis man is not created as an image of God but rather as an image of the image of God, the *Logos,* which is seen by Philo as an intermediate figure, located between God and the sensible world.[68] It was Philo's eventual position that the two different accounts of the creation of man in Genesis represented not two separate creations of one man but two separate creations of first the heavenly man and then the sensible man. Drawing upon the Platonic ideas of paradigm and copy, Philo envisioned the creation of solely the intelligible world on day one of creation and the sensible world coming into being only with the beginning of the second day through the activity of the *Logos.*[69] This *Logos* figure in Philo, however, is not solely relegated to the figure of the paradigm for the heavenly man. For Philo the figure of the *Logos* was highly complex and took various forms. Drawing upon Stoic models, Philo conceives the *Logos* alternatively as that which binds the divine plant (φυτὸν θεοῦ) together, [70]or as that which puts on the world as a garment,[71] or as "the one who fills up all things with its being,"[72]all of which are very much in line with the Stoic belief of the *Logos* as the principle of rationality that pervades the universe.[73]

Central to our current investigation, however, is the connection between the image of the *Logos* in Philo with that of the image of Divine Wisdom, *Sophia.* Philo presents us with a very standard picture of Divine Wisdom in *de Ebrietate*:

> Accordingly wisdom is represented by some one of the beings of the divine company as speaking of herself in this manner: "God created me as the first of his works and before the beginning of time did he establish me." (Prov 8:22) For it was necessary that all things which came under the

[67] Tobin, *Creation of Man,* p.20.
[68] Op. 24-24. L. A. 3.95-96, Her. 230-231, Spec. 180-181, as referenced Tobin, *Creation,* p.21.
[69] Tobin, *Creation,* p.21.
[70] *Plant.* 1-31.
[71] *Fug.* 110.
[72] *Her.* 188.
[73] Tobin, *Creation,* p. 63.

head of creation must be younger than the mother and nurse of the whole universe.

(Philo, de Ebrietate 31)

This image of Divine Wisdom preserves the notion that she was somehow distinct from God ("one of the beings of the divine company") and at the same time the first created entity. Yet this image of personified Wisdom akin to that found in Prov. 8.22-31, i.e. that of a female divine entity, is rare in Philo, only found in one other place, *de Fuga et Inventione*:

> *For we say that the high priest is not a man, but is the word of God, who has not only no participation in intentional errors, but none even in those which are involuntary. For Moses says that he cannot be defiled neither in respect of his father, that is, the mind, nor his mother, that is the external sense; because, I imagine, he has received imperishable and wholly pure parents, God being his father, who is also the father of all things, and Wisdom being his mother, by means of* (δι' ἧς)[74] *whom the universe arrived at creation.* (Philo, *de Fuga et Inventione* 108-109)

These feminine characterizations of Wisdom, however, are overshadowed by Philo's other depictions of Wisdom in which she is identified with the *Logos* with no allusions to feminine aspects. We see this most clearly in *Fug.*[75]:

> *The man who is capable of running swiftly it bids stay not to draw breath but pass forward to the supreme Divine Word* (λόγον θεῖον) , *who is the fountain of Wisdom* (ὃς σοφίας ἐστὶ πηγήν) *in order that he may draw from the stream and, released from death, gain life eternal as his prize.*
> (Philo, *Fug.* 97)

Our best example of where Philo identifies the *Logos* with Wisdom without feminine attributes occurs in Cher. 125-127. This example is important not only for the clear identification by Philo of the *Logos* with Wisdom/*Sophia*, an idea present in Platonic philosophy from at least the time of Antiochus of Askelon (130 BCE – 68 BCE), but also because it demonstrates that Philo chose to employ the language of the aforementioned "metaphysics of prepositions" in his

---

[74] The importance of this prepositional usage will be addressed presently.
[75] Also *L.A.* 1.65, 2.86, *Somn.* 1.65-66, 2.242-245, *Fug.* 109, *Post.* 122, *Deus.* 134-135.

discussion. In his allegorical interpretation of Cain's statement, "I have gotten a man through (διὰ τοῦ θεοῦ) God, Philo states the following:

> Because God is the cause not the instrument, and that which comes into being is brought into being through (δι᾽) an instrument, but by a cause. For to bring anything into being needs all these conjointly, the "by which" (τὸ ὑφ᾽οὗ), the "from which" (τὸ ἐξ οὗ), the "through which" (τὸ δι᾽οὗ), the "for which"(τὸ δι᾽ὅ), and the first of these is the cause, the second the material, the third the tool (τὸ ἐργαλεῖον), and the fourth the end or object.

> If we ask what combination is always needed that a house or city should be built, the answer is the builder, stones or timber, and instruments. What is the builder but the cause "by which"? What are the stones and timber but the material "from which"? What are the instruments but the means "through which"? And what is the end or object of the building but shelter and safety, and this constitutes the "for which."

> Let us leave these merely particular buildings, and contemplate the greatest of houses or cities, this universe. We shall see that its cause is God, by whom it has come into being, its material the four elements, form which it was compounded, its instrument (ὄργανον) the Word of God (λόγος τοῦ θεοῦ), through which (δι᾽οὗ) it was framed, and the final cause of the building is the goodness of the architect. It is thus that truth-lovers distinguish, who desire true and sound knowledge. But those who say that they possess something through God, suppose the Cause, that is the Maker, to be the instrument, and the instrument, that is the human mind, they suppose to be the cause. (Philo, *Cher.* 125-127)

Thus, in our final example from Philo we see an intermingling of the "metaphysics of preposition" with discussion of the *Logos*. With these examples from Middle-Platonic philosophy before us, we can now turn to the Christological hymnic fragments under investigation which describe the pre-existent Christ and Christ the Creator.

Implications for Understanding the Christological Hymnic Fragments

We have endeavored in this chapter to trace the evolution of the concept of Wisdom from her origins in Proverbs through the start of the Christian era when these images of Divine Wisdom from the Hebrew scriptures began to be blended with Hellenistic philosophical concepts, most importantly the *Logos*. Now that we have traced this evolution we can see a bit more clearly the connections between the Christological hymnic fragments and similar images contained in both Jewish wisdom literature and Hellenistic Middle Platonic philosophy. We ended our first chapter by isolating the possible provenance of the two key images of the pre-existent (or pre-Creation) Christ and that of Christ the Creator. It is now possible to expand upon this discussion and indicate more clearly where the authors of these hymns may have been getting these images.

Three of our Christological hymnic fragments contained images of the pre-existent or pre-Creation Christ: Phil 2:6, Col 1:17 and John 1:1-2:

Philippians 2:6

> ὃς ἐν μορφῇ θεοῦ
> ὑπάρχων οὐχ ἁρπαγμὸν ἡγήσατο τὸ εἶναι ἴσα θεῷ,
> ἀλλὰ ἑατὸν ἐκένωσεν...

> *Who, though he was in the form of God, did not regard equality with God something to be grasped, but he emptied himself...*

In the case of the image of Christ found in Phil 2:6, we noted in our second chapter that the only clear parallel we have in the works of Hellenistic Judaism comes from Philo's *Leg* 2.4 in which he compared "heavenly man" and "earthly man," for it is only here that we find a heavenly entity engaging in thought processes. (*For the man made after the image it is not good to be alone, because he yearns* (ἐφίεται) *after the image)* If one follows Philo's line of argumentation outlined above and links this "heavenly man" to the *Logos* we are clearly dealing with a pre-existent entity engaging in this thought process, an engagement which we do not see elsewhere. In previous examples from Jewish Wisdom literature, Wisdom is allowed to speak, reflect on creation, the world of men and, in the case of the images contained in *The Wisdom of Solomon,* even given specific tasks. Even in the case of Sirach, where she is described as compassing the vault of heaven and the deep abyss alone (Sir 24:5), we are not given even the barest glimpse of her thoughts. When we are given a glimpse of the inner workings of the mind of Wisdom, i.e. when she expresses delight in Prov 8:30-31, she never contemplates her own existence, solely the work of the Creator. Wisdom is never given an introspective moment. It is only in Philo where we see a link, albeit a somewhat tenuous one, to the image of Christ that we have in Phil 2:6, namely in a pre-creation entity engaged in thought.

Colossians 1:17a

καὶ αὐτός ἐστιν πρὸ πάντων...

He himself is before all things...

In our discussion of the hymnic fragment contained in Col 1:17 we isolated one image which speaks to the pre-existent or pre-Creation Christ, namely the idea that "he is before all things." This image, unlike Phil 2:6 examined above, has much clearer connections to depictions of Wisdom in the various texts from Jewish wisdom speculation (Prov 8:22-23, Sir 24:9) where Wisdom is clearly described as a pre-creation entity. We have also seen that Isis was also described in a similar fashion as "first offspring of the ages," although we must admit the lexical similarities to what we find in both Proverbs and Sirach are stronger than what we see in Apuleius.[76]

John 1:1-2

Ἐν ἀρχῇ ἦν ὁ λόγος, καὶ ὁ λόγος ἦν πρὸς τὸν θεόν, καὶ θεὸς ἦν ὁ λόγος. οὗτος ἦν ἐν ἀρχῇ πρὸς τὸν θεόν.

In the beginning was the Word, and the Word was with God, and the Word was God. He was in the beginning with God.

---

[76] Apuleius, *Metamorphoses*, J. Arthur Hanson trans., Cambridge: Harvard University Press, 1989, XI, 5.

As with the image from Col 1:17, the image of Christ in John 1:1-2 also seems to be clearly originating in part from within Jewish Wisdom literature as Divine Wisdom is similarly described as existing "from the beginning" in Prov 8:23 and Sir 24:9. In addition, we have here the concept of the *Logos*, with its connection to the eternal world of ideas from both Middle Platonism and Stoic thought, demonstrating a subtle interweaving of biblical and philosophical imagery. However, when we examine the subsequent image contained in the hymnic fragment from the prologue of John's Gospel below, it will become clear that the philosophical language employed in describing the creative functions of the *Logos* owes more to Middle Platonic concepts than to similar ideas in Jewish wisdom literature.

Thus, the images of the pre-existent/pre-creation Christ that we find in Phil 2:6, Col 1:17 and John 1:1-2 seem to have their closest parallels to Hellenistic Jewish wisdom speculation, albeit from different aspects of this thought world. In the case of Phil 2:6, the idea of the pre-existent Christ engaging in "regarding" his own equality with God has a clear parallel to Philo's discussion of the "heavenly man," which he eventually equates with the *Logos*. Similarly, the image from Col 1:17 of Christ "before all things" has clear parallels with not only the Book of Proverbs but also with the Wisdom of Solomon which we have endeavored to show was also influenced by Hellenistic philosophy. The final images from John 1:1-2, in its' combination of *Logos* speculation with wording akin to what we see in Proverbs, Sirach and the Wisdom of Solomon, also seem to most probably originate within Hellenistic Jewish circles.

Our second image, that of Christ the Creator found in 1 Cor 8:6, John 1:3, 10, Col 1:16, 20 and Heb 1:3 offer us perhaps our clearest link to Hellenistic Jewish wisdom speculation, and in turn the Middle Platonic philosophy that it was in conversation with, owing to both its use of the metaphysics of prepositions and the clear creative role associated with Wisdom. It is this description of Wisdom as having unambiguous creative powers, as opposed to the unclear creative role Wisdom plays in Proverbs 8, which is the clearest influence from the world of Hellenistic philosophical thought.

1 Corinthians 8:6

ἀλλ᾽ ἡμῖν εἷς θεὸς ὁ πατὴρ ἐξ οὗ τὰ πάντα
καὶ ἡμεῖς εἰς αὐτόν, καὶ εἷς
κύριος Ἰησοῦς Χριστὸς δι᾽ οὗ τὰ πάντα
καὶ ἡμεῖς δι᾽ αὐτοῦ.

Yet for us there is one God, the Father, from whom all things are and for whom we exist and one Lord, Jesus Christ, through whom all things are and through whom we exist.

In the case of 1 Cor 8:6 we are confronted with our only case of a hymnic fragment which seems to be composed entirely out of prepositional phrases which draw heavily upon the philosophical language of the "metaphysics of prepositions." Unfortunately, we seem to have a blending of philosophical schools in this short hymnic fragment. We have a clear example of δι᾽ οὗ being used in reference to Christ to indicate the instrument of agency, in this case to describe how all things exist "through Christ," i.e. a Middle Platonic usage. However, in this fragment we also have ἐξ οὗ being used to describe the actions of God. If we use Philo's *Cher.* 125-127 as an example of how a Middle Platonist would have used described the actions of God we would expect τὸ ὑφ᾽ οὗ as a means of indicating God as the cause of creation. For a Middle Platonist like Philo, the material and not the primal cause would be described as the "from whom" (ἐξ οὗ). [77] Whichever philosophical school contributed to the language of this hymnic fragment, however, it is clear that we are clearly within the realm of Hellenistic philosophical discourse that does not seem to be tethered in any way to the Hebrew Scriptures.

---

[77] Gregory Sterling, *Studia Philonica Annual,* 9, (Atlanta, Georgia: Scholars Press, 1997), believes this usage of ἐξ οὗ in 1 Cor 8:6 bears a closer affinity to Stoic than Middle Platonic usage, p. 235-236.

John 1:3, 10

πάντα δι'αὐτοῦ ἐγένετο, καὶ χωρὶς αὐτοῦ ἐγένετο οὐδὲ ἕν

All things came to be through him and without him nothing came to be.

ἐν τῷ κόσμῳ ἦν, καὶ ὁ κόσμος δι'αὐτοῦ ἐγένετο, καὶ ὁ κόσμος αὐτὸν οὐκ ἔγνω.

He was in the world, and the world came to be through him, but the world did not know him.

There is no inconsistency in the way the "metaphysics of prepositions" is used in John 1:3 and John 1:10 as only the instrument of agency (δι'αὐτοῦ) is used to describe Christ who had already been designated the *Logos* in v. 1. This is in contrast to the combined use of Stoic and Middle Platonic usage that we say in 1 Cor 8:6. Only the Middle Platonic usage seems to be employed here.

Colossians 1:16a,c, 17

ὅτι ἐν αὐτῷ ἐκτίσθη τὰ πάντα ἐν τοῖς οὐρανοῖς καὶ ἐπὶ τῆς γ ῆς...τὰ πάντα δι'αὐτοῦ καὶ εἰς αὐτὸν ἔκτισται.

For in him were created all things in heaven and on earth; all things were created through him and for him.

καὶ αὐτός ἐστιν πρὸ πάντων καὶ τὰ πάντα ἐν αὐτῷ συνέστηκεν.

He is before all things, and in him all things hold together.

The image of Christ the Creator in Col 1:16-17 exhibits similar Middle Platonic prepositional usage with the phrase all things were created "through him" (δι'αὐτοῦ).[78] In addition to this Middle Platonic use of prepositions we also see echoes of an all pervasive Divine Wisdom similar to Wis 7:23. In the Wisdom of Solomon she is described as one who "penetrates and pervades"

---

[78] Col 1:20 as well uses δι'αὐτοῦ ("through him to reconcile all things").

(διήκει δὲ καὶ χωρεῖ) whereas Christ in Col 1:17 is seen as "holding all things together" (τὰ πάντα ἐν αὐτῷ συνέστηκεν). It is description similar to what we have seen previously in Plutarch's depiction of Isis, which, like Wis 7:23, uses διῆκον. Thus, we seem somewhat in an area of overlap where it is difficult to discern whether the author of the hymnic fragment in Col 1:17 was drawing upon the Jewish Wisdom tradition, Platonic philosophy, or perhaps a combination of both.

<u>Hebrews 1:3c</u>

φέρων τε τα πάντα τῷ ῥήματι τῆς δυνάμεως αὐτοῦ

And who supports all things through the word of his power.

Our final Christological hymnic fragment under investigation, like our first, defies easy categorization. As with Col 1:17, we have the image of Christ somehow supporting all things (φέρων τε τα πάντα...). It is an idea similar to what we previously saw in both the Wisdom of Solomon as well as in Plutarch, yet, φέρω, "to endure, bear, put up with or yield", has a somewhat different meaning than συνίστημι in Col 1:17 which means "to hold together." However, the two ideas are conceptually similar.

It seems clear that both Hellenistic Jewish wisdom speculation often influenced by Middle Platonic thought contributed significantly to the images we see in the images of both the Pre-Existent/Pre-Creation Christ (Phil 2:6, Col 1:17, John 1:2) and the image of Christ the Creator (1 Cor 8:6, John 1:3, 10, Col 1:16-17, Heb 1:3). In essence, the image of Wisdom found in Proverbs that had been expanded upon in the Hellenistic period in works such as Sirach and the Wisdom of Solomon offered fertile ground for authors wishing to describe another divine presence alongside the Lord, namely Christ. Divine Wisdom, transformed in her encounters with *Ma'at*, Isis, and the *Logos* from Greek Philosophical thought, presented a ready palate for those seeking to describe the relationship between

God and Christ. By the time of the writing of the New Testament Christological hymns, using Philo as only one example, even the feminine side of *Sophia* had given away before the masculine *Logos* in philosophical discussions, albeit a masculine *Logos* who maintained creative aspects from earlier depictions of Isis. Thus, at the dawn of the Christian era, the stage was set for literary creations which extolled the image of the all pervasive, permeating *Logos*, who had been with the Lord from the beginning of time. Although it is difficult to determine whether the New Testament authors were drawing upon Greek philosophical thought directly or Greek philosophical thought as mediated through Hellenistic Judaism it is clear that such philosophical discussions were the source for these images. Knowing this, we can then speculate a bit further on the authors, and to some extent the communities, that embraced these literary creations. Such speculations must wait, however, until we examine the final and, to a great extent, the most problematic image in the hymnic fragments, Christ the Incarnate Divinity. As neither Divine Wisdom nor the Middle Platonic *Logos* ever took human form in either Hellenistic Jewish wisdom speculation or Hellenistic philosophy, those two bodies of literature will not prove fruitful as a source for this image. We must, therefore, look beyond the walls of the Academy, outside of the Synagogue, beyond the philosophical confines of Alexandria. We must look to the one place where gods taking human form and serving as a slave would have seemed commonplace. We must look to the literature of Greco-Roman religion, specifically the language of Greek and Roman myth.

Chapter Four

The God as Flesh

The images of the pre-existent Christ and that of Christ the Creator originated clearly from within the world of both Hellenistic Judaism and the world of Greek philosophical thought. The clear parallels to both Wisdom speculation and the Middle Platonic philosophy of Jewish writers like Philo demonstrate that as far as these particular images are concerned we are on fairly firm Hellenistic Jewish ground, albeit a Hellenistic Judaism that that has been heavily influenced by Greek philosophy. The next image, however, that of Christ the Incarnate Divinity does not easily fit into the either the Hellenistic Jewish or Greek philosophical thought world examined in our last chapter. Few ideas would have been as unpalatable to writers like Philo as the incarnation of God in human form. For the Jews, the idea of the supreme deity taking human form, becoming enfleshed, would be blasphemy. The voice of God could be heard, whether in the stentorian tones surrounding the burning bush or the still small voice heard by Elijah, but God could not be seen, much less seen in the guise of a human. In a similar fashion, the philosophically minded Greeks in the Hellenistic period would also have recoiled at the incarnation of a deity, no doubt ascribing such ideas to the "lies of the poets" which they saw as permeating ancestral religion. The same holds for Middle Platonic Greek writers concerned with the *Logos*. Although Greek writers could wax loquacious concerning the powers and attributes of the *Logos*, none ever went so far as to ascribe to it human characteristics much less embodiment.

The opposite is true in the Greco-Roman religious thought world where the human form of the gods is the starting point for all discussions of divinity. For a Greek or Roman the idea of a hymn which states a god existed or took human form would have been unsurprising to say the least. In the Greco-Roman religious tradition the gods may elect to assume other forms as the situation dictated, such as a bull or swan or shower of rain, but the primary form in which the gods existed and interacted with humans was in the human form itself. The anthropomorphic nature of the Greek pantheon was accepted *a priori*.

The decidedly physical nature of Christ is expressed in our last three images under consideration, namely, Philippians 2:6-7, John 1:14 and 1 Timothy 3:16. Each, however, opts to describe the human aspect or appearance of Christ in differing ways. In the Philippians image, we see Christ coming in human likeness and appearance and assuming the form of a slave, whereas the images in John and 1 Timothy express the human nature of Christ using the term "flesh." This chapter will investigate two distinct aspects of the Greco-Roman literary tradition in this regard. First, we shall examine the historical literary trajectory of gods who transform themselves. Starting with Homer and working to just beyond the time period of the Christian hymns under investigation, we shall place the images found in Philippians 2:7, John 1:14 and 1 Tim 3:16 within proper context in regards to the language of transformation. Secondly, we shall examine the endpoint of these transformations, namely that of slave and flesh and put them as well in their proper literary context. This will be quite easy to do with the image of slave that we see in the fragment from Philippians and a good deal more difficult with the image of the god as "flesh" that we see in the Gospel of John and First Timothy. Our Greek and Roman writers, like their Jewish contemporaries, rarely describe their divinities in such a way.

Before we get to our examples a word must be said about the method that will be employed in the subsequent section. What we are attempting to do is place images in literary context, a somewhat loaded term as the examples put forth can very easily determine what context we are aiming at. Therefore, representative examples from Homer onward will be examined and compared to the images we have concentrated upon in the Christ hymns. In this endeavor, as with the examples put forth in the preceding chapters, the net is cast wide. These examples, however, are not meant to be exhaustive but rather representative. A full catalogue of every example of a god transforming himself or herself in classical literature would run to volumes, as Ovid could attest.

The God in Human Form

The Greeks, from their earliest known writings, assumed their divinities existed in human form as we see in this excerpt from the opening chapter of Hesiod's *Theogony*[1]:

> *From the Heliconian Muses let us begin to sing, who hold the great and holy mount of Helicon, and dance on soft feet about the deep-blue spring and the altar of the almighty son of Cronos, and, when they have washed their tender bodies in Permessus or in the Horse's Spring or Olmeius, make their fair, lovely dances upon highest Helicon and move with vigorous feet. Thence they arise and go abroad by night, veiled in thick mist, and utter their song with lovely voice, praising Zeus the aegis-holder, and queenly Hera of Argos who walks on golden sandals, and the daughter of Zeus the aegis-holder bright-eyed Athena, and Phoebus Apollo, and Artemis who delights in arrows, and Poseidon the earth holder who shakes the earth, and revered Themis, and quick-glancing Aphrodite, and Hebe with the crown of gold, and fair Dione, Leto, Iapetus, and Cronos the crafty counselor, Eos, and great Helius, and bright Selene, Earth, too, and great Oceanus, and dark Night, and the holy race of all the other deathless ones that are for ever.[2]*

In one of the earliest examples of Greek literature, we see gods who have children, bodies with which to dance, sing, give praise, walk, and shake the earth. There is no question that they are of a different substance than humankind, their deathless nature attests to this. But they are, at least in terms of their form, appearance, and actions, decidedly human. From time to time, however, the gods of the Greeks and Romans could take other forms as the situation dictated. Often, in the case of Zeus in pursuit of one of his many conquests, the thunder god would assume various forms to obtain the object of his affections. Whether in the

---

[1] Unless otherwise indicated all translations are from the Loeb Classical Library.
[2] Hesiod, *Theog.*1.4-21(Evelyn-White, LCL).

form of a bull or swan or any other number of countless metamorphoses, the father of the gods regularly changed his human form for another, more often than not a powerful or majestic animal.

The closest parallels in Classical literature to the images of incarnate divinity in the New Testament, however, occur when we examine those instances when the gods of the Greeks and the Romans chose to take the form of *specific* humans, usually to convey messages or to deceive those around them. From Homer to Virgil, the gods of the Greek and Roman pantheon often descended from Olympus to appear in the guise most comfortable to human observers, a trusted friend, a beloved relative, a comrade in arms, a non-descript stranger, etc. The way this process was described, however, differs somewhat between authors and over time. What we are concerned with in our investigation of these images is the manner by which the transformation from god to human occurred in these works, for the images in the New Testament hymns stress this action, this movement from one state to another. Specifically, we are concerned with the particular words used to convey the idea of transformation as they occur in the following hymnic fragments:

Philippians 2:7b

> ἐν ὁμοιώματι ἀνθρώπον γενόμενος και σχήματι εὑρεθεὶς ὡς ἀνθρώπος
>
> *... coming in human likeness and found human in appearance.*

John 1:14

> Καὶ ὁ λόγος σάρξ ἐγένετο κάι ἐσκήνωσεν ἐν ἡμῖν
>
> *And the word became flesh and made his dwelling among us.*

1 Timothy 3:16a

> Ὃς ἐφανερώθη ἐν σαρκί...
>
> *Who was manifested in the flesh...*

The first two images under investigation are specifically concerned with the action, the change of state from divinity to human, and as such give us fertile points of comparison with the world of Greco-Roman literature. Paul, in quoting the hymn found in Philippians 2:6ff, stresses this change of state "coming in human likeness and found human in appearance." However, the words used in the hymnic fragment to describe the final state of Christ, ὁμοιώμα (likeness) and σχῆμα (outward form, likeness) allow for a certain amount of elasticity in regards to interpretation. In the case of ὁμοιώμα, it is a word which is very rare in secular Greek,[3] normally translated as "what is made similar" or simply "a copy."[4] It can rarely be used synonymously with εἰκών,[5] but can also be distinguished from εἰκών, seen as object, with ὁμοιώμα translated as "similarity'.[6] In the LXX, it is most often translated as "copy" or "form"[7] and in only one instance is used for םלצ,[8] thereby allowing for it being also seen as a synonym for μορφή. There is somewhat less ambiguity as to the meaning of σχῆματι, as it almost always denotes the outward form or structure perceptible to the senses and never the inward principle of order accessible only to thought in Greek literature,[9] i.e. solely the outward appearance or demeanor.[10] Yet, one is left with a certain amount of ambiguity in regard to this final state, i.e. was Christ truly human in form or simply likened to a human, an ambiguity which fueled debate for roughly the next three centuries. This elasticity of language in regard to describing the god who was transformed did not begin with the New Testament authors, however, having a long literary history stretching back to Homer.

---

[3] Plato, *Parm.*, 132d, 133d; *Phaedr.* 250a, 250b, *Soph.* 266d, Aristotle, *Rhet.* I.2.1345a.31, *Ditt. Or.* 669.52, P. Fay., 106.20.
[4] J. Schneider, "ὁμοιώματι," *TDNT* 5.191-192.
[5] Plato, *Phaedr.* 250b.
[6] J. Schneider, *TDNT*, 5.192.
[7] J. Schneider, *TDNT*, 5.192.
[8] Deut 4:16ff
[9] A. Spicq, σχῆματι, TDNT, 7.955-956.
[10] Lucian, *Som.* 13, *Dial. Mort.* 10.8.

A. Homer

The epic poet Homer, writing some seven to eight hundred years before the author of the Philippians hymn, often recounted how a god or more often a goddess would appear in the guise or form of someone else. This transformation was usually undertaken to aid in one intrigue or another in the world of humans. One example from the Iliad has the goddess Aphrodite assuming the form of an old woman:

> Then with her hand the goddess laid hold of her fragrant robe, and plucked it, and spoke to her in the likeness (ἐικυῖα) of an ancient dame, a wool-comber, who had been wont to card the fair wool for her when she dwelt in Lacedaemon, and who was well loved of her; in her likeness (ἐεισαμένη) fair Aphrodite spoke.[11]

This example from the Iliad demonstrates the somewhat fluid language of transformation employed by Homer. In the first instance, a participial form of ἔοικα is used, a verb which is normally translated as "to be like." In the second instance we see a participial form of εἴδω, a verb normally translated as "to be seen." The use of εἴδω to describe transformed gods is quite common in Homer as when Athena takes the form of Phoenix,[12] Mentor,[13] Dymas' daughter,[14] or one of Alkinoos' servants.[15] On occasion, however, Homer deviates from using εἴδω and uses the aforementioned ἔοικα as in the example above. A similar example occurs when Odysseus, finally back home in Ithaca encounters Athena is the guise of a woman:

> Then she took the form of a woman (δέμας δ᾽ ἤικτο γυναικὶ), fair, stately, and wise, "He must be indeed a shifty and deceitful person," said she, "who could surpass you in all manner of craft.[16]

---

[11] Homer, Il., 3.388 (A. T. Murray, LCL).
[12] Homer, Il., 17.550.
[13] Homer, Od., 2.393
[14] Homer, Od., 6.15
[15] Homer, Od., 8.1
[16] Homer, Od., 13.288 (Merry, LCL).

As with the previous example which used this form of ἔοικα, i.e. to be like, Homer has given a hint at a somewhat less elastic meaning, i.e. the god no longer simply looks like but *is* alike in form to someone else.[17] However, one would not wish to push this interpretation too far as both terms seem to be suitably elastic to allow for various interpretations.

B. The Homeric Hymn to Demeter

Written at roughly the same time as the *Iliad* and the *Odyssey*,[18] the *Homeric Hymn to Demeter* also describes a god in the state of transformation. This hymn in dactylic hexameter is important to our study for two reasons. First, it sheds light on the inherent difficulty in seeing the true "form" of a god or in this case goddess. In one of the first descriptions of the appearance of Demeter we are told the following:

> *There the daughters of Celeus, son of Eleusis, saw her as they were coming for easy drawn water, to carry it in pitchers of bronze to their dear father's house: Four were they and like goddesses in the flower of their girlhood, Callidice and Cleisidice and lovely Demo and Callithoë who was the eldest of them all. They knew her not-for the gods are not easily discerned by mortals.* (χαλεποὶ δὲ θεοὶ θνητοῖσιν ὁρᾶσθαι).[19]

What is important about this passage is the idea that the true form of a god or goddess is something not easily perceived by the human observer. It was an a priori assumption during an encounter with a deity that there is and always will be in the mind of the observer a difficulty in terms of perception. Thus, what humans see when they gaze upon Demeter, in this case an old woman, is not the true form of the goddess but simply an appearance. We shall see this ambiguity in terms of human perception often.

---

[17] W. B. Stanford has commented that this example is particularly interesting in that this particular transformation could indicate the "true" form of Athena, i.e. the young woman *sans* her armor as in Archaic Greek art. *The Odyssey of Homer*, W. M. Stanford, Ed. (London: Macmillan & Co. Ltd., New York: St. Martin's Press), 1965, p. 210, notes 288-289.

[18] Apostolos N. Athanassakis, *The Homeric Hymns*, (Baltimore/London: Johns Hopkins University Press, 1984), pp. xii-xiii.

[19] *The Homeric Hymn to Demeter*, lines 105-111, (Evelyn-White, LCL).

Secondly, *The Homeric Hymn to Demeter* gives us yet another early example of a god or goddess transforming. When Metaneira, the mother of Demophoön, surprises the goddess as she thrusts the infant into the purifying fire, the goddess transforms herself:

> *Thus speaking, the goddess changed her size and appearance*
> (μέγεθος καὶ εἶδος ἄμειψε) *thrusting off old age. Beauty breathed about her and from her sweet robes a delicious fragrance spread; a light beamed far out from the goddesses' immortal skin, and her golden hair flowed over her shoulders. The well built house flooded with her radiance like lightening.*[20]

In this passage we are confronted with a more active idea of transformation through the use of the verb ἀμείβω, meaning to change or exchange. The verb is paired with εἶδος, normally translated as that which is seen, form, shape or figure. We are again dealing with the *appearance* of the goddess, no mention is made of her "true" form. However, there is a subtle shift in this transformation relative to the examples from Homer in that the author of the Homeric Hymns is ascribing a greater deal of activity to the deity, i.e. it is the deity who changes her appearance.

C. Euripides

In the works of Euripides, we see a similar approach to the god taking human form with the use of verbs which convey greater action. We see this most clearly in the following example from Euripides'*Bacchae* in the opening lines where the god Dionysus recounts his origins:

> *I am come, the son of Zeus, to this Theban land, Dionysis, to whom the daughter of Kadmos gave birth, Semele, midwived by lightening born fire. And having changed my form from god to mortal* (μορφὴν δ' ἀμείψας ἐκ θεοῦ βροτησιάν) *I am here at the streams of Dirke and the water of Ismenus.*[21]

---

[20] *The Homeric Hymn to Demeter,* Helene P. Foley Ed., (Princeton: Princeton University Press, 1994), lines 275-280.
[21] Euripides, *Bacch.* Richard Seaford, Ed., (Warminster, England: Aris & Phillips, Ltd., 1996), lines 1-4.

A similar preference for words which convey more action is seen in Euripides' *Helen*, where the heroine similarly recounts her parentage:

> For me, not fameless is my fatherland Sparta: My sire was Tyndarus. The
> tale telleth that to my mother Zeus flew, who had stolen the likeness of a
> swan (κύκνου μορφώματ᾽ ὄρνιθος λαβών), and fleeing from a
> chasing eagle, wrought by guile his pleasure, if the tale be true.[22]

Euripides, unlike Homer and closer to the usage in the *Homeric Hymn to Demeter*, seems to prefer greater action (λαβών, ἀμείψας) in recounting the transition from god to mortal or god to animal. Whereas Homer most often prefers words which at least imply the act of observation by another (εἴδω), more often than not in the middle voice, Euripides stresses the action of the god and emphasizes the transition from one state to another. This may stem from the necessity of crafting dialogue for the stage or may simply be the preference of the great playwright. Whether the transformation is actively described or not, however, the end result is always the same, i.e. it is simply the outward form or appearance that is transformed.

D. Apollodorus, Isidorus, Plutarch, Pausanias

When Apollodorus recounted the same myth as the one recounted in Euripides' *Helen* in his *Library* sometime in the second century B.C., we find still yet another way of describing the transformation of Zeus from god to swan in that he uses the aorist passive participle from ὁμοιόω, ὁμοιοθέντος meaning to be made like or be like:

> But Zeus in the form of a swan consorted with Leda (Διὸς δὲ Λήδᾳ
> συνελθόντος ὁμοιωθέντος κύκνῳ)...But some say that Helen was a
> daughter of Nemesis and Zeus; for that she, flying from the arms of Zeus
> changed herself into a goose (εἰς χῆνα τὴν μορφὴν μεταβαλεῖν) but
> Zeus in his turn took the likeness of a swan (ὁμοιωθέντα δὲ καὶ Δία
> κύκνῳ συνελθεῖν) and so he enjoyed her.[23]

---

[22] Euripides, *Hel.* lines 16-21 (Way, LCL).
[23] Apollodorus, *Lib.* 3.10.7 (Frazer, LCL).

As with the previous examples, we are still dealing with a god (and in this case also a goddess) transforming themselves. However, Apollodorus has described the transformation somewhat differently than his literary forbears opting for participial formations of ὁμοιόω to convey his meaning in addition to words which convey this active transformation (μορφὴν μεταβαλεῖν).

One of the more interesting examples of a god, or in this case god-king, assuming mortal form comes from the *Hymns of Isidorus*.[24] The author of these hymns, 80 B.C.E., recounts in primitive hexameter the salvific acts attributed to Isis. In the fourth hymn, however, the author digresses to praise a certain Porramanres, a god-king considered to have been the XIIth Dynasty Pharaoh, son of Senosis, who was the center of a popular folk cult in the Fayyum area during the Ptolemies[25]:

> *A certain one, they say was born (γενέσθαι) a divine king of Egypt,*
> *he appeared (ἐξεφάνη) on earth as Lord of All the World,*
> *rich, righteous and omnipotent. (lines 7-9)*
> *When the Egyptians say his name (in their language) they call (him)*
> *Porramanres, the Great, Deathless. (ἀθάνατον) (lines 33-34)*

This example is important for several reasons. First, we have here an example of a hymn to a divine personage, in this case a Pharaoh, whose divinity, like Heracles, is clearly stated in the hymn. It is an example which comes relatively close to the period of the New Testament. Secondly, we have the birth of this divine character described using a form of γίνομαι. Finally, we have an example where the entry of this personage onto the scene of the mortal world is expressed via a derivative of the Greek verb φαίνω, akin to the usage in 1 Timothy 3:16 outlined above.

As we get closer to the time of the writing of our hymnic fragments we find that the variety in describing the transformation from god to mortal, whether human or animal, has continued unabated. It must be noted, however, that with

---

[24] Vanderlip, *Four Greek Hymns of Isidorus*, "The Hymn to Porramanres, lines 7-9 and lines 33-34.

[25] Vanderlip, *Four Greek Hymns of Isidorus*, p. 66-67, note 6.

115

these later Greek writers one gets the impression that the authors regarded such miraculous transformations as bordering on fable. In each case greater emphasis seems to be placed on the perceptions of those relaying the information, perceptions that each author is clear to assign to someone else. Plutarch (45-125 AD) in recounting the divine origins of Alexander describes the process in this manner:

> However, after his vision, as we are told, Philip sent Chaeron of Megalopolis to Delphi, by whom an oracle was brought him from Apollo, who bade him sacrifice to Ammon and hold that god in greatest reverence, but told him he was to lose that one of his eyes which he had applied to the chink in the door when he espied the god, in the form of a serpent (ἐν μορφῇ δράκοντος), sharing the couch of his wife.[26]

Plutarch, although using the common word for form (μορφή), nevertheless fails to recount the actual transformation of the god. Pausanias writing in the early to mid 2nd century AD recounts the similar circumstances surrounding the birth of a little known Messenian, Aristomenes:

> Of the young men who had grown up in Messenia the best and most numerous were round Andania, and among them was Aristomenes, who to this day is worshipped as a hero among the Messenians. They think that even the circumstances of his birth were notable, for they assert that a spirit or a god united with his mother, Nicoteleia, in the form of a serpent (δράκοντι εἰκασμένον συγγενέσθαι λέγουσι).[27]

Pausanias, perhaps echoing Homer, has opted for a somewhat more subtle depiction, choosing a form of εἰκάζω which means to make like or portray. Finally, Cassius Dio (165 – 229 AD) relegates reports of the miraculous birth of the future Emperor to the fevered incubations of his mother in the temple of Asclepius. The transformation of the god into the form of a snake is not detailed, simply alluded to by recounting the perceptions of Attia, the mother of Augustus:

> He was influenced largely by Attia's emphatic declaration that the youth had been engendered by Apollo; for while sleeping once in his temple, she

---

[26] Plutarch, *Alex. 3.4-6* (Perrin, LCL).
[27] Pausanias, *Descr.* 4.14.7 (Jones/Omerod, LCL).

*said, she thought she had intercourse with a serpent, and it was this that
caused her at the end of the allotted time to bear a son.*[28]

E. Latin Writers: Suetonius, Virgil, and Ovid

We would be remiss in our investigation if we did not examine, however
briefly, some of the Latin sources of our time period. Historians like Suetonius
(A.D. 69-122) often describe gods in human or animal form, yet one gets the
impression that they treat the occurrences as at best fable at worst hearsay. In
recounting the circumstances surrounding the birth of Augustus, Suetonius
describes his divine birth in this manner:

> *I have read the following story in the books of Asclepias of Mendes
> entitled Theologumena. When Attia had come in the middle of the night to
> the solemn service of Apollo, she had her litter set down in the temple and
> fell asleep, while the rest of the matrons also slept. On a sudden a serpent
> glided up to her and shortly went away. When she awoke, she purified
> herself, as if after the embraces of her husband, and at once there
> appeared on her body a mark in colours like a serpent, and she could
> never get rid of it; so that presently she ceased ever to go to the public
> baths. In the tenth month after that Augustus was born and was therefore
> regarded as the son of Apollo. Atia too, before she gave him birth,
> dreamed that her vitals were borne up to the stars and spread over the
> whole extent of land and sea, while Octavius dreamed that the sun rose
> from Attia's womb.*[29]

Suetonius does not recount that Apollo in the form of a serpent slept with Attia
the mother of Augustus. Instead he relates that as a result of a visitation of a
serpent in a dream and a subsequent mark on her body, the mother of the future
Emperor believed she had been visited by Apollo. These later Latin historians
tend to eschew language which implies the transfer from one state to another by
simply stating that individuals thought or simply believed that they had been
touched by a god in another form. When we turn to the Latin epic poets such as
Vergil and Ovid, however, we see similar language to that which we have seen
before, namely, an emphasis on the active transformation of a god from one state

---

[28] Cassius Dio, *Roman History*, 15.2 (Cary, LCL).
[29] Suetonius, *Aug.* 94.4 (Rolfe, LCL).

to another. As both authors were conscientiously modeling themselves on earlier Greek models, however, this should surprise no one.

Vergil's *Aeneid*, written between 29 - 19 B.C., in telling the exploits of Aeneas on his journey home after the Trojan war recounts gods taking human form:

> *Then he changes the fashion of his features to those of aged Butes*
> (Forma tum vertitur oris antiquum in Buten), *who aforetime was armour-bearer to Dardan Anchieses, trusty watcher at his gate.* [30]

Using a form of *verto*, "to turn up, turn, turn back, direct," Vergil opts for a similar way of describing this transformation as some of the more active depictions examined above. The change is clearly in the hand of the god.

Finally with Ovid, we find perhaps a work uniquely suited to our current task. It is an epic poem which is concerned expressly with transformations from one state to the other. In *Metamorphoses*, written between 2 - 8 A.D., we find countless examples of gods changing into mortal and animal form as well as mortals changing into gods, fertile ground for our investigation. In his retelling of the myth of Apollo's servitude, which will be examined more fully in the next section, we read:

> *There, Apollo saw Laomedon building the foundations of the new city of Troy. The great undertaking prospering with difficulty, and demanding no little resources, he, and Neptune, trident-bearing father of the swelling sea, put on mortal form* (mortalem induitur forma), *and built the walls of the city for the Phrygian king for an agreed amount in gold.* [31]

As with the transformation in Vergil, the emphasis is on the action of the god who "puts on, assumes, or dresses in" the form of a mortal.

The Language of Transformation: New Testament Hymnic Fragments

The language which surrounded the transformation of a god in classical literature can be described as decidedly ambiguous. Authors from Homer to Ovid

---

[30] Virgil, *Aen.* 9.645 (Fairclough, LCL).
[31] Ovid, *Metam.* 11. 196-197 (Miller, LCL).

never really came down on one side or the other as to the final state of the god post-transformation. In general the classical authors were content to describe the transformed god as something that only "seemed like" or "looked like" this new form, whether human or animal. In the later classical period with Euripides, even though the transformation takes on a more active timbre with the use of words such as μεταβαλεῖν, "to throw into a different position," we are still confronted with simply the form of the god or goddess as we the audience perceive it. When we turn to our examples from the New Testament we can see that these authors as well left a certain amount of ambiguity in their depictions of the transformed Christ.

Philippians 2:7b

> ἐν ὁμοιώματι ἀνθρώπον γενόμενος και σχήματι εὑρεθεὶς ὡς ἀνθρώπος

The author of the Philippians hymnic fragment describes the "likeness" of man as the end result of the transformation similarly to the way Apollodorus described the transformation of Zeus (ὁμοιώματι/ὁμοιωθέντος). Similarly, it is the outward appearance (σχήματι) in which Christ is found as man. In both cases, the elasticity of the language concerning what exactly has occurred is maintained as we are not dealing unambiguously with the transformation of the god, simply how that likeness is perceived by the onlookers. Similarly, the author of the hymnic fragment found in 1 Tim 3:16 makes use of a similar verb (φαίνω) to describe the manifestation of Christ as what we find in Isidorus:

1 Timothy 3:16a

> Ὅς ἐφανερώθη ἐν σαρκί...

We are dealing here with the "manifestation" of the god alone, and "manifestation" normally deals in the realm of the perception of the onlookers, preserving the ambiguity. Yet, this ambiguity is tempered to a great extent by other words used in close proximity to the descriptions of transformation and it is here where our New Testament authors begin to diverge from their Greek and Roman literary forbears to a great extent. Two places in particular in our hymnic fragments, Phil 2:7b and John 1:14, tend to eschew the language of ambiguity by the use of γίνομαι, to be. In the case of Phil 2:7b γίνομαι is used near the aforementioned ὁμοιώματι ("being in the likeness of man") and allows room for interpretation, but there is a sense here of a greater existential element to the description. We are at least approaching the idea of "being" as opposed to "seeming." In the second instance of John 1:14 we have the deceptively simple "the word became flesh" (ὁ λόγος ἐγένετο σὰρξ) which also opts for the more concrete γίνομαι and, unlike the Philippians example, does not combine this word with any of our aforementioned elastic terms such as ὁμοιώματι ("likeness"). Our final example, 1 Tim 3:16 similarly pairs an elastic term such as ἐφανερώθη (was manifested) alongside the decidedly inelastic term ἐν σαρκί (in flesh).

What then can we say about these descriptions? It appears that our New Testament authors, in describing the transformation of Christ from God to man drew upon language common to the Greek literary tradition yet modified these descriptions of transformation through either the use of γίνομαι which tempers the ambiguity greatly or by describing the endpoint of the transformation as flesh (σὰρξ). As we have seen before in our examination of how Jewish writers appropriated what they felt useful in the various literary traditions they were exposed to and modified it to fit their own reality, our Christian authors seem to be following in the same vein. They can use similar ideas, constructed of similar language, yet add something new, something different, something subtle, but which changes the meaning greatly from what had come before. Prior to investigating the problematic end point of transformation, the god as σὰρξ, we need to briefly examine the other end stage of the process, the transformation of the god into a slave that we see in our fragment from Philippians. In this example, at least, our Christian authors seem to have kept literary novelty to a minimum.

The God as Slave

Now that we have examined the mechanism whereby a god transforms, specifically the way the ideas were expressed in Greek and to a lesser extent in Latin, we have to examine the end result of this transformation. Our examples offer up two very different end results in this regard: Philipians 2:7 has Christ taking the form of a slave (μορφὴν δούλου) and both John 1:14 and 1 Timothy 3:16 have Christ becoming flesh (ἐγένετο σὰρξ) or being manifested in the flesh (ἐφανερώθη ἐν σαρκί). As we have discussed previously, the idea of God serving as a slave or becoming enfleshed are ideas which the Jews and philosophically minded Greeks and Romans would have found extremely unusual but more the norm for those who adhered to the ancestral religion surrounding the Greco-Roman pantheon. In the case of a god becoming a slave, for example, we find a long and established history stretching back to Homer and Hesiod and continuing up to the time period of the writing of our hymns. In the case of god becoming flesh, σὰρξ in our examples, although we have copious examples of gods taking human form we have, with one exception, no examples of Jews, Greeks or Romans ever using this term for the state of the final divine transformation. The final section of this chapter will examine the literary history, or in the case of σὰρξ ("flesh") literary paucity, of these two images.

A. Apollo

The idea of Apollo having to live as a slave for a specific time is a myth which reaches back at least to the time of Homer. Yet, as we find with many of the Greek myths, there seems to be numerous versions of exactly why Apollo was committed to servitude. The retelling of these myths from the time of Homer onward offer us ample examples of how the Greco-Roman world viewed the god as a slave as a common story. Poets, tragedians and historians all retold these myths up to and beyond the time of the writing of our hymns, albeit in differing ways. Homer briefly recounts the enslavement of Apollo to Laomedon in the *Iliad*. In this section Poseidon recollects the punishment meted out to both him and Apollo for their attempted coup against Zeus:

> *Begin, for you are the younger; for it is not good for me, since I am the elder-born and know the more. Fool, how senseless is the heart you have! Do you not remember all the ills that we two alone of all the gods suffered at Ilios, that time when we came at the command of Zeus and served (θητεύσαμεν) the lordly Laomedon for a year a fixed wage, and he was our taskmaster and laid on us his commands?*[32]

Another story concerning the enslavement of Apollo comes from Euripides' *Alcestis* (438 B.C.) which describes the tasks that the god was made to perform as punishment for the slaying of the Cyclops, again at the behest of Zeus:

> *Halls of Admetus, hail! I stooped my pride here to browse fare of serfs (ἔτλην ἔγω θῆσσαν τράπεζαν) yea I, a God! The fault was the fault of Zeus: he slew my son Asclepius-hurled the levin through his heart. Wroth for the dead, his smiths of heavenly fire, the Cyclopes, I slew; for blood atonement Allfather made me serf (θητεύειν) to mortal men. To this land I come, I tended my hosts kine (ἐβουφόρβουν) and warded still his house unto this day.*[33]

Both Homer and Euripides use variants of θετεύω, meaning to be a serf or laborer, with Euripides[34] adding the extra descriptive of Apollo serving as ἐβουφορβουν (one who pastures herds or flocks of any kind). Apollodorus in his retelling of the myth tells the tale in a way very similar to Euripides:

> *But Zeus, fearing that men might acquire the healing art from him and so come to the rescue of each other, smote him with a thunderbolt. Angry on that account, Apollo slew the Cyclopes who had fashioned the thunderbolt*

---

[32] Homer, *Il.* 21.439-445 (A. T. Murray, LCL).

[33] Euripides, *Alc.* 1.1-9 (Way, LCL).

[34] In Euripides, *The Trojan Women*, line 1-2, the playwright also alludes to the Homeric myth of Apollo and Laomedon: *Lo! From the depths of salt Aegean floods I, Poseidon, come, where choirs of Nereids trip in the mazes of the graceful dance; for since the day that Phoebus and myself with measurement exact set towers of stone about this land of Troy and ringed it round, never from my heart hath passed away a kindly feeling for my Phrygian town, which now is smouldering and o'erthrown, a prey to Argive prowess.*

for Zeus. But Zeus would have hurled him to Tartarus; however, at the intercession of Latona he ordered him to serve as a thrall (θητεῦσαι) *to a man for a year. So he went to Admetus, son of Pheres, at Pherae, and served* (λατρεύων) *him as a herdsman* (ἐποίμαινε), *and caused all the cows to drop twins.*[35]

Although Apollodorus opts for different words to denote servitude as well as for occupation, the meaning is essentially the same, i.e. that is he uses words to specify that Apollo must serve another and that this menial service is one normally reserved for servants/slaves. Lucian of Samosata (120-180 A.D.) similarly recounted Apollo's period of servitude but with one important modification:

They say too that you gods fall in love and get wounded and sometimes become slaves (δουλεύειν) *in the households of men as did your brother (Poseidon) in the house of Laomedon and Apollo in the house of Admetus.*[36]

What is notable here is that we have an infinitival form of the Greek verb δουλεύω, to serve as a slave, a subtle but important change from θετεύω or λατρεύω (both which are normally translated as to serve for hire or for wages) used earlier. We find a similar use of δοῦλος in addition to the usual variants of θετεύω and λατρεύω in Clement of Alexandria (80-140 A.D.) who, in his *Exhortation to the Heathen*, links the slavery of the Greek gods to their enslavement to their passions:

It would seem natural, therefore, for gods like these of yours to be slaves (δοῦλοι[37]), *since they have become slaves* (δοῦλοι) *of their passions. What is more, even before the time of the Helots, as they were called, among the Lacedaemonians, Apollo bowed beneath the yoke of slavery* (δούλειον) *to Admetus in Pherae, and Heracles ti Omphale in Sardis. Poseidon and Apollo were serfs* (ἐθήτευε) *to Laomedon, Apollo like a worthless servant* (οἰκέτης) *not having been able, I suppose, to obtain the*

---

[35] Apollodorus, *Lib.* 3.122 (Frazer, LCL).
36 Lucian, *Jupp. conf.*, 8.11-15. (Harmon, LCL).
[37] This first δοῦλοι was an insertion into the text by Schwartz and maintained in the Butterworth translation in the Loeb to make up for a lacunae in the manuscript. It seems a fair insertion given the presence of δοῦλοι in the second half of the sentence.

gift of freedom from his former master...Panyasis, too, relates in addition very many other instances of gods becoming servants (λατρεῦσαι) to men[38]

As with our previous section on how the transformation from god to another state took place, here too we need to incorporate, however briefly, a few examples from Latin. Lucan (39 A.D. – 65 A.D.), in his epic poem about the Roman civil war, *The Pharsalia*, recounts the myth of Apollo's slavery in his description of the land around Thessaly:

Evenus purpled by the Centaur's blood wanders through Calydon: in the Malian Gulf thy rapids fall, Spercheius: pure the wave with which Amphrysos irrigates the meads where once Apollo served.
(et flumine puro irrigat Amphyrysos famulantis pascua Phoebi)[39]

Perhaps in imitation of the epic poets which served as his models, Lucan opts to describe the servitude of Apollo without recourse to naming the occupation, using a form of *famulare,* to work as a slave or servant, and conveying very much the same meaning as θετευώ, λατρεύω or δουλεύω.[40]

B. Heracles

As important as the evidence brought forth to illustrate the tradition of god as slave in the above examples concerning Apollo appear to be, one other personage from classical literature is even more important to our discussion, namely Heracles. In Heracles we have a character who is at once mythic and historical, both god (or at the very least demi-god) and mortal. The historical literary tradition of Heracles, therefore, is of the utmost importance if we endeavor to show parallels between Christ as slave in Philippians 2:7 and the Greco-Roman literary tradition.[41] The stories about Heracles, however, will only

[38] Clement of Alexandria, *Protr.* 2.30, (Butterworth, LCL). with an English translation by G. W. Butterworth, *The Exhortation to the Greeks, The Rich Man's Salvation,* and the fragment of an address entitled *To the Newly Baptized,*(London: William Heinemann, New York: G. P. Putnam's Sons, 1919).
[39] Lucan, *Pharsalia* 6.367-368 (Duff, LCL).
[40] Similarly, Publius Papinius Statius' *Thebaid*, line 96 and Minucius Felix, *Oct.* 22.12-18
[41] As David E. Aune has pointed out, connections between the life of Herakles and the life of Jesus have been made since the middle of the second century A.D. with the writings of Justin Martyr.

illumine our hymnic images if we can find clear parallels between the two. In the case of the image of the god as slave, we must first establish that Heracles was perceived as divine, a fairly easy task given the wide ranging literary and archaeological data available to us. Secondly, we must show that Heracles was indeed perceived as a slave in the various recounting of his labors, a task which is a bit more difficult.

We must start, as we did with Apollo, with our earliest epic poets, in this case Hesiod (700 B.C.E). The story concerning the divine origins of Heracles is well known.[42] Zeus, impersonating Amphytrion, bedded Alcmena who eventually gave birth to two sons, Heracles and Iphicles. The peculiar nature of this birth is recounted by Hesiod in his *Shield of Heracles:*

> *Though they were brothers, these were not of one spirit; for one was weaker but the other a far better man, one terrible and strong, the mighty Heracles. Him she bore through the embrace of the son of Cronos, lord of the dark clouds, and the other, Iphicles, of Amphytrion the spear-wielder-offspring distinct, this one of union with a mortal man, but that other of union with Zeus, leader of all the gods.[43]*

Herodotus (484 B.C.E. - 425 B.C.E), writing two centuries later, affirmed the divinity of Heracles in his description of the religious practices of the Egyptians and Greeks:

> *Therefore, what I have discovered by inquiry plainly shows that Heracles is an ancient god. And further: those Greeks, I think, are most in the right, who have established and practice two worships of Heracles, sacrificing to one Heracles as immortal, and calling him the Olympian, but to the other bringing the offerings of a dead hero.[44]*

Aune, David E. Aune, "Heracles and Christ: Heracles Imagery in the Christology of Early Christianity," in *Greeks, Romans and Christians: Essays in Honor of Abraham J. Malherbe,* (Minneapolis: Fortress Press, 1990), pp. 3-19.

[42] On the divinity of Herakles in Homer see *Il.* 14.249-262

[43] Hesiod, [*Scut.*] 50-56 (Evelyn-White, LCL).

[44] Herodotus, *Hist.* 2.44 (A. D. Godley, LCL). Godley notes this dual nature of Herakles in the Odyssey, XI, 601, where an εἴδωλον of Herakles is seen in the world of the dead; but "he himself" is an immortal among the gods of heaven.

It is notable that in the time of Herodotus, Heracles is worshipped both as a god, an immortal, as well as a hero, an idea which we see persisting in the cults of the first century.

The divine origins of Heracles and great deeds provided ample fodder for the lyric poets and historians. It was the tragedians, however, who turned the labors of the great hero into the stuff of drama, for these labors offered a rich mine for theatrical productions. Euripides (480 B.C.E. - 406 B.C.E.) in his *Madness of Heracles*, has Amphitryon recount Heracles' many labors at the opening of the play:

> *And all his marriage-kin, my son forsook, yearning for Argos' giant builded*
> *burg Mycenae, whence I am outlawed, since I slew Electryon: he, to lighten*
> *mine affliction and fain to dwell in his own fatherland, proffered Eurystheus*
> *for our home-return-or spurred by Hera's goads, or drawn by fate-a great*
> *price, even to rid the earth of pests. And, all the other labours now achieved,*
> *for the last, down the gorge of Taenarus he hath passed to Hades, to bring up*
> *to light the hound three-headed, whence he hath not returned.*[45]

In *The Madness of Heracles,* Euripides recounts the sad tale of the slaughter of children of Heracles by his own hand. Prior to the murder of the children, the chorus recounts the twelve labors (πόνους) which include Heracles' time in service to Eurysteus. Nowhere in *The Madness of Heracles* is our protagonist described as a slave (δοῦλος). The only time one encounters the mention of slaves in this play by Euripides is in reference to Lycus' highly negative view of the citizenry of Thebes.[46] Similarly, in Sophocles' (496 B.C.E.- 406 B.C.E.) *Trachiniae,* the character of Heracles is treated the way a slave would be treated, i.e. sold to another to perform manual labor, but is never designated as such.[47]

The first century B.C.E. *Library and Epitome* attributed to Apollodorus of Athens offers us a prose account of the twelve labors of Heracles. In Apollodorus, Apollo sends Heracles on his twelve labors as a result of the murder

---

[45] Euripides, *Herc. fur.*, 14-25 (Way, LCL).

[46] Euripides, *Herc. fur.*, line 250 and 270.

[47] Sophocles, *Trachiniae,* line 275, "... the father of all, Olympian Zeus, sent him away to be sold," (Storr, LCL).

of his children whereas in Euripides these tasks are demanded of the son of Zeus as a condition for the recall of Amphytrion from exile. As with Euripides and a majority of our other authors, although some of the labors of Heracles are tasks normally associated with a slave, most notably the cleaning out of the stable of Augeas, the vast majority of the time when this story is recounted we find words other than derivatives of δουλός/δουλεύω being used:

And she told him to dwell in Tiryns, serving (λατρεύοντα) Eurystheus for twelve years and to perform the ten labours (ἄθλους) imposed on him, and so, she said, when the tasks were accomplished, he would be immortal.[48]

A close parallel to what we see in Philippians 2:6 occurs in Apollodorus' *Library* when the oracle at Delphi informs Heracles how he is to atone for the murder of Iphitus:

When they had thus been parted, Heracles received an oracle, which declared that the remedy for his disease was for him to be sold and to serve for three years (τρία ἔτη λατρεύσαντι), and to pay compensation for the murder to Eurytus. After the delivery of the oracle, Hermes sold Heracles, and he was bought by Omphale, daughter of Iardanes, queen of Lydia, to whom at his death her husband Tmolus had bequeathed the government. Eurytus did not accept the compensation when it was presented to him, but Heracles served Omphale as a slave (δουλεύων), and in the course of his servitude he seized and bound the Cercopes at Ephesus.[49]

As with our other authors, Heracles is described as doing slaves work using a variant of λατρεύω, but for the first time we see a variant of δουλός/δουλεύω being used. This use of a variant of δουλός/δουλεύω persists when the same story is told by Plutarch (46-120 C.E.) in his *Lives:*

And when Heracles met with calamity and, after the slaying of Iphitus, removed into Lydia and for a long time did slave's service (ἐδούλευε) there in the house of Omphale, then Lydia indeed obtained great peace and security.[50]

---

[48] Apollodorus, *Lib.* 2.4.12 (Frazer, LCL).
[49] Appolodorus, *Lib.* 2.131.1-132.4 (Frazer, LCL).
[50] Plutarch, *Thes.* 6.1.15 (Perrin, LCL).

C. Athena in Herodotus' *Histories*

We would be remiss in our investigation if we failed to include at least a brief mention of the description of a goddess taking human from Herodotus' *Histories*. Although this description of the manifestation of the goddess tells us nothing about the language by which Greeks described the act of transformation, it speaks volumes to the idea that descriptions of gods taking human form was an idea not solely consigned to the time of myth. Writing sometime between 446 and 425 B.C.E., Herodotus (485 B.C.E. – 425 B.C.E.) describes the spectacle that accompanied the return of the disgraced Pisistratus:

> *The Greeks have never been simpletons; for centuries past they have been distinguished from other nations by superior wits; and of all Greeks the Athenians are allowed to be the most intelligent: yet it was at the Athenians' expense that this ridiculous trick was played. In the village of Paeania there was a handsome woman called Phye, nearly six feet tall, whom they fitted out in a suit of armor and mounted in a chariot; then, after getting her to pose in the most striking attitude, they drove into Athens, where messengers who had preceded them were already, according to their instructions, talking to the people and urging them to welcome Pisistratus back, because the goddess Athene herself had shown him extraordinary honour and was bringing him home to her own acropolis. They spread this nonsense all over the town, and it was not long before rumour reached the outlying villages that Athene was bringing Pisistratus back, and both villagers and townsfolk, convinced that the woman Phye was indeed the goddess, offered her prayers and received Psistratus with open arms.*[51]

Thus, the idea that a goddess could appear to mortals was an idea very much alive in mid-sixth century Athens, albeit an idea that was looked down upon as foolish by Herodotus. It does show, however, that the Greeks were at least somewhat familiar with the manifestation of gods and goddesses in human form occurring in historical as opposed to mythological time.

---

[51] Herodotus, *The Histories,* Aubrey de Sélincourt trans. (Middlesex, England: Penguin Books, 1972). 1.61.

The God as Slave: Philippians 2:6

ὃς ἐν μορφῇ θεοῦ ὑπάρχων...μορφήν δούλου λαβων

Now that we have made our examination of a select examples from the Greco-Roman literary tradition concerning the god as slave a few observations can be made concerning what we find in the hymnic fragment from Philippians 2:6. It becomes clear from the above examples that the god as slave was a recurring theme in Greco-Roman literature, being seen most notably in the myths surrounding both Apollo and Heracles. In addition, it is also clear that in the myths associated with both Apollo and Heracles we find the same word being used for slave that we find in Phil 2:6 (δοῦλος) with Heracles being designated as a δοῦλος from the time of Apollodorus, 2nd - 1st century B.C. Thus, in describing Christ as a δοῦλος (slave) in Philippians 2:6, the author of that hymn was standing squarely in a literary tradition which had described two gods in particular, Apollo and Heracles, in much the same way. In addition, if I may borrow a bit of argumentation from the previous section, the use of a form of λαμβάνω, "to take, receive, grasp or understand," to describe the transformation to a slave is identical to the way Euripides described the transformation of Zeus into a swan in *Helen*. Clearly, in this one instance of Christ taking the form of a slave that we have in Philippians 2:6, our author was on well trod literary ground.

The God as Flesh

We are left then with our final description of the transformation from god to man, the transformation which results in the god becoming manifest as σάρξ (flesh). Unlike our previous examples, however, we do not have a long and established mythological and historical literary inheritance to draw upon as the god as σάρξ (flesh) is an idea relatively uncommon in the Greek literary tradition. God's appear in various forms in Greco-Roman literature, but the God as σάρξ is all but unattested. We must venture forth from the literary world of myth, albeit temporarily, and examine how the term σάρξ (flesh) came to be used in Greek philosophy.

The Greek word σάρξ most often translated as flesh pertaining to the body or more simply meat, is a word which is somewhat common in Greek prose and with one exception, Euripides, rather scarce in drama, rhetoric or tragedy. Outside of its' 146 appearances in the New Testament, the author who most frequently uses σάρξ is Plato, followed by Aristotle and lastly the aforementioned Euripides. Outside of the literature of the classical period, the only authors to use σάρξ significantly are Epictetus and Josephus. In order to properly situate the use σάρξ in the hymns under investigation we need to examine how these authors used this word in the centuries leading up to the writing of the New Testament.

A. Plato, Aristotle, Euripides

Plato uses σάρξ in two distinct ways either describing sustenance or food or as an anatomical designator,[52] signifying the muscles, skin and bones that make up the human body which surrounds the soul. There is a not so subtle negative connotation attached to the use of the word σάρξ in Plato owing in part, no doubt, to his adherence to the dichotomy between body and soul. We get a hint of this negative connotation in these two quotes from the *Laws* and the *Symposium*:

> *...so that when living his life might have been as just and holy as possible, and when dead he might be free during the life which follows this life from the penalty for wickedness and sin. This being so, one ought never to spend extravagantly on the dead, though supposing that the carcass of flesh (σαρκών) that is being buried is in the truest sense one's own relative; but one ought rather to suppose that the real son or brother--or whoever else it may be that a man fancies himself to be mournfully burying--has departed in furtherance and fulfillment of his own destiny, and that it is our duty to make a wise use of what we have.*[53]

> *But tell me, what would happen if one of you had the fortune to look upon essential beauty entire, pure and unalloyed; not infected with the flesh*

---

[52] Plato, *Tim.* 60 a, 61c, 62 b, 65 a, 67 d, 73 b, 74 a, e, d, 75 a, c, 76 c, 77 d, 80 e, 82 c,d,e, 83 a,c e, 84b, 84 e, 85 d, *Gorg.* 518 c, *Leg.* 6.78 2 c, 7.797 e, *Phaed.* 96 d, 98d, *Resp.* 8.556d, *Symp.* 207 d, 211 e. Plato. *Platonis Opera,* ed. John Burnet. Oxford University Press. 1903, Plato. *Plato in Twelve Volumes*, Vol. 9 translated by W.R.M. Lamb. Cambridge, MA, Harvard University Press; London, William Heinemann Ltd. 1925.

[53] Plato, *Leg.* 12.959c (W. R. M. Lamb, LCL).

(σαρκῶν) *and color of humanity, and ever so much more of mortal trash?*
What if he could behold the divine beauty itself, in its unique form? [54]

Aristotle, like Plato, seems to concentrate on two similar meanings of
σάρξ with the primary definition in Aristotle describing a part of a human body.[55]
As these quotes from the *Metaphysics* will show, however, at times Aristotle will
use σάρξ to mean the entire human body, "the human" as opposed to simply a
part. Unlike Plato, however, there does not seem to be any negative connotation
attached to σάρξ, with Aristotle concentrating   primarily on an anatomical
meaning:

> *For even if the line is divided and resolved into its halves, or if the man is*
> *resolved into bones and muscles and flesh (σάρκας), it does not follow*
> *that they are composed of these as parts of their essence, but as their*
> *matter; and these are parts of the concrete whole, but not of the form, or*
> *that to which the formula refers.*[56]
> *For the material generation of one thing from another cannot go on in an*
> *infinite progression (e.g. flesh (σάρκα) from earth, earth from air, air*
> *from fire, and so on without a stop); nor can the source of motion (e.g.*
> *man be moved by air, air by the sun, the sun by strife.*[57]

Euripides also maintains two general meanings for σάρξ, meanings
similar to those put forth by Aristotle,[58] namely meaning either the entire body,

---

[54] Plato, *Symp.* 211, (W. R. M. Lamb, LCL).

[55] Aristotle, *Poet,* 1458 b, *Metaph.* 1.993, 5.1024 a, 6.1026, 7.106 b, 7.1034, 7.1036 a, 8.1035 a b,
8.1041 b, 8.1042, 11.106 a, 12.1070 a b, 12.1071, 14.1092 b, *Eth. nic.*, 1129 a, J. Bywater,
Aristotle's *Ethica Nicomachea*. Oxford, Clarendon Press. 1894, Aristotle. *Aristotle in 23 Volumes*,
Vols.17, 18, translated by Hugh Tredennick. Cambridge, MA, Harvard University Press; London,
William Heinemann Ltd. 1933, 1989

[56] Aristotle, *Metaph.* 7.1035a. (H. Tredennick, LCL).

[57] Aristotle, *Metaph.* 2.994a. (H. Tredennick, LCL).

[58] Euripides, *Bacch.* line 605, 746, lines 1127-1130, line 1135, *Cycl.* line 380, line 342, line 402,
El. line 385, lines 819-824, *Hec.* line, 1056, *Hel.* line 301, line 330, *Heracl.* line 1151, *Hipp.*
line 1021, line 1235, line 1342, *Med.* 1181, *Suppl.* line 48, *Phoen.* line 1285, line 1577, *Tro.*
line 440, line 775, Clarendon Press, Oxford. 1913. *The Complete Greek Drama*, edited by
Whitney J. Oates and Eugene O'Neill, Jr. in two volumes, 1938, *Hecuba*, translated by E. P.
Coleridge. New York. Random House. *Helen*, Euripides. *Euripidis Fabulae*, ed. Gilbert Murray,
vol. 3. Oxford. Clarendon Press, Oxford. 1913, *Medea*, Euripides. *Euripides*, with an English
translation by David Kovacs. Cambridge. Harvard University Press. Forthcoming, *Trojan Women*,
Euripides. *The Plays of Euripides*, translated by E. P. Coleridge. Volume I. London. George Bell

the human, or the fleshy part of the body as distinct from blood and bone. As one would expect from his chosen subject matter, Euripides emphasizes the more visceral and graphic aspects of flesh:

> *No more was seen her eyes' imperial calm, no more her comely features: but the gore dripped from her head's crown flecked with blended fire. The flesh flakes from her bones* (σάρκες δ' ἀπ' ὀστέων)...[59]

There is one instance in Euripides, however, where the meaning attached to σάρξ differs subtly from the above, namely when it is used to describe not simply the body but the body in a particular stage, in this case young adulthood. In Euripides' the *Madness of Heracles*, the demi-god ponders both his divine parentage and the fate that has befallen him since birth:

> *For truer father thee I count than Zeus. When I was yet a suckling, Zeus' bride sent gorgon-glaring serpents secretly against my cradle, that I might be slain, soon as I gathered vesture of brawny flesh.* (ἐπεὶ δὲ σαρκὸς περιβόλαι' ἐκτησάμην)[60]

Whether Heracles is referring here to his own birth or, what seems more likely, that period of young adulthood when he began his labors, this example stands out as the only instance where the word σάρξ is used in connection to someone of divine parentage in Greek literature outside of the New Testament. Granted, it is an example some five to six centuries distant from our New Testament examples, however, it is at least an indication that the term σάρξ could be used to describe a god in some stage of his or her existence.

B. Epictetus and Josephus

Epictetus (55-135 A.D.) heir to the Stoic, and hence aspects of Platonic doctrines concerning the dichotomy between flesh and soul discusses the nature

---

and Sons. 1891, *Suppliants*, Euripides. *Euripidis Fabulae*, ed. Gilbert Murray, vol. 2. Oxford, 1913.

[59] Euripides, *Med.* 1197-1200 (Way, LCL).

[60] Euripides, *Herc. fur.* 1265-1269 (Way, LCL).

132

of life much in the same way as Plato. Σάρξ for Epictetus means both "the body" as well as a distinct part of the human anatomy[61]:

> God is helpful; but the good also is helpful. It would seem, therefore, that the true nature of the good will be found to be where we find that of God to be. What, then is the true nature of God? Flesh? (σάρξ) Far from it.[62]

> But if a man who has entered a philosopher's lecture does not know what he himself is he deserves to be in a state of fear, and also to flatter those whom he used to flatter before; if he has not yet learned that he is not flesh (σάρξ), nor bone, nor sinews, but that which employs these, that which both governs the impressions of the senses and understands them[63].

Finally, we turn to Flavius Josephus (37-100 A.D.),[64] who maintains three distinct uses for the word σάρξ, namely flesh, as in the flesh of animals, flesh as in the soft parts of a human and flesh as in body distinct from soul. This flesh/soul dichotomy seems to be borrowed from Greek philosophy as is evident in his discussion of the Essenes:

> For it is a fixed belief of theirs that the body is corruptible and its constituent matter impermanent, but that the soul is immortal and imperishable. Emanating from the finest ether, these souls become entangled, as it were, in the prison-house of the body, to which they are dragged down by a sort of natural spell; but once they are released from the bonds of flesh (σάρκα), then as though liberated from a long servitude, they rejoice and are born aloft.[65]

Josephus, always the good historian with an eye to detail, is not above using more visceral images of flesh on occasion, especially when it shows his own ingenuity:

---

[61] Epictetus, *Diatr.* 1.20.18-19, 2.8.1-3, 2.9.19, 2.22.19, 2.23.21, 3.7.1-5, 3.7.24, 4.7.31-32, *Epicteti Dissertationes ab Arriano digestae*. Epictetus. Heinrich Schenkl. editor. Leipzig. B. G. Teubner. 1916
[62] Epictetus, *Diatr.* 2.8.1-3 (Oldfather, LCL).
[63] Epictetus, *Diatr.* 4.7.31-32 (Oldfather, LCL).
[64] Josephus, *A.J.* 6.120, 6.186, 19. 325, 12.211-212, 15.236, *B.J.* 2.254, 3.271-274, 5.4, 6.47, 6.45 Flavius Josephus. *The Works of Flavius Josephus*, Translated by. William Whiston, A.M. (Auburn and Buffalo:NY, John E. Beardsley. 1895), Flavius Josephus. *Flavii Iosephi opera*, (B. Niese. Berlin. Weidmann. 1892).
[65] Josephus, *B.J.* 2.154 (H. St. J. Thackeray, LCL).

> *In this critical situation, Josephus, taking counsel from necessity - ready as she is in invention when stimulated by despair – ordered boiling oil to be poured upon this roof of close-locked shields. His men had it ready, and at once from all quarters deluged the Romans with large quantities, flinging after it the vessels still scalding hot. This broke their formation; the Romans, burning and in excruciating agony, rolled headlong from the ramparts. For the oil instantaneously penetrated beneath their armour from head to foot, spreading over the entire surface of their bodies (σώματος) and devouring the flesh (σάρκα) with the fierceness of a flame.*[66]

Thus, it becomes clear that the word σάρξ had two basic meanings in Greek literature in the period directly leading up to the writing of our hymnic fragments. The first is concerned with flesh as meat. This can refer to the meat of an animal, most often in reference to a feast or meal, or it can refer to the meaty or fleshy parts of a human. It is this latter usage that is used most often in describing wounds, the horrors of battle or any other such violent images. The second definition, that of flesh as referring to the entire human body as distinct from soul, seems to be the most prevalent, especially when it is encountered in Plato, Aristotle or later Epictetus and Josephus. It may or may not have a negative connotation, but often, as in the case with Plato and others, a dichotomy is preserved in which the flesh of this mortal realm pales in comparison to the higher soul.

The New Testament usage of Σάρξ

With the exception of our two examples, John 1.14 and 1 Timothy 3.16, the usage of σάρξ in the New Testament never approaches ideas of incarnation. The few examples we have from the Synoptic Gospels and the Acts of the Apostles fall into the categories outlined above. Some are quotations from/allusions to the OT (Mark 10:8/Genesis 2:24 and par., Luke 3:6/Is 40:3-5, Mk 13:20/Dan 9:37, Acts 2:17/Is 2:2, Acts 2:26/Ps 16:8-11) corresponding to the idea of flesh as a synonym for the human person as distinct from the soul.[67] The

---

[66] Josephus, *B.J.* 3.271-275 (H. St. J. Thackeray, LCL).
[67] Also Matt 16.17, Mark 14.38, Luke 24.39, Acts 2.31

134

preponderance of evidence for σάρξ in the NT comes from both Paul and the Gospel of John, however, with two exceptions (John 1:14 and 1 Tim 3:16), nowhere do we see σάρξ being used to unambiguously describe the incarnation of Jesus. As you would expect from the thoroughly Hellenized Paul, σάρξ more often than not simply designates the human body or earthly life.[68] As with previous authors, the designation of σάρξ in Paul can often take on negative connotations in an oppositional relationship to πνεῦμα (spirit).[69] We see this negative connotation often as well in John 8:15 where the visible is negatively compared to the spiritual, i.e. unseen. When σάρξ is used in a positive sense in John, such as in John 6:51-58, it is used in regards to the words of institution, where the flesh and blood of Jesus which gives eternal life is compared to the bread eaten by the Hebrews in the dessert. Only the Johannine prologue uses σάρξ in describing the act of the incarnation.

It becomes clear when examining our two instances of the use of σάρξ in John 1:14 and 1 Tim 3:16 that we are clearly seeing σάρξ used to describe the body, as opposed to simply a part of the body, of Jesus. In that regard it is more or less in line with the definitions of σάρξ examined previously. Yet, we must admit the context of how σάρξ is used in these two instances, in reference to someone who is clearly divine, is an odd one and one almost without precedent. With the aforementioned exception of Heracles in the play by Euripides, flesh/σάρξ is not a word one encounters in Greek literature in reference to a divinity. In the vast majority of examples from literature it is more often than not solely consigned to the mortal realm. One can only surmise why the authors of these hymns chose σάρξ when other words would have sufficed such as σόμα. We can only assume that the authors wished to leave no doubt as to the mortal state of Christ after the incarnation.

---

[68] ex. Gal 4.13, 1 Cor 7.28, 15.9, 2 Cor 4.11, 12.7, Phil 1.22, 24
[69] ex. Phil 3.3, Rom 8.13, Gal 4.23, 5.18

In our examination of the language of transformation we have seen that the manner by which the New Testament authors described the shift from divine to mortal bears a close affinity to the way in which similar transformations were described in both Greek and Latin literature. The elasticity of language allowed by the use of ὁμοίωμα (likeness) and σχῆμα (outward form, likeness) that we find in Phil 2:7 is mirrored by the preponderance of Greek and Roman authors who allowed for the true form of the god to be unknown, and preferred simply the "appearance" of a god in human or animal form to be perceived by onlookers. In addition, authors like Euripides and Apollodorus embraced the action of transformation, describing the change of form as something that was actively taken or "put on" by the god. In this sense as well the authors of our New Testament hymnic fragments were standing fore square within the Greco-Roman literary tradition. Finally, in the case of the transformation of Christ into slave that we see in Philippians 2:6, one is wont to see any major differences with the Greco-Roman literary tradition with similar depictions in how later authors described the transformations of Apollo and Heracles.[70]

As we have seen, however, the ambiguity attached to the transformation of Jesus in the hymnic fragments is ameliorated somewhat by verbs such as γίνομαι ("to become") which calls for a somewhat more concrete interpretation. In the case of Philippians 2:7, Christ "comes" in a human likeness. Granted, we are still dealing with a final state that is concerned with simply "appearance" but the choice of verb here differentiates it slightly. In John 1:14 and 1 Tim 3:16 the ambiguity of the transformation that is maintained in the Philippians example disappears for in both Christ "becomes" flesh and not simply the appearance of something else.

The god as flesh, however, was all but non-existent in the Greek and Roman literary record. In this regard it appears that with the image found in John 1:14 and 1 Tim 3:16 we are venturing into new literary ground. The god as flesh,

---

[70] Aune, David E., "Heracles and Christ," p. 4.

σάρξ, in having no literary antecedents save one scant reference in Euripides would seem to be a Christian invention. Clearly, these early Christian authors wanted to emphasize the true humanity of Christ, so human in fact that he took on the flesh which surrounds us all and which forever differentiates us from those who are solely immortal and who can only appear mortal when the situation dictates.

Chapter Five

The Appropriated God and the People of the Hymns

The original aim of our investigation was to examine the core images of Christ as they appear in the Christologic hymnic fragments of the New Testament (The Pre-Existent/Pre-Creation Christ, Christ the Creator and Christ the Incarnate Divinity), with an eye to discovering more about the authors that produced them and the communities that received them. As we were consigned to solely literary evidence, the conclusions that we can now draw illuminate the most probable literary environments that that may have contributed to their production. Spread out over six separate works in the New Testament, these hymnic fragments tell us not only how the earliest Christians chose to describe Christ but also how they chose to borrow from the culture around them to give meaning to these images.

This chapter is separated into two distinct sections. The first section summarizes the most probable literary backdrop for the images contained in the hymnic fragments under investigation and posits the literary influences that may lay behind such images. As part of this piece we will also discuss briefly how such images may have been received by the communities that first heard them. The second section outlines some areas of further investigation that the previous sections have pointed towards. As we have alluded to in the previous chapters, some hymnic fragments, such as John 1.1-18, offer up numerous images allowing for in depth discussions of probable literary antecedents. Others, such as the decidedly fragmentary fragment found in Heb 1.3-4, give us very little to go on. We shall lay out our findings in roughly chronological sequence in an attempt to demonstrate how the core images of Christ expanded and changed in that all important first Christian century.

Philippians 2:6-11

Arguably our earliest hymnic fragment, the core images contained in Phil 2:6-11 center upon the ideas of Christ as a divine, thinking entity prior to his incarnation, and the circumstances surrounding that incarnation. The idea of a god "regarding" or contemplating his or her own existence prior to descending to the world of mortals seems to bear at least some similarity to Philo's concept of the heavenly man, in that both Christ and the divine man engage in thought processes in some pre-creative time frame. The second image of Christ taking the form of a slave and coming in human form, on the other hand, seem most probably to be coming from the world of Greco-Roman religion owing to its close similarities to what we saw in Homer, Hesiod, Euripides, and Plutarch. When this Greco-Roman religious image is coupled with images which had to have originated in the Jewish thought world, the aforementioned allusion to Ps. 110 as well as the similarities to Philo's "heavenly man," we can surmise that the author or community which produced this hymnic fragment was most probably influenced by Hellenistic Judaism. It is somewhat surprising, then, that we find this hymnic fragment in not only in one of our earliest Pauline letters, but in a community that was, in the mind of most commentators predominantly Gentile.[305]

---

[305] Joseph H. Hellerman, *Reconstructing Honor in Roman Philippi*, (Cambridge: Cambridge University Press, 2005), p. 64-72, Martin, Ralph P., *Philippians*, p. 3-7, Melick, *Philippians, Colossians and Philemon*, Nashville, pp. 24-25, H. C. J. Moule, *Philippian Studies*, (London: Pickering and Inglis, 1962), p. xi – xiv, Peter Pilhofer, *Philippi*, (Tübingen : J.C.B. Mohr, 1995), p. 85-91, Bonnie B. Thurston and Judith Ryan, *Philippians and Philemon*, (Collegeville, Minn: Liturgical Press, 2005), p. 7-9.

As with all our hymnic fragments, there is no way of telling whether this was produced by the Philippian community or if Paul simply imported it into his *Letter to the Philippians* from elsewhere, perhaps some other community that he had encountered. What we can surmise, however, is that the earliest hymnic fragment we possess appears to draw not only upon images culled primarily from Hebrew Wisdom literature but from the aforementioned world which produced Homer, Euripides and Plutarch as well. Only this world offers us examples of divine personages assuming human form and serving as or being designated as a slave. It is an image in all probability readily accepted by a Gentile audience well versed in the mythology surrounding Apollo and Herakles. Whether the audience may have been able to pick up on the subtle links to the philosophical concept of the "heavenly man" that we see in Philo is uncertain. It is possible that the author of the hymn may have been drawing on similar language to what we see in Philo but the evidence is scarce.

1 Corinthians 8:6

Our second hymnic fragment under investigation, 1 Cor 8:6, like Heb 1:3-4, offers us very little indeed to go on, simply one verse. Yet, in this one verse we are offered yet another image that bears no affinity to anything seen specifically in Jewish Wisdom literature. There is no reference to the *Logos*, no allusions to Divine Wisdom and no images or ideas which originated in the Hebrew scriptures. With no descriptions of pre-Creation divinities, and hence no allusions to Divine Wisdom, 1 Cor 8:6 offers us solely a statement about Christ's relationship to the Father and the role he plays in the life of the community. This image is described using language that could only have originated in Hellenistic philosophy, although whether from Middle Platonic or Stoic circles is unclear as we have indicated. Unlike Phil 2:6-11, the hymnic fragment contained in 1 Cor 8:6 seems to be originating in a non-Jewish literary environment, or at least this particular fragment gives no indication of being influenced by the Jewish literary world. One could posit that the community which produced the hymnic fragment found in 1 Cor 8:6 might have had exposure to a "higher" literature, i.e. eschewing talk of gods talking human form in favor of more metaphysical descriptions, but that might be making too much of a few verses. There is nothing in 1 Cor 8:6 which strikes one as hailing from a Jewish literary context, although one could posit that Hellenized Jews would have been a possible source for discussions of the one God using Greek philosophical language. Again, the evidence is not conclusive.

Colossians 1:15-20

With the images found in Col 1:15-20 we are, for the first time, encountering images that could have unambiguously originated in the world of Hellenistic Jewish literature, specifically Hellenistic Jewish wisdom speculation as influenced by Middle Platonic philosophy. Although one cannot date the writing of the "Colossians Hymn" with anything approaching specificity, even allowing for authorship during the lifetime of Paul, the general consensus is that we are dealing with something that came together after either the *Letter to the Philippians* or the *First Letter to the Corinthians.* We see that by the time of the writing of the hymnic fragment contained in Col 1:15-20 we have a community which was drawing upon not solely Hellenistic philosophy, but which was also in conversation with the Wisdom tradition as well. As with Philo in works such as *de Fuga et Inventione* 108-109 and *de Cherubim* 125-127, images of Wisdom, under either the guise of Divine Wisdom or the *Logos,* appear alongside the oft cited Middle Platonic "metaphysics of prepositions." As with the community that produced the hymnic fragment contained in 1 Cor 8:6, Hellenistic philosophy undoubtedly influenced the author of Col 1:15-20 but it was a Hellenistic philosophy as seen through the eyes of the wisdom tradition of the Jews.

John 1:1-18

The hymnic fragment represented by John 1:1-18 offers us all three of the core images under investigation and is, in fact, the only hymnic fragment to contain all of these images. It is the only hymnic fragment which exhibits

Hellenistic Jewish philosophical images of the *Logos*, and as such is the closest parallel to similar treatments in Philo of Alexandria mentioned above. However, in addition to these philosophical speculations which draw upon the Hellenistic Jewish wisdom tradition, we also have the decidedly non-Jewish image of Christ the Incarnate divinity appearing in the flesh (John 1:14). We have then, at least at the time of the writing of John 1:1-18, an early Christian community which was well versed in not only the language of philosophy but somewhat familiar with the language of incarnate divinities. However, it must be noted that the use of σάρξ in terms of an incarnate divinity as put forth in John 1:14 is extremely rare in Greco-Roman literature. The only example which even approximates this usage comes from Euripides *Herakles*, where the demigod describes how he took on "a cloak of youthful flesh" (Euripides, *Her.fur.* 1265-1269). Unfortunately, this evidence is not enough to unequivocally show that the language of Greco-Roman religion influenced the author of the hymnic fragment found in John 1:14. When left with such little evidence we must then eliminate alternatives to arrive at our best guess. Clearly, the language of gods becoming flesh does not occur in Jewish literature. It is equally clear that neither Middle Platonic or late Stoic thought would have entertained such a notion. In addition, we find nothing of the sort in our chief example of Hellenistic Jewish thought, namely, Philo of Alexandria. Finally, as we have indicated, the use of σάρξ in an incarnational sense in John 1:14 does not resemble anything that we see elsewhere in the New Testament, specifically in Paul. Thus, our only alternative is to posit that in the use of σάρξ that we find in John 1:14 we are seeing some echo, however faint, of the image of gods taking human form that was so prevalent in Greco-Roman religion. It must be noted, however, that the concept of the *Logos* as σάρξ defies any neat characterization.

What then can we say about the author or community which produced the core images found in John 1:1-14? Clearly, we are dealing with an individual or community well versed in Hellenistic Jewish wisdom speculation as the parallels to similar ideas in Philo will attest. However, it is a community which also knows something, how much we cannot ascertain, about incarnate divinities. We are potentially dealing then with Hellenized Jews who were so thoroughly Hellenized that incarnate divinities posed no serious problems for them.

As for the reception of this image of Christ as *Logos* incarnate by the community what then can we say? Clearly the image would have resonated with those in the audience with some background in the Greek philosophical tradition surrounding the *Logos*. However, for those not so well versed in such traditions, and this would have to be the majority of the first hearers of the hymn, the idea of the word of God as existing in the beginning of creation would have been a comfortable image to any acquainted with the book of Genesis. Finally, although the God as σάρξ would have appeared odd to most all who first heard it, it is clear that the image behind the image of god as flesh, namely the idea of an incarnate divinity, would have been a welcome one to any Greek in the audience.

Hebrews 1:3-4

As we discussed in the third chapter, the hymnic fragment under investigation in Heb 1:3-4 offers parallels to both Hellenistic Jewish wisdom literature and Greco-Roman descriptions of Demeter, owing to the odd choice of Christ being described as "bearing" (φέρων) all things by his word. It is close to the idea we see in both the *Wisdom of Solomon* (Wis 7.24), used to describe the actions of Divine Wisdom and in Plutarch (*De Iside et Osiride*, 367) when used to describe the powers of Demeter, her daughter and Poseidon. Yet, in both of the above descriptions, the context argues for either Divine Wisdom or Isis to have some creative function, whereas in Heb 1:3b the creative aspect appears to be lacking. However, as there is general consensus that the first part of the verse ("who is the refulgence of his glory, the very imprint of his being") is a direct allusion to Wis 7:26,[2] one can postulate that the first part of the verse which

---

[2] Attridge, *Hebrews*, p. 42, F.F. Bruce, *Epistle to the Hebrews*, (Grand Rapids, MI: Eerdmans, 1990), p. 5, Robert P. Gordon, *Hebrews*, (Sheffield, Sheffield Academic Press), 2000, p. 39,

speaks to Christ "bearing" all things could also be an allusion to Wis 7:24 in which Divine Wisdom "penetrates and pervades." As our investigation of the influences of Isis imagery in the Wisdom of Solomon indicates, it is uncertain whether the author of Heb 1:3 was accessing Isis imagery as filtered through Wis 7:26 or whether he or his community had access to the Isis cult directly. As with our discussion of John 1:14 above, once we eliminate influences that are clearly not in this hymnic fragment, i.e. there is no evidence of Greco-Roman religious language about incarnate divinities nor examples from Hellenistic philosophy elsewhere in the verses under consideration, Jewish wisdom speculation would seem to have to be the most probable source. We are dealing with an author or community of Hellenized Jews who, drawing upon similar ideas in Hebrew literature such as the Wisdom of Solomon, have chosen to depict Christ with images that just as easily could have been used of Divine Wisdom in her feminine guise.

1 Tim 3:16

Our final hymnic fragment under investigation is, arguably, chronologically the last to be written. It is a hymnic fragment solely concerned with the life of Christ, giving no depictions of either his life with the Father prior to his own incarnation nor putting forth any images of creation. Thus, it is in all probability not drawing upon Hellenistic Jewish wisdom speculation at least as represented from the time of the Wisdom of Solomon onwards. In addition, we are also free from any images which could be being drawn from Hellenistic philosophy as witnessed by the absence of either the "metaphysics of prepositions" or any discussion of the *Logos*. Thus, the core image contained in 1 Tim 3:16 would most probably have to originate in the world of Greco-Roman religious thought as it deals expressly and solely with the incarnation. However,

---

Héring, Jean, *Hebrews*, p. 5, Victor C. Pfitzner, *Hebrews*, (Nashville, Tenn: Abingdon Press, 1997), p.51.

as we indicated with the image in John 1:14, the image of the god incarnate as σάρξ is indeed a peculiar one.

Conclusions

Thus, if we look at each of the above hymnic fragment we seem to be dealing with images from two literary worlds which often overlapped, the literary world of Hellenistic Jewish wisdom speculation and the literary world of Greco-Roman religion. On the one hand you have the image of the god becoming man and serving as a slave which had to come from Greco-Roman religion as exemplified by the hymnic fragment in Philippians 2:6-11. Yet, along with such incarnational imagery, Phil 2:6-11 also contains images which may have borrowed from Hellenistic Jewish wisdom speculation as well. Thus, in what is arguably the first Christian hymnic composition, these two literary worlds seem to be thoroughly intermingled. At roughly the same time, however, you have the Corinthian community, or at least a community familiar to the Corinthian community, writing a decidedly small hymn to Christ lacking any clear indications of influence from Hellenistic Judaism, a hymnic fragment which, for all intents and purposes would appear to be hailing solely from the Greek philosophical world. Sometime after the writing of these hymnic fragments you have clear and unmistakable influences from Hellenistic Jewish wisdom speculation occurring in the hymnic fragments contained in Col 1:15-20, John 1:1-18 and Heb 1:3-4, with the aforementioned blending of both Hellenistic Jewish wisdom speculation and Greco-Roman religious ideas in the hymnic fragment found in John. Finally, you have a community, as represented by the hymnic fragment found in 1 Tim 3:16, which seems to be writing clearly from the Greco-Roman side of the spectrum, having no recourse to the images normally found in Hellenistic Jewish wisdom, such as those which are patterned after feminine Wisdom, and lacking any clear indications of influence from the world of Hellenistic philosophy, concentrating solely on Christ as "flesh." Whether the author of 1 Tim 3:16 was drawing upon Greco-Roman religious imagery for incarnational divinities or perhaps, and this is more likely, simply drawing upon early Christian kerygma and other hymns, is unclear.

As we indicated in our first chapter, the image of the pre-existent or pre-creation divinity is difficult to separate from the image of the creator standing alongside the Lord. Divine Wisdom, although only definitively given creative powers in the Wisdom of Solomon, was at the very least present with God when these actions were undertaken. It is odd that the first Christians would have seized upon this image as one of the most important in their descriptions of Christ. Appearing as it does in three of the six hymnic fragments under investigation, it was clearly central to the earliest beliefs about Christ. Yet, the fact remains that what originally was a feminine aspect of God became, in the first Christian century, the preferred image to describe God's son in the earliest hymnic fragments we possess. True, it is feminine Wisdom re-imagined and mediated via Middle Platonic thought which can now speak of the male *Logos*, but her feminine origins are never that far below the surface.

The image of Christ as somehow responsible for the created world is even more striking when one considers it alongside descriptions of his incarnate nature, and gives us a clear indication that although we are dealing with language from Greco-Roman religion we are on decidedly new ground. Greek gods did take human form but their actions and responsibilities while in this sphere of existence were decidedly pedestrian. We find a petty intrigue here, a romantic dalliance there, but nowhere do we see a Greek god taking human form and maintaining the created order. It is when you take these core images together, most easily seen in the one hymnic fragment that contains all three images, John 1.1-18, that we truly see the break with either Hellenistic Jewish thought or the thought world of Greece and Rome. In the hymnic fragments to Christ, or more correctly in the combination of images taken from these two thought worlds, we are dealing with something new.

Theological Appropriation and the Christological Hymnic Fragments

Although the resultant image of this combining of ideas from Greco-Roman religion and Wisdom speculation, i.e. the idea of Christ the Incarnate Creator, was novel, the process by which ideas from disparate literary traditions were combined had a long provenance. Beginning with the appropriation of images of the Egyptian goddess *Ma'at*, Jewish authors from the time of the writings of Proverbs 9 onwards were amenable to incorporating other religious traditions and making them decidedly their own. In this way the decidedly pagan *Ma'at* could be incorporated into the ostensibly monotheistic tradition of the Jews. Thus, an aspect of the Lord could have Egyptian characteristics but could also be subordinated to the one God of the Jews. This process continues when we see clear echoes of the Isis traditions in the depictions of Divine Wisdom in the *Wisdom of Solomon.* As with Proverbs, the characteristics of a feminine pagan divinity could be incorporated into the now Hellenized depictions of Divine Wisdom all the while maintaining the primacy of the Lord. By the time of the Christian authors under consideration here, this long tradition of incorporating characteristics from the religious world outside of Judaism was employed in creating the images found in the Christological hymns. The descriptions of the distinct yet subordinate divine entity represented by Divine Wisdom could be modified and used also of Christ for the treatment of Divine Wisdom in the wisdom literature of the Hellenized Jews offered a ready palate for a means to describe a divine entity distinct from the Lord.

The use of Middle Platonic and to a lesser extent Stoic language also offered the Christian authors of the hymnic fragments ready made language to describe the new reality represented by Christ. The relationship between the Lord and the *Logos/Sophia* as represented by the Hellenistic Jewish wisdom speculation exemplified by Philo as well as the relationship between God and the *Logos* in Greek philosophical discourse could easily be used as a model to describe the relationship between God and His Son. Even when Middle Platonic language had not already been filtered through Hellenistic Jewish wisdom speculation, as potentially the case of 1 Cor 8.6, the language of Middle Platonic philosophy as represented by the "metaphysics of prepositions" offered early Christian authors a template to describe the relationship between God and Christ. Finally, we should not be all that surprised that formerly pagan Greeks in the first century looked to their own religious tradition to describe the incarnation of Jesus. Phil 2:6, John 1:14 and 1 Tim 3:16 all indicate a close familiarity with the great works of Greco-Roman literature, specifically those which deal with the cosmos such as Homer and Hesiod and the myths of the gods which inhabited the mythic world of the Greeks and Romans.

We are left, then, with a collection of hymnic fragments which give us a glimpse on these early Christians who appear to be both educated Hellenized Jews and highly literate former pagans. Both groups wrote and spoke in Greek and both groups were in all probability familiar with the great literary works of their day. As the example of John 1:1-18 attests, however, the dividing lines between Jew and Greek might not be all that firmly drawn. They were educated people of the Hellenized east, making use of the literary traditions before them to describe a new reality; a new reality in which the figure of *Logos/Sophia* had taken human form and walked among them. As to what the non-educated members of the audiences of these hymns would have made of this odd collection of Middle Platonic philosophical discourse coupled with allusions from Jewish wisdom speculation it is decidedly difficult to surmise. Clearly, these images resonated with many as they were passed down from community to community over the generations. Whether they resonated because of parallels to what the audience had already been exposed to in their own literary or religious traditions or whether they persisted in the first Christian communities simply because they expressed the reality of Christ as God in a way which described what these communities knew from their own experience is impossible to know.

The transmittal of these hymnic fragments by Early Christian communities, however, does pose a problem. Although one could argue that the authors of these hymnic fragments had access to Homer, Hesiod, Plato and the like, it is highly doubtful that the vast majority of the audience in the first hundred years of Christianity would have been able to pick up on allusions to Euripides or the subtleties of Alcinous. Why then were these hymns revered and transmitted by these first communities? It must be true that they resonated with the first hearers or else we would not have them today. However, there is no clear answer as to why the vast majority of the first Christians, who in all probability lacked the education to truly appreciate the philosophical subtlety of these hymns, nonetheless revered them enough to repeat them and pass them on to other communities.

In essence what we are witnessing in our examination of the core images found in the Christological hymnic fragments of the New Testament is a continuation of the process of theological appropriation of images which began with the writing of Proverbs half a millennia or more before the Christian era. Beginning with the subtle appropriation of images from the Egyptian goddess *Ma'at,* the Jews displayed an affinity for borrowing from neighboring polytheistic cultures images which they could adjust and modify greatly to make their own. In the case of Proverbs, monotheists like the Jews could borrow descriptions of one of the minor deities in the Egyptian pantheon and sublimate this feminine divinity to the one god, Yahweh. *Ma'at* could be domesticated, as it were, and used to augment descriptions of the Lord, giving him a partner during His acts of creation. As Jews speculated upon the role of Wisdom in the Hellenistic era (most notably in Sirach and the Wisdom of Solomon) they borrowed again from Egyptian religion, this time from the cults of Isis. However, by this time the language of Middle Platonic philosophy, with its discussion of the *Logos* and the use of the "metaphysics of prepositions" was also influencing the images of Wisdom, producing now a feminine aspect of the Lord's creative power that nevertheless had a more defined role to play in the creative process than anything seen in Proverbs.

It was this image of Wisdom, by now imbued with creative powers owing to her connection to both the *Logos* and Isis imagery that the Christian authors inherited. Not content, or perhaps not able, to simply appropriate all that was said of Wisdom and re-direct these images toward Christ, these early Christian authors now had to contend with the fact of the incarnation. It was in the hymnic fragments which describe the incarnation of Christ that we see our final instances of theological appropriation. The Christian authors, like the Jewish authors before them, could now borrow language and imagery from the myriad of myths surrounding gods taking human form. However, in a fashion similar to their Jewish forebears, these Christian authors modified these images and altered the language to make them decidedly Christian. The language surrounding the myths of Apollo and Herakles could now be put to use in describing the similar transformation undergone by Christ.

However, as with every stage in the theological appropriation outlined in the preceding chapters, these Christian authors made the images their own. In the case of the Christological hymnic fragments which dealt with the incarnation, this language now contains elements not found in the literary antecedents which may have formed their models, specifically the insistences in which Christ is described as flesh (σάρξ). These Christian authors were dealing with a new reality. A new reality which could be described using language from other religious traditions, but which had to embrace the fundamental truth of the Christian message, i.e. that God had become a man not found in myth but a historical personage known to the communities which continued to praise him in their hymnody.

Questions for Further Study

As with all investigations of scripture this one has raised several questions that cannot be adequately answered given the scope of the work, chief among them is the education level and social status of the people producing the hymnic fragments. One of the fundamental tenets of the social science method as it is currently practiced in relationship to the New Testament is the idea that an understanding of peasant society is integral to the understanding of much of the literature. Honor and shame, limited goods, patron/client relations and other terms taken from studies of both modern and ancient anthropology form the background of this system which aims to understand the cultural matrix which produced the literature of the Christian scriptures. Although these models may illuminate the cultural milieu of Jesus and his first followers, a social scientific model which concentrates solely on the peasantry may miss the influence of elites during the formative years of early Christianity (35 C.E. - 110C.E.). As evidence for the influence of these elites allow me to cite three examples from early Christian hymnody: 1 Cor 8:6, John 1:3, 10, Col 1:16-17. Each of these hymnic fragments clearly contains evidence of the influence of either Middle Platonic or Stoic philosophy, influence which would not have been available to the peasantry.

There is no question that ideas such as patron-client and honor-shame apply to elites as well as to peasantry in the first century. Profs. J. Neyrey and B. Malina have, through countless literary parallels and examples from the field of anthropology,[3] shown that such concepts fit the world of the first century that we know. However, might there not be some aspects of early Christianity that are getting overlooked by a concentration on the peasant side of the social science equation? I understand that the social science method and the corresponding concentration on the social anthropology of peasant society acted as a correction upon earlier scholarship which was disproportionately influenced by classical studies and heavily weighted in favor of elites and the literary record they produced. Yet, something seems decidedly odd about using the peasant model as the lens whereby we examine much of early Christianity. In the above examples,

---

[3] Bruce J. Malina, *Christian Origins and Cultural Anthropology,* (Atlanta: John Knox Press, 1986), *The New Testament World: Insights from Cultural Anthropology,* (Atlanta: John Knox Press, 1981), *The Social Gospel of Jesus: The Kingdom of God in Mediterranean Perspective,* (Minneapolis: Fortress Press, 2001), and Jerome H. Neyrey, *An Ideology of Revolt: John's Christology in Social-Science Perspective,* (Philadelphia: Fortress Press, 1988), *Honor and Shame in the Gospel of Matthew,* (Louisville, KY: Westminster John Knox Press, 1998), *Paul in Other Words: A Cultural Reading of His Letters,* (Louisville, KY: Westminster John Knox Press, 1990), *Social World of Luke-Acts,* (Peabody, Mass: Hendrickson Publishers, 1991).

clearly we are dealing with individuals who have had the benefit of not just an adequate education, but quite a good one. Peasants do not write in Greek, employ the "metaphysics of prepositions" or wax loquacious on the multiple aspects of the *Logos*. This is not to say that the social science method is not useful, and indeed it is extremely useful in deciphering the social matrix in which the sayings of Jesus were received or perhaps in discerning how the first Christian communities received these hymns. Indeed, an understanding of peasant agrarian society is probably the only way by which these sayings and hymns can be properly situated within early Christian communities as the average person singing "hymns to Christ as to a god" probably lacked all but the most rudimentary education. Also, categories such as "honor and shame" transcend social strata and are as applicable when applied to John the Baptist as Seneca. However, other aspects of the literary tradition found in the New Testament do not seem to so easily fit into the peasant model. One could conceivably argue that although some of the material contained in the New Testament originated in a peasant societies, the authors of the hymnic fragments and at least a small proportion of the first hearers (as witnessed by the conflicts evident between rich and poor of 1 Cor 11:17-22 will attest) may not have hailed from the agrarian peasantry. If nothing else this investigation has shown the need for a more nuanced understanding of these first Christians and demonstrated the complex character of these first Christian communities.

A second area of investigation has to do with the use of imagery taken from Greco-Roman myth, specifically the myths of Apollo and Heracles that the author of Phil 2:6-12 seems to be drawing upon. How prevalent were the worship of these two gods in the first century in the areas where Paul was active, specifically in the area around Philippi? This is a question for archaeology. If it can be shown that there were greater concentrations of shrines to one or both of these particular gods in areas traditionally associated with Paul such as Philippi or

Corinth, a stronger case could be made for parallels between the Philippians hymn and the myths surrounding these gods.

Third, there is clearly influence coming from Hellenistic philosophy in several of our hymnic fragments (1 Cor 8:6, Col 1:16-17, John 1:1-3, 10). In the case of 1 Cor 8:6 we seem to be dealing with a pagan author, well versed in the language of Middle Platonism or Stoic thought who lent his considerable philosophical talents in the composition of a short hymn to Christ. Do we have any evidence, anywhere in the first half of the first century, of such well educated pagans being attracted to Christianity? If our conjectures about the educational background of the author of 1 Cor 8:6 are correct, what does it say about Christian origins if one of the earliest Christian authors was well educated in Greek philosophy?

An additional question which needs to be examined deals with the concept of Hellenization specifically as it applies to the Jews in the first century. The hymnic fragment represented by John 1:1-18 seems to be giving us a little bit of everything: Middle Platonic thought, Hellenistic Jewish wisdom speculation and talk of incarnate divinities "taking flesh." How Hellenized could a Jew be in the first century before he is no longer considered a Jew? What were the dividing lines? Clearly, talk of an incarnate divinity would seem to disqualify one from being a Jew, yet talk of the *Logos*, of a mediating aspect of reality distinct from the Lord would not, as we see in Philo. Clearly, in many of the hymnic fragments examined above we are dealing with folks who lived on the periphery of Hellenized Judaism, i.e. individuals who could make the move to the incarnate Christ while maintaining all the language normally reserved for the Hellenized *Sophia*. In the period after the destruction of Jerusalem in 70 C.E., where would one find such Jews in Asia Minor and were there similar Christian communities near by?

The Appropriated God

This work is entitled "The Appropriated God" to show that if one thing characterized religious thought in the half-millennia prior to and including the Christian era it was the borrowing of ideas from one religious tradition by another. Whether described as assimilation or theological appropriation, it is clear that Jews, Greeks and Romans often went to other religious traditions to augment what they wanted to say about their own. This is perhaps most remarkable in the Jewish context for even a cursory examination of the Pentateuch or the Deuteronomistic History would indicate that borrowing from the surrounding cultures is something that is never, ever lauded. Yet find this borrowing we do and in some fairly sensitive places, specifically the creation of the world and God's role in it. Once the wall of monotheism was breached by the incorporation of *Ma'at* theology in Proverbs, and a great breach it was indeed, lesser incursions such as the incorporation of Greek thought in Sirach or Isis imagery in the Wisdom of Solomon are easier to understand. Once Hellenistic philosophy supplied the necessary language to talk about this troublesome relationship between the One God and another divine entity, the literary ground was suitably prepared for similar depictions of the relationship between Christ and His Father. This theological appropriation continued when these first Christian authors had to describe the Incarnation in language their hearers could understand. However, at this point it is hard to talk about theological appropriation for these first Christian authors were drawing water from a stream in which they were clearly standing in already. These former pagans were shaping their new reality with images and ideas from their old reality. The Hellenized Jews among them, too, were trying to express the difficult concept of Wisdom as flesh drawing upon their traditions but also adding new elements. Luckily for them, and for us, the truth about Christ could be expressed so beautifully because the literary ground had been properly prepared.

Appendix A

Proverbs and the Creative Role

The concentration on the Hellenistic period in the investigation of the creative role of *Divine Wisdom* falters if it can be shown that depictions of *Divine Wisdom* in Proverbs were indeed creative centuries before Alexander. As with the answer to so many questions in biblical scholarship, the answer hinges upon the translation:

Prov 8:30-31

וָאֶהְיֶה אֶצְלוֹ, אָמוֹן : וָאֶהְיֶה שַׁעֲשֻׁוּעִים,

יוֹם יוֹם; מְשַׂחֶקֶת לְפָנָיו בְּכָל־עֵת.

מְשַׂחֶקֶת, בְּתֵבֵל אַרְצוֹ; וְשַׁעֲשֻׁעַי, אֶת־בְּנֵי

אָדָם.

I was with him as his confidant, a source of delight every day, rejoicing before him at all times, rejoicing in his inhabited world, finding delight with mankind.

...ἤμην παρ᾽ αὐτῷ ἁρμόζουσα.
ἐγὼ ἤμην ᾗ προσέχαιρε. καθ᾽ ἡμέραν, δὲ εὐφραινόμην ἐν προσώπῳ

αὐτοῦ ἐν παντὶ καιρῷ, ὅτι ἐνευφραίνετο τὴν οἰκουμένην συντελέσας, καὶ ἐνευφραίνετο ἐν υἱοῖς ἀνθρώπων

> *I was by him, suiting myself to him, I was that wherein he took delight; and daily I rejoiced in his presence continually. For he rejoiced when he had completed the world, and rejoiced among the children of men.*

This connection to creation and the creative act, however, rests upon one verse and in particular one word that we encounter in Prov. 8:30a, the Hebrew word normally translated as "artificer", "craftsman" or "architect", אמון . This matter of translation is made all the more sensitive when various theological considerations influence the enterprise, namely, if one posits "craftsman/architect" as the best translation, *Divine Wisdom* is elevated from being a presence at God's side before and during the creation of the word to an active participant.

As you would expect, significant problems arise when one attempts to translate אמון as it appears nowhere else in the Hebrew Bible. When we look to Prov. 8:30 in the LXX we find the feminine participle of ἁρμόζειν, ἁρμόζουσα, normally translated as "in harmony with, suitable to, arranger or joiner."[1] If one interprets ἁρμόζουσα as synonymous with craftsman, i.e. one who arranges or joins together, it would appear that the question is fairly settled. Problems arise here, however, owing to the fact it would appear that the LXX translators took a Hebrew masculine noun and substituted a Greek feminine participle. When the LXX translators encountered a similar masculine noun elsewhere, such as אמן in Cant. 7:2, they opted for another noun, a form of τεχνίτης. Although we cannot demand too high a level of consistency from our LXX translators, this peculiarity has led to a spate of theories as to the word that might have existed in the original Hebrew text. Some posit that the word was

---

[1] Clifford, *Proverbs*, p. 99.

simply misvocalized[2] by the Masoretes and put forth alternatives such as אוֹמֵן
[3](uniting, binding together). Unfortunately, this form is unattested in Hebrew.[4]
Others try to read אמון adverbially to mean "true or faithful,"[5] yet this form is
also extremely difficult to find in Hebrew as it is not productive in this particular
stem. The same goes for reading אמון as a passive participle meaning "ward or
one who is raised" as this form also is unattested in Hebrew.[6]

M. V. Fox[7] examines the above possibilities and eliminates most of the
traditional readings based on context and lack of attestation in Biblical Hebrew
and bases his translation of אמון upon both context and a similar, but not
exact form, found in Esth. 2:20b בְּאָמְנָה ("being brought up by or growing up").
Although Fox's argument rests upon only slightly stronger attestational evidence
than those who would see Cant 7:2 as the best alternative, the strength of his
argument lies in the way the idea of "being brought up by or growing up" fits in
with the remainder of the verse. It is far easier to accommodate the idea of *Divine
Wisdom* growing up in the presence of the Lord and then playing before him all
the while than the idea of *Divine Wisdom* creating alongside the Lord and then
doing the same. [8] For these reasons I have operated from the premise that a
creative role does not indeed exist for *Divine Wisdom* at the time of the writing of
Proverbs and that subsequent creative activity on her part in the literary record
only appears when Jewish authors were coming under Hellenistic influences,
most notably Isis theology, which allowed for a feminine divine presence to have
a creative role.

---

[2] Clifford, *Proverbs*, p. 100.
[3] R.B.Y. Scott, "Wisdom in Creation: The 'Amon of Proverbs VIII 30," VT 10 (1960), 213-223.
[4] Michael V. Fox, 'AMON Again, *Journal of Biblical Literature* 115.4 (Winter 1996), p.700
[5] R. B. Y. Scott, *Proverbs – Ecclesiastes,* (New York: Doubleday, 1960), p. 72.
[6] Fox, M.V., 'AMON Again, p. 701
[7] Fox, M.V., 'AMON Again, pp. 699-702.
[8] It must be noted, however, that if one were to adopt the noun (nursling or child) as opposed to
the infinitive absolute (growing up) the overall sense of the passage would remain fairly similar,
i.e. *Divine Wisdom* being is some way like a child. This position is seen by Clifford as
"semantically odd".

159

BIBLIOGRAPHY

Primary Sources

Aelius Aristides, *The Complete Works, Vol. I and II,* Trans. Charles A. Behr. Leiden: E. J. Brill, 1986.

Alcinous, *The Handbook of Platonism,* Trans. J. Dillon. Oxford: Clarendon Press, 2001.

Apollodorus, *The Library,* Loeb Classical Library, Trans. Sir J. G. Frazer. London: W. Heinemann, New York: G. P. Putnam's Sons, 1921.

Apuleius, *Metamorphoses,* Loeb Classical Library, Trans. J. Arthur Hanson. Cambridge: Harvard University Press, 1989.

Aristotle, Loeb Classical Library, 17 Volumes, Trans. H. P. Cooke, E. S. Forster, J. H. Freese, W. K. C. Guthrie, W. S. Hett, H. D. P. Lee, A. L. Peck, H. Treadennick, P. H. Wicksteed and F. M. Cornford. Cambridge: Harvard University Press, 1966-1987.

Cassius Dio, *Roman History,* Loeb Classical Library, 9 Volumes, Trans. E. Carey and H. B. Foster. Cambridge: Harvard University Press, 1955 – 1961.

Cicero, *De Natura Deorum,* Loeb Classical Library, Trans. H. Rackham. Cambridge: Harvard University Press, 1961.

Clement of Alexandria, Loeb Classical Library, Trans. G. W. Butterworth. London: W. Heinemann and New York: G. P. Putnam's Sons, 1919.

Diogenes Laertius, *Lives of the Eminent Philosophers,* Loeb Classical Library, Trans. R. D. Hicks. London: W. Heinemann and New York: G. P. Putnam's Sons, 1938.

Epictetus, *The Discourses,* Loeb Classical Library, 2 Volumes, Trans. W. A. Oldfather. London: W. Heinemann and New York: G. P. Putnam's Sons, 1926 – 1928.

Euripides, Loeb Classical Library, 8 Volumes. Trans. D. Kovacs and A. S. Way. Cambridge: Harvard University Press, 1912 – 2002.

_____, *Bacchae*, E. R. Dodds, Ed. Oxford: Oxford University Press, 1960.

_____, *Bacchae*, Richard Seaford, Ed. Warminster, England: Aris and Phillips Ltd., 1996.

_____, *Alcestis,* A. M. Dale, Ed. Oxford : The Clarendon Press, 1966.

Herodotus, Loeb Classical Library, 4 Volumes. Trans. A. D. Godley. Cambridge: Harvard University Press and London: W. Heinemann, 1920 - 1925.

Hesiod, *Hesiod, The Homeric Hymns and Homerica,* Loeb Classical Library, Trans. G. Evelyn-White. Cambridge: Harvard University Press, 1974.

Homer, *The Illiad,* Loeb Classical Library, 2 Volumes, Trans. A. T. Murray. Cambridge: Harvard University Press, 1999.

_____, *The Odyssey,* Loeb Classical Library, Volume 1, Trans. A. T. Murray. Cambridge: Harvard University Press, 1984.

_____, *The Odyssey of Homer,* Loeb Classical Library, Volume 2, Trans. A. T. Murray. London: Macmillan & Co. Ltd. and NewYork: St. Martin's Press, 1965.

The Homeric Hymns, Helene P. Foley, Ed. Princeton: Princeton University Press, 1994.

Josephus, Loeb Classical Library, 9 Volumes, Trans. L. H. Feldman, R. Markus and H. St. J. Thackeray. London: W. Heinemann and New York: G. P. Putnam's Sons, 1926 – 1965.

Lucan, Loeb Classical Library, Trans. J. D. Duff. Cambridge: Harvard University Press and London: W. Heinemann, 1928.

Lucian, Loeb Classical Library, 8 Volumes, Trans. A. M. Harmon, K. Kilburn, and M. D. Mcleod. Cambridge: Harvard University Press, 1913 – 1967.

Ovid, *Metamorphoses,* Loeb Classical Library, Trans. F. J. Miller. Cambridge: Harvard University Press and London: W. Heinemann, 1984.

Pausanias, *Description of Greece,* Loeb Classical Library, 5 Volumes. Trans. W. H. S. Jones and H. A. Omerod. Cambridge: Harvard University Press, 1918 – 1935.

Philo Alexandrinus, Loeb Classical Library, 12 Volumes, Trans. F. H. Colson, G. H. Whitaker, and P. Wendland. Cambridge: Harvard University Press, 1929 –1962.

Plato, Loeb Classical Library, 12 Volumes, Trans. R. G. Bury, H. N. Fowler, W. R. M. Lamb, and P. Shorey. Cambridge: Harvard University Press, 1914 -1935.

Plutarch, *Lives,* Loeb Classical Library, 9 Volumes. Trans. B. Perrin. Cambridge: Harvard University Press, 1968 – 1988.

Sophocles, *Trachiniae.* Loeb Classical Library. Trans. F. Storr. London: W. Heinemann and New York: The Macmillan Co., 1912 – 1913.

Stoicorum Veterum Fragmenta, 4 vols, Ed. H. von Arnim. Leipzig: Teubner, 1905-1924.

Suetonius, *The Lives of the Caesars,* Loeb Classical Library, 2 Volumes, Trans. M. Ihm and J. C. Rolfe. Cambridge: Harvard University Press and London: W. Heinemann, 1964 – 1965.

Virgil, Loeb Classical Library, 2 Volumes, Trans. H. R. Fairclough. London: W. Heinemann, 1965.

Secondary Sources

Albright, J. N., "Some Canaanite-Phoenician Sources of Hebrew Wisdom," *VT* Suppl. 3, 1955, pp. 16-25.

Athanassakis, Apostolos N., The Homeric Hymns, Baltimore/London: Johns Hopkins University Press, 1984.

Attridge, Harold W., *Hebrews,* Philadelphia: Fortress Press, 1989.

Aune, David E., "Heracles and Christ: Heracles Imagery in the Christology of Early Christianity," in *Greeks, Romans and Christians: Essays in Honor of Abraham J. Malherbe,* Minneapolis: Fortress Press, 1990.

Barclay, John M. G., *Jews in the Mediterranean Diaspora: From Alexander to Trajan (323 BCE – 117 CE),* Berkeley: University of California Press, 1996.

Barth, Markus and Helmut Blanke, *Colossians,* New York: Doubleday, 1994.

Beasley-Murray, George Raymond, *John,* Waco, Texas: Word Books, 1987.

Berger, Klaus, *Formgeschichte des Neuen Testaments,* Heidelberg: Quelle & Meyer, 1984.

Bergman, Jan, *Ich Bin Isis: Studien Zum Memphitischen Hintergrund Der Griechischen Isisaretalogien,* Uppsala: Almqvist und Wiksell, 1969.

Böhlig, Alexander, *Koptissch-gnostiche Apokalypsen aus Codex V von Nag Hammadi,* Halle-Wittenberg, 1963.

Bremer, Jan Maarten, and William D. Furley, *Greek Hymns,* Tübingen: Mohr Siebeck, 2001.

Brown, Raymond Edward, *The Gospel of John,* New York: Doubleday, 2003.

Bultmann, Rudolph C., *The Gospel of John,* Philadelphia: Westminster/John Knox Press, 1971.

_____,"Der religionsgeschichtlilche Hintergrund des Prologs zum Johannes-Evangelium," *Eucharisteriion, Festschrift für Hermann Gunkel,* ed. Hans Schmidt, vol. II, Göttingen, 1923.

_____,"Die Bedeutung der neuerschlossenen mandäischen und manichischen Quellen für das Verständnis des Johannesevangeliums," ZNW, vol. XXIV, 1925.

_____,"Johanneische Schriften und Gnosis," *OLZ* 43 (1940), pp. 150-175.

_____, *The Theology of the New Testament,* New York: Scribner, 1965.

Cerfaux, Lucien, 'L'hymmne au Christ-Serviteur de Dieu,' *Miscellanea historica in honorem Alberti de Meyer,* Louvain, 1946.

_____, *Christ in the Theology of St. Paul,* English translation by Geoffrey Webb and Adrian Walker, New York: Herder and Herder, 1959.

Charlesworth, James H. *The Old Testament Pseuedepigrapha and the New Testament,* Cambridge: Cambridge University Press, 1985.

_____, "A Prolegomenon to a New Study of the Jewish Background of the Hymns and Prayers in the New Testament," *Journal of Jewish Studies 33,* Spring/Autumn, 1982 .

Clifford, Richard J., *Proverbs*, Louisville, KY.: Westminster John Knox Press, 1999.

Collins, John J., *Between Athens and Jerusalem,* Grand Rapids, MI: W.B. Eerdmans, 2000.

_____, *Jewish Wisdom in the Hellenistic Age,* Louisville, KY: Westminster John Knox Press, 1997.

Collins, Raymond F., *1 Corinthians,* Collegeville: Liturgical Press, 1999.

_____, *I and II Timothy and Titus,* Louisville: Westminster John Knox Press, 2002.

Colpe, Carsten. *Die religionsgeschichtliche Schule: Darstellung und Kritik ihres Bildes vom gnostischen Erlösermythus,* FRLANT 78, Göttingen, 1961.

Conzelmann, Hans, *1 Corinthians,* Philadelphia: Fortress Press, 1975.

_____, "The Mother of Wisdom," in *The Future of Our Religious Past,* New York: Harper & Row, 1971.

Daniélou, Jean, "Judéo-christianisme et gnose," in *Aspects du Judéo -christianisme,* Paris, 1965.

_____, *Théologie du judéo-christianisme,* Tournai, 1958.

Davies, W. D. *Paul and Rabbinic Judaism,* London: SPCK Publishers, 1970.

Deutch, Cecilia M. *Lady Wisdom, Jesus and the Sages,* Valley Forge, PA: Trinity Press International, 1996, pp. 9-41.

Dibelius, Martin, *An die Klosser, Epheser, an Philemon,* Tübingen: Mohr, 1953.

_____, *The Pastoral Epistles,* Philadelphia: Fortress Press, 1972.

Di Lella, Alexander, *The Hebrew Text of Sirach,* London, The Hague, Paris: Mouton & Co., 1966.

Dillon, John, *The Middle Platonists,* Ithaca, N.Y. : Cornell University Press, 1996.

Dodd, C. H. *The Interpretation of the Fourth Gospel,* Cambridge: Cambridge University Press, 1953.

_____, *The Bible and the Greeks,* London: Hodder and Stoughton, 1935.

Doresse, Jean, *The Secret Books of the Egyptian Gnostics,* New York: Viking Press, 1960.

Dunn, J. D. G., *Christology in the Making,* Philadelphia: Westminster Press, 1980.

Durr, Lorenz, *Die Wertung des göttlichen Wortes im Alten Testament und im Antiken Orient,* Leipzig, 1938.

Fitzmyer, Joseph A., "The Aramaic Background of Philippians 2.6-11," *CBQ* 50.3, July 1988.

_____, *The Gospel According to Luke,* Garden City, New York: Doubleday & Co., 1981.

Fox, Michael V., 'AMON Again, *Journal of Biblical Literature*, 115.4, Winter 1996.

_____, *Proverbs 1-9,* New York: Doubleday, 2000.

Furley, William D., "Praise and Persuasion in Greek Hymns, "*The Journal of Hellenic Studies*, Vol. 115, 1995.

Garland, David E., *Colossians*, Grand Rapids, MI: Zondervan, 1998.

Georgi, Dieter, "Der vorpaulinische Hymnus Phil. 2.6-11," *Zeit und Geschichte. Dankesgabe an Rudolf Bultmann zum 80. Geburstag,* Tübingen, 1964. pp. 263-93.

Gordon, Richard L., "Syncretism," Oxford Classical Dictionary, Oxford/New York: Oxford University Press, 1996.

Grant, Frederick C., *Hellenistic Religions and the Age of Syncretism,* Indianapolis: Bobbs-Merrill/Liberal Arts Press, 1953.

Harrington, Daniel J., *Invitation to the Apocrypha,* Grand Rapids, MI: W.B. Eerdmans, 1999.

Harris, Margaret J., *Colossians and Philemon,* Grand Rapids, MI: Eerdmans,

1990.

Hellerman, Joseph H., Reconstructing Honor in Roman Philippi, Cambridge: Cambridge University Press, 2005.

Helyer, L., "Arius Revisted: The Firstborn over All Creation (Col. 1:15)," *JETS 31,* 1988.

Héring, Jean, "Kyrios Anthropos,' *RPHR*, vol. VI, 1936.

Hooker, Morna D., *Jesus and the Servant: The Influence of the Servant Concept of Deutero-Isaiah in the New Testament,* London: SPCK Publishers, 1959.

Jeremias, Joachim, *The Servant of God,* London: SCM Press, 1957.

_____, *Die Briefe an Timotheus und Titus* (NTD, 9), Göttingen, 1947.

Jervis, L. Ann, "Paul the Poet in First Timothy 1:11-18, 2:3b-7; 3:14-16," *Catholic Biblical Quarterly* 61.4, October 1999.

Johnson, Luke Timothy, *The First and Second Letters to Timothy,* New York: Doubleday, 2001.

Jonas, Hans, *The Gnostic Religion,* Boston: Beacon Press, 1963.

Käsemann, Ernst, *Das wandernde Gottesvolk: Eine Untersuchung zum Hebräerbrief,* Forschungen zur Religion und Literatur des Alten und Neuen Testaments, Göttingen, 1961.

Kayatz, Christa, *Studien zu Proverbien 1-9: Eine Form-und Motivgeschichtliche Untersuchung unter Einbeziehung ägyptischen Vergleichsmaterial* (WMANT 22), Neukirchen-Vluyn: Neukirchener Verlag, 1966.

Kelber, Werner, "The Birth of the Beginning: John 1: 1-18, " *Semeia* no 52, 1990.

Kloppenborg, John S., "Isis and Sophia in the Book of Wisdom," *Harvard Theological Review,* 75.1.

Knox, W. L., "Divine Wisdom," *Journal of Theological Studies*, 38, 1937.

Kroll, Joseph. *Die christliche Hymnodik bis zu Klemens von Alexandreia,* Königsberg, 1921, Darmstadt, 1968.

Lamp, Jeffrey S., "Wisdom in Col 1:15-20: Contribution and Significance,"

166

Journal of the Evangelical Theological Society, 41/1, March 1998.

Lane, William L., *Hebrews,* Waco, Texas: Word Books, 1991.

Lang, Bernhard, *Wisdom and the Book of Proverbs,* New York: Pilgrim Press, 1986.

LaPorte, Jean, "Philo in the Tradition of Wisdom," in *Aspects of Wisdom in Judaism and Early Christianity,* Robert L. Wilken ed., Notre Dame/London: University of Notre Dame Press, 1975.

Lattke, Michael, "Hymnische Materialeien zu einer Geschichte der antiken Hymnologie", *NT und Orbis Antiquus 19,* Freibourg: Universitatsverlag: Gottingen: Vandenhoeck & Ruprecht, 1991.

Lohmeyer, Ernst, Die *Briefe an die Kolosser und an Philemon,* Göttingen: Vandenhoeck & Ruprecht, 1961.

_____, *Kyrios Jesus: Eine Untersuchung zu Phil. 2, 5-11, Sitzungsberichte der Heidelberger Akademie der Wissenschaften,* Jahrgang 1927/8, 4. Abhandlung; reprinted Darmstadt, 1961.

Lohse, Eduard, *Colossians and Philemon: A Commentary on the Epistles to Colossians and Philemon,* Philadelphia: Fortress Press, 1971.

MacDonald, Margaret Y., *Colossians and Ephesians,* Collegeville, Minn.: Liturgical Press, 2000.

Mack, Burton L., *Logos und Sophia,* Göttingen: Vandenhoeck & Ruprecht, 1973.

Malina, Bruce J., *Christian Origins and Cultural Anthropology,* Atlanta: John Knox Press, 1986.

_____, *The New Testament World: Insights from Cultural Anthropology,* Atlanta: John Knox Press, 1981.

_____, *The Social Gospel of Jesus: The Kingdom of God in the Mediterranean,* Minneapolis: Fortress Press, 2001.

Martin, Ralph P., *Carmen Christi,* Downers Grove, IL: InterVarsity Press, 1999.

_____, 'Μορφή in Philippians 2.6,' *ExpT* 70, 1958-1959.

_____, *Colossians and Philemon,* London: Oliphants, 1974.

Martone, Corrado, "Ben Sira Manuscripts from Qumran and Masada," *The Book of Ben Sira in Modern Research: Proceedings of the First International Ben Sira Conference,* 28-31 July 1996.

McLeod, David J., "The Eternality and Deity of the Word: John 1:1-2," *Biblica Sacra,* 160, January-March 2003, pp. 48-64.

_____, "Christology in Six Lines: An Exposition of 1Timothy 3.16," *Biblica Sacra* 159, July-September 2002.

Melick, Richard R., *Philippians, Colossians, Philemon,* Nashville, Tenn.: Broadville Press, 1991.

Michaels, J. Ramsey, *1 Peter,* Waco, TX: Word Books, 1988.

Middendorp, Theophilus, *Die Stellung Jesu Ben Siras zwischen Judentum und Hellenismus,* Leiden: Brill, 1973.

Moffatt, James, *Hebrews,* New York: Scribner's Sons, 1924.

Moule, C. F. D., *Colossians and Philemon,* Cambridge: Cambridge University Press, 1957.

Muddiman, John, *Ephesians,* London/New York: Continuum, 2001.

Murphy, Roland, "Wisdom and Eros in Proverbs 1-9," *CBQ,* 50.4, 1988.

Murphy-O'Connor, Jerome, *Paul,* Oxford: Clarendon Press, 1996.

Neyrey, Jerome H., An Ideology of Revolt: John's Christology in Social Science Perspective, Philadelphia: Fortress Press, 1988.

_____, *Honor and Shame in the Gospel of Matthew*, Louisville, KY: Westminster John Knox Press, 1998.

_____, *Paul in Other Words: A Cultural Reading of His Letters,* Louisville, KY: Westminster John Knox Press, 1990.

_____, *The Social World of Luke-Acts*, Peabody, Mass: Hendrickson Publishers, 1991.

Norden, Eduard, *Agnostos Theos: Untersuchungen Zur Formengeschichte Religiöser Rede*, Darmstadt: Wissenschaftliche Buchgesellschaft, 1956.

_____, *Die Antike Kunstprosa*, Stuttgart: B.G. Teubner Verlagsgessellschaft, 1958.

Oesterley, W. O. E., *An Introduction to the Books of the Apocrypha,* London: The Society for the Promotion of Christian Knowledge, 1935.

O'Brien, Peter Thomas, *Commentary on the Philippians,* Grand Rapids, MI: Eerdmans, 1991.

O'Neill, J.C. "Who Is Comparable to Me in My Glory - 4Q491 Fragment 11(4Q491C) and the New Testament,"*Novum Testamentum* 42.1, Issue 1, 2000.

Osiek, Carolyn, *Philippians Philemon,* Nashville: Abingdon, 2000.

Parker, R. C. T., *"Greek Hymns, "* Oxford Classical Dictionary, Oxford: Oxford University Press, 2003.

Perkins, Pheme, *Ephesians,* Nashville: Abingdon, 1997.

Pfitzner, Victor C., *Hebrews*, Nashville: Abingdon Press, 1997.

Pokorny´, Petr, 'Epherserbrief und gnostische Mysterien,' ZNW, vol. LIII, 1962.

Pollard, T. E. "Colossians 1:12-20: A Reconsideration," *NTS* 27, July 1981.

Quinn, Jerome D. and William C. Wacker, *The First and Second Letters to Timothy,* Grand Rapids, MI: Eerdmans, 2000.

Reitzenstein, Richard, *Zwei religionsgeschichtliche Fragen,* Strassburg: Tübner, 1901.

Richter, Daniel S., "Plutarch on Isis and Osiris: Text, Cult, and Cultural Appropriation," *Transactions of the American Philological Associations,* 131, 2001.

Robinson, James M., "A Formal Analysis of Col. 1:15-20," *JBL* 76 (1957).

Rochais, Gerard, "La formation du prologue, " *Science et Esprit*, 37 My-S 1985.

Sanders, Jack T. *The New Testament Christological Hymns,* Cambridge: Cambridge University Press, 1971.

_____, *Ben Sira and Demotic Wisdom,* Chico: Scholars Press, 1983.

Schenke, H. M., *Der Gott 'Mensch' in der Gnosis,* Göttingen, 1962.

Schlier, Heinrich, *Christus und die Kirche im Epheserbrief,* Beiträge zur Kontroverstheologie, Münster-Westphalen, 1930.

Schmithals, Walter, *An Introduction to the Theology of Rudolf Bultmann,* London: SCM Press, 1968.

Schnabel, E. J., *Law and Wisdom from Ben Sira to Paul,* WUNT: Tübingen: J.C.B. Mohr, 1985.

Schnackenburg, Rudolph, *The Epistle to the Ephesians,* Edinburgh: T&T Clark, 1991.

Schüssler-Fiorenza, Elisabeth, "Wisdom Mythology and the Christological Hymns of the New Testament," in *Aspects of Wisdom in Judaism and Early Christianity,* ed. R.L. Wilken; Notre Dame: University of Notre Dame, 1975.

Schweizer, Eduard, *The Letter to the Colossians,* Minneapolis: Augsburg, 1982.

_____, *Erniedrigung und Erhöhung bein Jesus und seinen Nachfolgern..* Abhandlungen zur Theologie des Alten und Neuen Testaments, 28, Zurich, 1962.

Scott, R. B. Y., "Wisdom in Creation: The 'Amon of Proverbs VIII 30," *VT* 10, 1960.

_____, *Proverbs – Ecclesiastes,* New York: Doubleday, 1960.

Senior, Donald, *1 Peter,* Collegeville, MN: Liturgical Press, 2003

Skehan, Patrick, *The Wisdom of Ben Sira,* New York: Doubleday, 1987.

Smothers, Thomas G, "A Superior Model: Hebrews 1.1-4.13," *Review & Expositor* 82.3, Summer 1985.

Soggin, J. Alberto, *Introduction to the Old Testament,* London: SCM Publishers, 1989.

Stanford, W. B., *The Odyssey of Homer*, London: Macmillan & Co. Ltd., New York: St. Martin's Press, 1965.

Stanley, David M., 'The Theme of the Servant of Yahweh in Primitive Christian Soteriology and its Transposition by St. Paul,' *CBQ*, vol 16, 1954.

Sterling, Gregory, *Studia Philonica Annual,* 9, Atlanata, Georgia: Scholars Press, 1997.

Strange, J. F., *Critical and Exegetical Study of 1 Timothy 3:16,* Madison, NJ: Drew University, 1970.

Thiselton, Anthony C., *The First Epistle to the Corinthians,* Grand Rapids: Eerdmans, 2000.

Thompson, Marianne Maye, *Colossians and Philemon,* Grand Rapids: Eerdmans, 2005.

Thraede, Klaus, "Hymnos," *Reallexicon fur Antike und Christentums*, Stuttgart: A. Hiersemann, 1993.

Thurston, Bonnie and Ryan, Judith, *Philippians and Philemon*, Collegeville, MN: Liturgical Press, 2005.

Tobin, Thomas, *The Creation of Man,* Washington, DC: The Catholic Biblical Quarterly Monograph Series, 1983.

_____, 'The Prologue of John and Hellenistic Jewish Speculation," *CBQ* Vol. 52, No. 2, April 1990

_____, "The World of Thought in the Philippians Hymn (Philippians 2:6-11)," paper presented at the Catholic Biblical Society annual meeting, Philadelphia, Pennsylvania, 2005.

Vanderlip, Vera F., *The Hymns of Isidorus,* Toronto: A.M. Hakkert, Ltd., 1972.

Von Rad, Gerhard, *Wisdom in Israel,* Nashville: Abingdon Press, 1972.

Webster, Jane S., "Sophia: Engendering Wisdom in Proverbs, Ben Sira and the Wisdom of Solomon," *JSOT,* 43.1, Feb 1998.

Warren, Carter, "The Prologue and John's Gospel: Function, Symbol and the Definitive Word," *Journal for the Study of the New Testament,* no 39 Je 1990.

Whybray, R. N., *The Book of Proverbs: A Survey of Modern Study,* New York: E.J. Brill, 1995.

Wilson, R., *Gnosis and the New Testament,* Philadelphia: Fortress Press, 1968.

Winston, David, *The Wisdom of Solomon,* Garden City, NY: Doubleday, 1979.

Yadin, Yigael, *The Ben Sira Scroll from Masada,* Jerusalem: Israel Exploration Society, 1965.

Yee, Gail, "I Have Perfumed My Body with Myrrh: The Foreign Woman in Proverbs 1- 9," *JSOT,* Feb 1989, pp. 53-68.

Index of Biblical and Ancient Sources

Hebrew Bible

Genesis

1:26	27, 40, 94
1:27	37, 40, 94
2:7	63, 94
2:24	133
9:29	47

Exodus

17:6	56

Deuteronomy

4:16	37

Judges

8:18	59

II Kings

11:18	37

II Chronicles

33:7	37

Ezra

7:20	37
8:5	37
16:17	37
23:14	37

Esther

2:20	157

Psalms

16:8-11	134
38(39):6	37
72(73):20	37

Proverbs

8:22-31	78, 82, 96,
8:22-23	99
8:23-24	11, 42, 44, 47, 48, 71, 72, 75, 100
8:30-31	11, 42, 43, 47, 48, 49, 71, 72, 73, 75, 80, 99, 155, 156
22:17-24	74

Song of Songs/Canticles

7:2	156, 157

Isaiah

2:2	134
3:17	59
40:3-5	133
40:19	37
44:13	59
45:23	36
52:12	40, 63
55:10	66

Job

4:16	59

Daniel

2:31	37
2:34	37
2:35	37
3:1-18	37
3:19	37
9:37	134

Hosea

13:2	37

Deuterocanonicals

Tobit

1:13   59

Wisdom

2:23	37
7:15-22	81
7:22	85
7:22-24	50, 70, 103
7:24	81, 85, 86, 142, 143
7:25-26	87
7:26	37, 142, 143
7:27	82
8:1	85, 86
9:1-2	45
13:13, 16	37
14:15, 17	37
14:16-20	79

15:5	37
17:21	37
18:1	59

Sirach

1:7, 13	78
17:3	37
19:17	78, 80
24:1-10	78
24:5	45, 77, 99
24:9	11, 42, 44, 47, 77, 80, 100
43:1-35	82
43:2	78
43:11-12	78
43:16	78
43:26	56, 78
43:35	78

New Testament

Matthew

16:17   134

Mark

6:9-13   18
9:2   38, 59
10:8   133
13:20   134
14:38   134
16:2   38, 59

Luke

3:6   133
11:2-4   18
20:42   17
24:39   134
24:44   17

John

1:1-18   2, 4, 7, 8, 10, 11, 12, 16, 24, 31, 58, 137, 140, 141, 145, 147
1:1   47
1:1-2   32, 33, 38, 40, 41, 98, 99, 100
1:3   32, 49, 50, 51, 100, 102, 103, 150
1:10   51, 102
1:14   32, 59, 61, 65, 106, 108, 118, 120, 133, 134,

1:14 (cont.)   135, 136, 141, 143, 144, 147
6:51-58   134
8:15   134

Acts

2:17   134
2:31   134
4:24-30   18

Romans

1:18-25   35
1: 3   59
3:23   35
5:12-19   35, 36, 63
7:7-11   35
8:3   59
8:13   134
8:19-22   35

I Corinthians

7:28   134
7:31   59
8:6   2, 4, 7, 8, 10, 11, 12, 16, 17, 24, 31, 32, 49, 50, 51, 54, 100, 101, 102, 103, 104, 139, 140, 147, 150
11:17-22   151
15:9   134
15:20-49   63
15:21-24   36
15:45-49   35, 36, 38

I Corinthians (cont.)

16:22   18

II Corinthians

4:4   35
4:11   134
12:7   134

Galatians

4:4   35
4:13   134
4:23   134
5:18   134

Ephesians

4:5-6   17, 25

Philippians

1:22-24   134

2:6-11   2, 4, 7, 8, 10,
             11, 12, 13, 16,
             17, 23, 24, 25,
             63, 64, 138,
             139, 144
             31, 58
2:6   32, 33, 34, 35,
             37, 38, 41, 44,
             47, 58, 62, 64,
             98, 99, 100,
             103, 106, 128,
             147
2:7   32, 40, 58, 62,

2:7 (cont.) 63, 65, 106,
             108, 118, 119,
             120, 123, 135
2:10   36
3:3   134

Colossians

1:15-20   2, 4, 7, 8, 10,
             11, 12, 16, 24,
             25, 31, 50,
             140, 144

1:16-17   32, 49, 52, 54,
             100, 102, 103,
             150
1:17   32, 33, 39, 40,
             41, 47, 56, 98,
             99, 100
1:20   103

I Timothy

3:16   2, 4, 7, 8, 10,
             11, 13, 16, 17,
             24, 25, 31, 32,
             58, 60, 66,
             106, 108, 118,
             119, 120, 133,
             134, 135, 136,
             143, 144, 145,
             147

Hebrews

1:3-4   2, 4, 7, 8, 10,
             11, 12, 16, 17,
             24, 25, 31,
             137, 142, 144
1:3   32, 49, 50, 52,
             55, 56, 87,
             103, 104, 139,

Hebrews (cont.)

1:3	142, 143

I Peter

1:20-21	33
3:18-22	17, 25

Revelation

14:3	17
15:3	17

Other Ancient Writers

Aelius Aristides

Her. XL	24

Alcinous

Did. IV, 8-22	92

Apollodorus

Lib. 3.10.7	113
Lib. 3.122	122
Lib. 2.4.12	126
Lib. 2.131.1-132.4	126

Aristotle

Eth. nic. 1129	130
Metaph. 1.993	130
Metaph. 2.994	130
Metaph. 5.1024	130
Metaph. 6.1026	130
Metaph. 7.106	130
Metaph. 7.1034-5	130
Metaph. 8.1035	130
Metaph. 8.1041-2	130
Metaph. 11.106	130
Metaph. 12.1070-1	130
Metaph. 14.1092	130

Poet. 1458	130

St. Augustine

Conf. 9.13	65

Clement of Alexandria

Protr. 2.30	123

Dio Cassius

Hist. 15.2	115

Diodorus Siculus

Lib. 1.27	83

Epicetus

Diatr. 1.20.18-19	132
Diatr. 2.8.1-3	132
Diatr. 2.9.19	132
Diatr. 2.22.19	132
Diatr. 2.23.21	132
Diatr. 3.7.1-5	132
Diatr. 3.7.24	132
Diatr. 4.7.31-32	132

Euripides

Alc. 1.1-9	121
Bacch. 1-4	112
Bacch. 605	130
Bacch. 746	130
Bacch. 1127-30	130
Bacch. 1135	130
Cycl. 342	130
Cycl. 380	130
Cycl. 402	130
El. 385	130
El. 819-24	130
Hec. 1056	130
Hel. 16-21	113
Hel. 301	130
Hel. 330	130
Her. fur. 14-25	125
Her. fur. 250	125
Her. fur 270	125
Her. fur. 1151	130
Her. fur. 1265-9	131, 141
Hipp. 1021	130
Hipp. 1235	130
Hipp. 1342	130
Med. 1181	130
Med. 1197-1200	131
Phoen. 1285	130
Phoen. 1577	130
Suppl. 48	130
Troj. 1-2	121
Troj. 440	131
Troj. 775	131

Herodotus

Hist. 1.61	127
Hist. 2.44	125

Hesiod

Scut. 50-56	124
Theog. 1.4-21	107

Homer

Il. 2.393	110
Il. 3.388	110
Il. 6.15	110
Il. 8.1	110
Il. 13.288	110
Il. 14.249-262	124
Il. 17.550	110
Il. 21.439-445	121
Od. 11.601	125

Homeric Hymns

Demeter 275-280	111

Hymns of Isidorus

Porramanres 7-9	114
Porramanres 33-34	114

Josephus

A.J. 6.120	132
A.J. 6.186	132
A.J. 12.211-112	132
A.J. 15.236	132
A.J. 19.325	132
B. J. 2.154	132
B. J. 2.254	132
B. J. 3.271-275	133
B. J. 5.4	132
B. J. 6.45-47	132

Lucan

Phars. 6.367-368	123

Lucian

*Dial. Mort.*10.8   109
Jupp. Conf. 8.11-15 122
Somn. 13   109

Marcus Aurelius

Medit. 4:23   56

Minucius Felix

Oct. 22.12-18   123

Ovid

Metam. 11.196-197 117

Pausanias

Desc. 4.14.7   115

Philo of Alexandria

Cher. 125-127   54, 96,
97,101,
140
Conf. 40-41   66
Conf. 62-3   66
Conf. 142   66
Ebr. 8.31   48, 95,
96
Fug. 97   96
Fug. 108-9   96, 140
Her. 281   56
Leg. 1.31   63
Leg. 1.165   46
Leg. 2.4   48, 98
*Op.*134   35, 63
Op. 146   87

Q.E. I.4   35
Somn. 1.241   56
Virt. 62   45

Plato

Gorg. 518   129
Leg. 3.700   20
Leg. 6.78   129
Leg. 7.797   129
Leg. 12.959   130
Phaedr. 96-98   129
Phaedr. 250b   109
Tim. 60-67   129
Tim. 73-85   129
Symp. 207   129
Symp. 211   129
Symp. 211   129

Plutarch

Alex. 3.4-6   115
De Isid. 367   87, 142
Thes. 6.1.15   127

Seneca

Ep. 31:10   55
Ep. 65:8-10   92

Sophocles

Trach. 275   126

Statius

Thebaid 96   123

Suetonius

Aug. 94.4   116

Virgil

Aen. 9.645   117

Index of Modern Authors

Allbright, J. N., 73
Atthanassakis, Apostolos N., 111
Attridge, Harold, 54, 56, 57
Aune, David, 124, 135
Barclay, John, M. G., 79, 80
Barth, Markus, 40
Beasley-Murray, George, 60, 65
Behr, Charles, 23, 24
Berger, Klaus, 2, 16, 17
Bergman, Jan, 83
Blanke, Helmut, 40
Bornkamm, G., 38, 65
Bremer, Jan, 15, 18, 19, 22
Brown, Raymond, 59, 65
Brunner, H., 75
Bultmann, Rudolf, 3, 25, 26, 28, 50, 59, 60
Cerfaux, Lucien, 3
Charlesworth, James, 27, 28
Clifford, Richard, 72, 73, 74, 156, 157
Collins, J. J., 80, 87
Collins, Raymond, 51, 60, 67
Colpe, Carsten, 27
Conzelmann, Hans, 50, 55, 77
Davies, W. D., 41
Deutch, Cecilia M., 75
Dibelius, Martin, 3, 25, 67
DiLella, Alexander, 77
Dillon, John, 90, 91, 92, 93
Dodd, C. H., 3, 26, 41, 47, 51
Dunn, J. D. G., 3, 34, 35, 36, 37, 39, 56
Dürr, Lorenz, 2, 41
Elliot, John, 33
Fox, Michael V., 75, 157

Furley, William, 15, 18, 19, 22
Garland, David E., 39
Georgi, Dieter, 40, 64
Gifford, E. H., 38
Godley, A. D., 125
Gordon, Richard, 5
Grant, Frederick C., 83
Harrington, Daniel J., 79
Harris, Margaret, 39
Hellerman, Joseph, 138
Helyer, L., 52
Héring, Jean, 3, 41, 143
Holtzmann, H. J., 34
Hooker, Morna, 3
Jeremias, Joachim, 3, 67
Jervis, L. Anne, 67
Johnson, Luke Timothy, 60
Käsemann, Ernst, 25, 38
Kayatz, Christa, 74, 75
Kelber, Werner, 42
Kloppenborg, John S., 81, 82
Knox, W. L., 82
Kroll, Joseph, 2, 25
Lane, William, 56
Lang, Bernhard, 73
LaPorte, Jean, 46
Lattke, Michael, 2, 16, 17, 18
Lightfoot, J. B., 38, 62
Lohmeyer, Ernst, 3, 25, 41
Lohse, Eduard, 39, 56
MacDonald, Margaret, 39
Mack, Burton, 82
Mackintosh, H. R., 38
Malina, B., 150
Martin, Ralph, 2, 9, 34, 37, 39, 138
Martone, Corado, 77
McCleod, David J., 40, 60
Melick, Richard, 39, 138

Michaels, J. Ramsey, 33
Middendorp, T., 77
Moffatt, James, 55, 56
Moule, H. C. G., 38, 39, 138
Murphy, Roland, 75
Murphy-O'Connor, 3, 34
Neyrey, J., 150
Norden, Eduard, 2, 15, 16, 24, 25, 55
O'Brien, Peter, 59, 62, 63, 65
Oesterley, W. O. E., 80
Parker, R. C. T., 22
Pfitzner, Victor C., 143
Pilhofer, Peter, 138
Pollard, T. E., 52
Quinn, Jerome, 20, 21
Reitzenstein, Richard, 82
Richter, Daniel, 86
Rochais, Gerard, 42
Ryan, Judy, 138
Sanders, Jack, 2, 25, 26, 34, 39, 40, 56, 64, 65, 66, 67, 77
Schenke, H. M., 27
Schlier, Heinrich, 25
Schmithals, Walter, 3
Schnabel, E. J., 52
Schneider, J., 109
Schüssler-Fiorenza, Elizabeth, 52
Schweizer, Eduard, 3, 25, 39, 65
Scott, R. B. Y., 73, 157
Senior, Donald, 34
Shumacher, H., 38
Skehan, P. W., 72, 77
Smother, Thomas, 56
Soggin, J. Alberto, 79
Spicq, A., 109
Spicq, Ceslas, 37
Stanford, W. B., 111
Stanley, David, 3
Sterling, Gregory, 102
Strange, James, 20, 21

Theiler, Willy, 90, 91
Thiselton, Anthony, 56
Thompson, Marianne, 40
Thraede, Klaus, 16
Thurston, Bonnie, 138
Tobin, Thomas, 3, 40, 45, 47, 54, 92, 94, 95
Vanderlip, Vera, 19, 114
Vincent, M. R., 38
Von Rad, Gerhard, 75, 76
Wacker, William, 20, 21
Webster, Jane S., 75
Whybray, R. N., 72, 73, 74
Wilson, R., 27
Winston, David, 79, 80, 85
Yadin, Yigael, 77
Yee, Gail, 75

Subject Index

Adam and Christ, 34, 35, 36,
37, 38, 39, 41, 49
Aelius Aristides, 23, 24
Aeneid, 117
Aëtius, 91
Alcinous, 70, 148
Alexander the Great, 69, 70,
115
Amenope, 74
Antiochus of Askelon, 96
Aphrodite, 110
Apollo, 13, 14, 68, 116, 117,
120, 121, 122, 123, 124, 128,
135, 139, 148, 152
Apollodorus, 13, 113, 118,
122, 126, 128, 135
Appropriated God, 5, 146, 153
Apuleius, 83, 84, 99
Aretalogy, 19, 82, 88
Aristotle, 15, 18, 24, 62, 93,
129, 130, 133
Asclepius, 24, 115
Athena, 24, 110, 127
Augustus, 79, 115, 116
Augustine, 65
Cleanthes, 23
Clement of Alexandria, 14, 122
Christ the Creator, 4, 31, 32, 49,
54, 55, 57, 59, 61, 67, 70, 98,
100, 103, 105, 137
Christ the Incarnate Divinity, 4,
5, 8, 11, 13, 31, 32, 57, 59, 67,
105, 137
Cicero, 86
Demeter, 87, 142
Demiurge, 91
Didorus Siculus, 83
Dio Cassius, 115
Dionysus, 24, 112

Diogenes Laertius, 86
δουλός, 122, 123, 125, 126,
127, 128
Εἰκων, 37, 38, 109
Epictetus, 129, 131, 132, 133
Essenes, 132
Eudorus of Alexandria, 91
Euripides, 14, 112, 113, 118,
121, 125, 126, 128, 129, 131,
134, 135, 138, 139, 148
Eusebius, 73
Fourth Ezra, 64, 65
Gayōmart, 41
God as Slave, 13, 58, 62, 63,
120, 122, 123, 124, 128
Gnosticism/Gnostic Redeemer,
25, 26, 27, 28, 29, 41, 62, 65
Greco-Roman Hymns, 2, 16, 17,
18, 19, 23, 28
Greco-Roman Religion, 7, 12,
120, 137, 141, 143, 145, 147
Hellenistic Jewish Wisdom, 3,
6, 11, 12, 13, 14, 18, 19, 23,
26, 28, 29, 40, 41, 47, 49, 53,
54, 56, 57, 61, 66, 67, 69, 85,
98, 100, 103, 139, 140, 142,
143, 145, 153
Heracles, 13, 14, 24, 68, 123,
124, 125, 126, 127, 131, 134,
135, 139, 141, 149, 151
Herodotus, 124, 125, 127
Hesiod, 13, 14, 107, 120, 124,
138, 147, 148
Hokmah/Sophia, 6, 12, 26, 40,
44, 45, 46, 47, 53, 57, 58, 66
68, 70, 75, 76, 80, 82, 88, 104,
153
Homer, 13, 93, 105, 106, 108,
109, 110, 113, 115, 120, 138,

Homer (cont.), 139, 147, 148
Homeric Hymn to Demeter, 111, 113
Homeric Hymns, 18, 19, 23
Illiad, 110, 111, 121
Isis, 6, 68, 71, 80, 81, 82, 83, 84 85, 86, 88, 99, 104, 143, 148, 149, 153
Isidorus, 13, 113, 114
Jewish Hymns, 2, 8, 16, 18
Josephus, 129, 131, 132, 133,
Logos, 12, 26, 35, 38, 39, 40, 41, 45, 46, 47, 49, 51, 52, 54, 57, 58, 60, 65, 67, 69, 70, 80, 89, 90, 91, 93, 95, 96, 98, 100, 102, 104, 105, 139, 140, 141, 142, 145, 146, 147, 148, 149, 151
Lucan, 123
Lucian of Samosata, 14, 122
Lukan Canticles, 23
Ma'at, 6, 68, 74, 75, 76, 104, 146, 148, 153
Marcus Aurelius, 55
Metaphysics of Prepositions, 55, 57, 89, 90, 91, 96, 101, 102, 140, 143, 147, 148, 151
Middle Platonism, 12, 13, 54, 57, 67, 69, 80, 87, 88, 90, 92, 94, 96, 100, 104, 105, 140, 141, 145, 146, 147, 148, 150, 151
Μορφή, 37, 38, 59, 62, 63, 120, 128
Nag Hammadi, 3, 24, 27
Neopythagoreans, 90
Odysseus, 110
Odyssey, 111
ὁμοιόω, 109, 113, 114, 119, 135
Osiris, 27
Ovid, 23, 116

Paul and Pauline Hymns, 1, 6, 21, 22, 28, 34, 35, 36, 63, 67, 134, 139, 141
Pausanias, 13, 113, 115
Philo, 3, 4, 6, 12, 26, 32, 34, 35, 45, 46, 47, 49, 54, 56, 57, 63, 66, 70, 71, 87, 91, 93, 95, 97, 98, 101, 105, 139, 140, 141, 142, 146, 151
Philo and the Creation of Man, 94, 100, 138
Plato and Platonic Philosophy, 23, 47, 65, 69, 71, 88, 89, 91 92, 93, 128, 130, 132, 133, 148
Plutarch, 13, 14, 86, 103, 113, 115, 126, 138, 139
Porramanres, 114
Poseidon, 87, 121, 122
Pre-Existent Christ/Pre-Creation Christ, 4, 10, 31, 32, 33, 38, 57, 59, 61, 67, 70, 98, 103, 105
Proverbs, 6, 11, 12, 46, 57, 66, 68, 69, 70, 75, 76, 88, 99, 100, 101, 104, 153, 155, 158
Pythagoreans, 91
Σάρξ, 11, 14, 59, 60, 61, 119, 120, 128, 129, 130, 132, 133, 134, 136, 141, 142, 145, 149, 151
Second Maccabees, 64, 65
Seneca, 55, 91
Serapis, 24
Similitudes of Ethiopian Enoch, 64, 65
Sirach, 6, 11, 12, 46, 57, 65, 68, 69, 76, 78, 80, 88, 99, 100, 104, 148, 153
Sirach at Qumran, Geniza and Masada, 77
Socrates, 93
Sophocles, 125, 126

Stoic Philosophy, 13, 54, 55, 57,
   67, 71, 80, 81, 85, 86, 88, 91,
   95, 100, 132, 141, 150, 151
Suetonius, 116
Theognis, 76
Timaeus, 90, 93
Trojan War, 117
Varro, 91
Virgil, 23, 108, 116, 117
Wisdom of Solomon, 6, 12, 66,
   68, 71, 79, 80, 81, 84, 85, 88,
   98, 100, 104, 143, 145, 146,
   148, 153
Xenocrates, 90
Zeno, 85, 86
Zeus, 23, 24, 45, 90, 107, 112,
   118, 121, 124, 131